STAND
ON
IT

STAND ON IT

Stroker Ace

Little, Brown and Company—Boston-Toronto

FIRST EDITION

T 11/73

Chapter 6 originally appeared in *Playboy* Magazine.

Library of Congress Cataloging in Publication Data

Ace, Stroker.
    Stand on it.

    I. Title.
PZ4.A168St [PS3551.C4]   813'.5'4   73-10414
ISBN 0-316-66870-2

Published simultaneously in Canada by Little, Brown & Company (Canada) Limited

PRINTED IN THE UNITED STATES OF AMERICA

THE MORAL
of this book is quick and easy:
If you're ever going to stand on it at all,
stand on it now. The longer you wait,
the slower you get.

I was thirty-one years old when I started writing this book. I was a whole lot smarter then, and now — a couple of years later — the big surprise is that I still have all my fingers and toes.

This is the way it happened, more or less, and I say that because I have a tendency to lie a lot and get facts and places wrong. Besides, I changed all the names. But, what the hell: essentially, this is all of it.

I wrote all this on ring binders in thirty-two motel rooms all across the country. That's because I live in motels. Hell, I really *like* motels and that ought to tell you a little bit about me before you start the book.

It may be too late for me to change now; I'm not sure. Oh, I can still be trotted right out in mixed company and all that — but I'm getting meaner and more closed-in. Right now I'm down to about one lady who will still have me, and she's a used lady. She is a nurse and she appears in Chapter 2.

She understands me and I've never admitted it to her until this very minute.

— Stroker Ace

STAND
ON
IT

one

oday I went out to qualify for the Indy 500. I did not make it. Definitely not. In fact, you might say that I made a hell of a mess out of it. For one thing, I came walking back into the pits carrying my goddam helmet in my hand, with the crowd giving me a lot of polite applause. The track announcer was saying something about ". . . tough luck, but a great display of bravery by the talented Stroker Ace." Bravery, my ass.

Remember now, the thing about a scene like this is that more than 250,000 people are watching you and I mean: watching your every move. A lot of photographers are taking your picture and at a time like this you must never show any emotion. *Never.* Never let anybody know that you are upset or that your stomach hurts — or that you are still so scared that your testicles have retracted up somewhere behind your goddam *breastbone.* None of that. In fact, you must look cool and professional and *pleasant,* for God's sake. And since the pits are full of spies, you have to talk very low so that nobody can overhear what you are saying.

First thing I got back to my pit, I mean the very *first* thing, my chief mechanic runs over and throws one big, hairy arm around my shoulder. He pats me on the back with the other hand, smiling widely at me. It is all very happy. He puts his big, smiling face right up next to mine and says, pleasantly, "What's the matter, prick, can't you *drive* that fucking car?"

I put my arms around him and hugged him and we stood there and chatted pleasantly for a few minutes, our heads together conspiratorially. I said: "Lissen, shithead, if you knew how to *set up* a car, I promise you I could drive that sumbitch." And he said, pleasantly, "It was set up perfect." And I said, pleasantly, "Bullshit it was set up perfect. You made the front suspension out of *toilet paper*, you lousy motherfucker, and you could hear it snap all the way to *Bloom*ington, for chrissakes."

And he smiled at me, because they were still taking our pictures, and he patted me on the shoulder again for the benefit of the cameramen and he whispered into my ear again, pleasantly, "Your ass. If you would go into the goddam turn *front*wards instead of ass-end-to, you would find that the suspension won't snap. Chrissakes, you would break the damn suspension in a *tank*, you cunt."

Now, then.

I have just given you, verbatim, the first exclusive report ever published on a real, actual pitside conference between driver and chief mechanic. Understand, while all this is going on, 500,000 eyes are looking at us (this is assuming that everybody at the track had two eyes, of course), and our every move is being recorded for history. People are crowded around looking at us: Everybody. And I am smiling and my chief mechanic is smiling and when I finally figure that I can pull it off without my hands shaking too hard, I get out a cigarette and light it up.

And here comes good old track announcer Chuck Mackey and his microphone.

"We're here at the pit of Stroker Ace," he says. "And while we have this brief break between qualifying runs — while they clean the wreckage off the track — let's talk now to Ace and his chief mechanic, Lugs Harvey. Hi, fellas."

We both smile pleasantly at good old Chuck.

"Tell us," says good old Chuck, "how do you feel right now, Stroker? Are you all right there?"

I nod and smile. "Fine. I'm *fine*," I say. I take a deep puff on the cigarette and swallow the smoke. Christ, my kneecaps are still shaking.

He turns to Lugs. "I'll bet you were really worried there for a minute about your boy, right, Lugs?"

And Lugs smiles broadly. "Golly, yes, Chuck," he says. "I sure was. Yessir, I was really worried there for a minute, uh-huh."

Now he turns to me. "Well, tell us: what exactly went wrong out there on the track, Stroker? You turned the first lap beautifully there. And then — well, what was it that went wrong?"

I smile. "Well," I say, "I hit the wall, for one thing."

"I'll *say* you did. Yessir. You certainly did hit that wall, and you certainly gave this splendid crowd here the thrill of their lives. And, naturally, they're all thrilled to see that you're all right ——"

"I'm all right," I say.

"Well, tell us, Stroker: what happened out there on the Number One Turn? Our spotter tells us that he thinks that the front suspension broke and threw you into a spin."

I shake my head no, smiling.

"Gosh, no, Chuck," I say. "No, no. The suspension is *perfect* and the car was set up beautiful. No, what happened was, I hit this oily spot there just going into the turn and then . . ."

"He hit this oily spot," Lugs says, smiling and nodding.

"Tough break. A tough, tough break. Tell us, Lugs, do you think you'll be able to fix the car in time to qualify it next weekend?"

Lugs nods, smiling fixedly.

"Oh, we'll sure try, Chuck," he says. "But it's not the *car* that counts. What really counts is that Stroker here is all right and safe after that awful, horrendous spin. He's a wonderful driver, as you know, and I sure was worried there."

"I know you were. Well, boys, better luck next time, as we always say in racing. And now, let's go back out on the track where . . ."

Lugs and I walk away, our arms around each other.

In the garage, we didn't speak. I yanked open the refrigerator door, got out a beer, and snatched the tabtop off it. I drank it all in almost one continuous swallow. Then I got out another beer for drinking more slowly and I started to pull off my clothes.

Lugs walked around for a few minutes, hands jammed into his back pockets, smoking his cigar. Finally he turned to me and said:

"You asshole."

"I don't want to talk about it."

"Chrissakes, I wish you had broken your goddam *head* out there and then maybe I could get me a-holt of a real driver."

"It ain't a driver you need. What you need is a course in elementary mechanics, is what you need. I *told* you the suspension was squirrelly. But, no. You ——"

"How's the car?"

"Car? The *car*? Lissen: I ended up sitting on my bare ass on the *track*, for God's sake. How's the car. Jesus Christ. There's not enough left of that car to put into a gunnysack."

He shrugged. "Well . . . uhhh. You, well, are you all right? I mean, you know. Really?"

"Oh, yeah, I suppose so. I mean, my pucker-string is yanked up so tight I won't be able to take a crap for a week. But I suppose I'm all ——"

"The fire burn you any?"

"No, not really. I had that goddam harness unsnapped just

about the time I first got *side*ways. Man, I could smell fire even before I hit the wall. You know how I am about fire."

He nodded. "Yeah, I know. And me, too. Well —— "

"Lissen: I'm sorry about all that —— "

"Me, too. Sorry. And, well, I figure that maybe that suspension really did —— "

"Forget it."

"Okay. Well, maybe next week. Lissen: what you gonna do, well, you know: now?"

"I'm going to go and get drunk and I'm going to get laid, in that order."

"Mmm, Shirley?"

"You mean Miss Firepants, Queen of All Racing? Well, I guess so. I mean, I'm not in much of a mood to go scrounging around for broads tonight. And Shirley is always, well, you know. She's always *there*."

"Lissen: does that friend of hers —— "

"They *all* do, for chrissakes. You want to come on along?"

He sort of nodded, wiping his hands on a rag. "Well, you know. Sure. I, uhhh —— "

"Come *on*. A little piece of tail will do you some good."

"Well, but what if her friend, uhhh, whatsername . . . I mean: what if she doesn't —— "

"Hell with her. I mean: if she does, well, fine. And if she doesn't, well, we can all screw Shirley."

"Both us?"

"Both of us? For chrissakes, both of *us* and the whole goddamned Firestone tire crew and maybe even Grandstand B, for God's sake."

"Well . . ."

"Besides, maybe you'll even learn something."

"Like what?"

"Well," I said, "for one thing, you ain't never, ever in your life seen a suspension system until you've seen old Shirley in action. Now, I mean: *there* is a girl who can go the full five hundred miles, I promise you."

"Really holds the old road on a tight turn, huh?"

"Uh-huh," I said. "And you can hear the rubber burn. Now, let's get the hell out of here."

Still, I dreamed about it that night. I always do.

I suppose we looked like a goddam tableau in an X movie.

I mean: I was lying there on the bed, all sort of splayed out, with a Speedway Motel towel draped across my stomach, staring up at the ceiling, and the bed looked like crocodiles had been mating in it.

Lugs and Shirley were over in the other bed: Lugs face up, naked, sound asleep, still holding a can of beer locked in one hand and a cigar stub in the other. Shirley was all curled up on her side, naked except for the knee-high white vinyl boots with real high heels. Shirley hardly ever takes off her vinyl boots. I suppose I ought to ask her about that some time.

Shirley's sequined, sparkly Miss Fire Injection costume was draped over the television set. The tail was hanging down on the floor.

The television was still on. No picture; just a test pattern and a hum.

The top of the dresser was full of beer cans.

In the bathroom, Charlie Heffer, the Goodyear tire buster, was sleeping in the tub. He had yanked the shower curtain down and had wrapped himself up in it to keep warm.

Heffer had arrived at, oh, about five o'clock after the fights down at the White Front on Sixteenth Street and he had all the skin scraped off both sets of knuckles and a pretty decent cut just behind his left ear. And he had done what he usually does: he had gone from door to door at the Speedway Motel, knocking until somebody let him in.

Charlie Heffer never gets a motel room of his own.

He had said, simply, " 'Lo, Shirley, 'lo, Lugs, 'lo, Stroker," and walked right past us and tore down the shower curtain and got in the tub. He also ripped the curtain rod right out of the wall doing it.

Altogether, a routine night.

And I lay there, waiting for sleep.

And I dreamed about the crash.

What they ought to do with the Indy 500, what they really ought to do, is take the whole goddam thing and hang it from the ceiling of the Smithsonian Institution in Washington. Maybe right up there with the *Spirit of St. Louis*, for God's sake. Dick Gail, a guy from Champion Spark Plugs, a guy who reads a lot and stuff like that, says that the Indy 500 is "Grant Wood at speed." He even suggested that somebody enter an American Gothic Racing Team.

Understand, I am all for Americana and all that bullshit, just like the next guy. But The Race has become so big, so full of awful pressures, that nobody is *sane* around here any more. Boy, it's not racing any more the way we used to. Those guys are out of their damn *heads*.

The race is something else.

But just to qualify — just to get *into* the race — you got to wheel four laps around that old track, balls-out, in a tricked-up, fragile-ass racecar that weighs maybe fifteen hundred pounds or so. Faster you drive, farther up on the starting grid you go.

Remember, that mother track was designed for a top speed of maybe 95 miles an hour in 1911 and here we are, going 195–200 on the thing.

I had been turning 190's in practice and, except for the front suspension, the car felt fine. So when I rolled out there in front of everybody to go for it, we all felt pretty confident.

Driving at speed is one of the great, all-time sensations in the world: it tightens up your gut and all your reflexes are at their absolute best and you are all sensitive. You can feel everything, hear everything clearer than before. The grandstands on both sides of the track are like a tunnel, a long blur going by. Inside the car, inside my helmet and my Nomex coveralls and inside the safety harness, I can hear *every*thing. Christ, I can hear the gears meshing into place with that distinctive "chink" and I can hear the rocker arms flexing and the tires wearing.

First lap: 189.4 miles an hour and I came off the Fourth Turn pretty much straightened out and right up alongside the outside wall where I was supposed to be. I hammered up the speed.

I have great peripheral vision.

I mention this only because one of the big things about qualifying is that you know that every other driver in the place is out there watching you. They stand there along pit row, one foot propped up on that little cement wall, and they watch your every move. In the actual race, they are all out there on the track with you and it isn't so bad. But in qualifying, you *know* they are watching you like a bunch of critics. And I can see them flash by. Rufus Smith, because I know where he likes to stand, usually, and because he is wearing a red Firestone jacket. My pit crew — because our sponsor this year has put us in purple. Purple, for chrissakes. But they're all watching and they are all holding their stopwatches.

All right, then, you critics. Watch this one.

I got the car all set up for the first turn. Right at the end of the pit wall, I eased back off the throttle and I muscled the steering wheel over to the left. The nose came around until I had a good line on the inside of the track and I could sight along the nose cone and see exactly where I wanted to go. Fine.

Then I hit the gas again, hard — and yanked the wheel back around to the right. And right away I was up to my goddam armpits in torque, man. I mean: all sorts of crazy engineering and physical forces were at work, pulling at the car, and my heart moved all the way over to the right side of my rib cage.

The front wheels are actually sliding now and not really biting at the track that much. And the rear end starts to come around a little bit and now the car is aimed pretty much where I want it to go. But it is still just a teensy bit sideways or caterwompus, if you follow me.

So I crank the wheel back left again and now I really get back on the gas pedal and all sorts of wonderful fucking things start happening to the engine. It suddenly has a hell of a lot more power going into it than it can use at just this second, and the goddam thing is just sitting there howling behind my head.

Then I wait. This is the longest moment in sports.

Sure enough, the push of the engine finally overcomes the torque and, suddenly, the car stops sliding and those rear wheels really grab. And — zing — I am halfway through the first turn, slightly off the gas again and going to beat hell.

A great goddam sensation and I love it.

Down the backstretch, which is where I let it run to pick up more time. Through Turns Three and Four, knowing that there is a little hump in the track coming out of the Number Four Turn where I will get all four wheels off the ground for just a split second there.

Down past the critics again. Satisfied that they know that I have got it all hung out.

Around again. All warmed up. I'm up into the high 190's.

This time I take my left hand off the wheel and hold it up, which means that I am ready and go ahead, you guys, put me on the official clocks.

And then it happened.

Too much oversteer. I get that son of a bitch cranked beautifully into the First Turn and — right now — I know that I have miscalculated. Understand now, a racecar does not forgive anybody. No-*body*. And the minute I rammed back down on the gas, I knew I was gone.

Sure enough, the rear wheels kept sliding and I knew God Damned Well that the car was going to come around on me.

There are three things you can do: crank the wheels right again, get the hell off that gas, and then resist any temptation to hit the brakes. Hope that you will whip around just once and then try to get on the gas just at the end of the spin — so that maybe you can come out of it.

You almost never do.

The car snapped around so fast that my eyes went blurry. Then it came around again and I knew I was going to hit the wall.

Then the suspension snapped. *Crack.*

Somebody, some radio announcer, once asked old Lee Roy Harber exactly what thoughts ran through his mind at a moment like that. There he was, spinning helplessly at top speed. Did his whole life flash before his eyes? Did he think of his mother, maybe? A flash image of a nice, gray-haired lady in an apron there at the kitchen door, perhaps just a little dab of flour at the tip of her nose? Did his mind go blank?

"No," Lee Roy said.

"Well, then. What did you say to yourself?"

"I said," Lee Roy said, " 'Oh, shit.' "

Exactly. I said: Oh, shit. And hunkered my head down.

There are four ways you can hit a wall, none of them any good. Worst way is to hit ass-on, because that usually puts the engine right into the bucket seat with you. Head-on is next worst. A side-shot is not good, but it is a whole lot better than the other alternatives.

SLAM! I hit that motherless wall and came back off it. The explosion of it made my head pop and knocked it up against the cowling, slicing one hell of a jagged cut just along the rim of my purple helmet. Half-inch lower and it would have knifed the top of my head right off.

Pieces flew away: I hit sideways and both right wheels popped free, bouncing high up into the stands, and I had a flash-image of spectators scrambling away. Well, screw the spectators. The whole right side of the car tore loose and went skittering down onto the track behind me. Then both the left wheels caved inward and the air was full of flying chunks of purple fiber glass and, all at once, I was down to the bare frame. The damned force of it all had stuck my hands to the steering wheel, but, finally, I lifted one thumb and hit the toggle switch to cut the engine.

They tell me that I spun around four times. Well, why not? I had been rolling at maybe 198 miles an hour, for God's sake. It was about on the third spin that the car started to burn.

I am afraid of fire. All drivers are afraid of fire.

Man, I had my harness loose after hitting the release so hard with the butt of my hand that I practically broke open my abdomen. The front cowling was down to where it was pinching my legs, so I rolled over on one hip and yanked them free. Then I just sort of threw myself out on the track and rolled over a few times, my hands up over my face.

And then I got up and patted out the little pieces of fire that were attached to my uniform.

And I sort of staggered down to the edge of the infield, trying to catch my breath.

Finally, I turned and looked back at the car.

Oh, shit.

two

That was last week. And several thousand dollars ago.

I did three things today. I qualified for the race in the backup car: new engine and turbocharger — with those exhaust pipes curled up there on top like steel spaghetti — new wheels and new everything front to back. We finished balancing that rascal on Friday and the fresh purple and gold paint was still half-wet when we rolled it out on Saturday and fired it up. Chrissakes, the sound of it made the cement pit walls ripple.

Two warm-up laps and then I cocked that bugger halfway left and then locked up my knee bone and held it that way for ten miles. I was rolling 181 the first time around and the car was just starting to gather itself up. And I came rolling in at 192 — enough to bump my way right up into the ninth row. I'm in the middle; there are twenty-five cars sitting ahead of me, and only six behind. Come race day I won't be able to see anything but big rear tail pipes and ass-ends and I'll be looking right into air that is all wavy and cloudy from exhausts. Well, that's just for the *pace* lap. Just about the time that flag goes down at the front of the pack I'm going to swing it out and point it upstream and a lot of the rookies back here with me are going to wish the hell they were somewhere up in the stands.

The second thing I did today was to go to the track doctor for my final pre-race physical.

"You are in excellent shape," he said. "Excellent. Bruises all healed from the crash; fine blood pressure, good reflexes. Marvelous muscle tone. Yes. I'd say you were in superb condition. Except, of course, for the clap."

Sometimes I wish that Shirley had maybe taken up school-teaching or library science or something like that instead of being a trophy queen.

"That's nothing," Lugs told me. "You remember when I got that dose down in Daytona? Well, I snuck into this drugstore downtown, see, and there was a lot of people in there and I was sort of embarrassed. So I kind of sidled up to the, uhhh, what do you call those guys? Uhh, the pharmacist, and I say to him: 'Lissen, what do I do for the clap?' "

"Uh-huh. What did he say?"

"Well, he sort of drew back and he held out both hands and he said to me: 'Well, first of all, don't touch anything.' "

Well, they tell this story about Bo Bo Findlay, who is both a good driver and a bad-ass. He drives stock cars.

Old Bo Bo flies his own plane and he had been down at Mexico City for some race, I don't know, and he flew back and landed at this little Texas border station to check in.

"Bring anything back with you?" asked the customs man.

"Christ, I hope not," says Bo Bo.

And the third thing I did today was this: I met a nurse. It was not exactly my Finest Hour.

Well, you got to understand that it is very hard to score any points with your whole ass hanging out; that is probably a pretty standard rule anywhere in life.

"Better unzip and drop your pants," the doctor had said,

"and I'll have my nurse give you a shot. One shot will take the edge off; two will cure you completely. I don't suppose you'd care to tell me where you picked this up."

"Probably off of a toilet seat in Gasoline Alley," I said.

He nodded. "You're the third driver who has told me that this week. Plus one mechanic and six members of the Firestone tire crew."

"I use Goodyear," I said.

"You mean the tires, not the condoms. All right, let's get on with it. God, I'll sure be glad when race day comes — all I get *then* is broken heads and bones."

I unzipped my driving uniform and shrugged off the arms and let the thing fall down around my ankles. And then I tugged down my fireproof Nomex longjohn underwear and sort of stood there, looking back over my shoulder, with no place to put my hands.

And fell in love. With everything hanging out. I do this a lot.

She was filling the needle, with the tip of it stuck up into this little bottle, making bubbles. And then she pulled it out and pushed on the plunger part until a little squirt of penicillin came jazzing out. "Now, then," she said.

"Hi, there," I said. "I'm Stroker Ace."

"I *know* who you are," she said. "I saw you qualify today. But I'm afraid that's not going to help you now. Would you bend over just a little, please?"

"Is this going to hurt?"

"I certainly hope so."

She was big for a girl, almost as big as I am, and her skin was tawny-colored, the same color as, mmmmm, Stuckey's coconut-honey-almond spread. She had very black hair, so black that it glistened, and it was parted in the middle and gathered up in a sort of bun-thing in back, with this dumb little nurse cap perched up on top and held there by a couple of hairpins.

"What's your name?" I said.

She was dabbing at the right cheek of my fanny with the cotton dipped in alcohol. "Polinos," she said. "Nurse Polinos. That's a Greek name, which is certainly appropriate, since I happen to be Greek. I am twenty-seven years old and, yes, I like racing and, no, I do not date race drivers. Now, are you going to bend over or not?"

"You're really pretty," I said. "I mean, really . . . Uuuugh! God *damn*, lady!"

"There," she said. "Now, what were you saying?"

She was all willowy, crinkly starched white on the outside, and when she moved, she *rustled*. But inside all of it, maybe just one layer down: she was all soft and creamy tan. And her bosoms came out independently: one on *this* side and one on *this* side, both of them straining hugely at the buttons in the middle — and after the great outcropping of breast she sloped down to a little waist and then began to swell out again into hips and long legs. I mean: long legs.

"The very minute you're through standing there looking at me," she said, "you may feel free to pull up your pants."

Uhhh, pants. "Where are you from?" I said. Jesus, I was really full of great lines like that. But what the hell.

She was disassembling the needle. "I'm from the hospital in Terre Haute. On loan down here for the race; we do this every year. It's really very exciting. I saw you when you won the race and you scared me half to death. You're really very reckless —— "

"The word is *good*."

"All right, then: you're really very good. And I saw you crash trying to qualify last week. I wasn't on duty when they brought you over for the checkup, but I'm glad you weren't hurt. Well, you may go now. We'll see you next shot."

I finished zipping up my driving suit. This is really a better view of me.

And we stood there and looked at each other a lot, memorizing.

She had brown eyes and sort of heavy, wolf-girl eyebrows. Full, pouty lower lip like a tiny, warm pillow. I wanted to reach over and touch it with a fingertip; maybe pull it down a little and look inside it.

"Be careful out there," she said.

"Can't win races being careful," I said.

"I mean *off* the track."

So much for falling in love.

Back to the damn racecar.

This week we're trying to pump maybe another twenty-five horses into the backup car before the race. Lugs is grouchy.

I feel fine. I sleep late in the mornings and then I drive over here and sit around on top of the workbench and drink beer. Now and then I give Lugs a bit of advice on timing the engine or something. Lugs does not take this very well.

Shelley Hansen just stuck his head in the door to see how we are doing. Shelley is a great help to Lugs in his Hour of Need.

"Can't you get that shitpot put together?" Shelley asks.

Shelley Hansen is a sponsor; owns two racecars and campaigns them on the circuit. Well, mostly he owns a string of hamburger stands around the Midwest and he has an awful lot of money and he is a racing nut. The only reason he sponsors racecars is so that he can get an owner's credential to come into Gasoline Alley and wander around and kick tires and talk to the guys. He loves to wear that racing jacket — it has his name embroidered in white script across the top front pocket and it has SHELLEYBURGERS in big red letters across the back of the shoulders. Wearing that jacket is costing old Shelley hundreds of thousands, but it's his thing.

Lugs half-straightens over the car, wiping his hands on an oily rag.

"Even now," says Lugs, "even *now*, in this shape, my car will run better than that goddam tractor of yours." Then Lugs turns to me: I am sitting on the counter top, cross-legged, with my note pad in my lap.

"Hide the fucking dogs," Lugs says, "the goddam hamburger man is here."

"Come on," Shelley says, looking hurt. "I put only the finest ground beef in my —— "

"What are you calling your car this year?" says Lugs. "The Ptomaine Flyer?"

Hansen nodded at us. "I would like to point out to you, *gentlemen,* that we qualified ahead of you clowns."

"Is that what you came here to tell me?" Lugs said.

"Well, no. What I came here to tell you was to come around my garage after work tonight. We're going to show some training films."

(You might as well face this right now. Training films is Gasoline Alley code for dirty movies. Pictures of folks copulating and kissing each other between the legs and a lot of other interesting things like that.

(Lissen: Shelley Hansen sponsors a racecar just so he can show dirty movies in some lousy garage at night and stand around with a bunch of mechanics, swearing and spitting on the floor and drinking beer and commenting on the movies. The most common comment is: "Will ya *look* at that guy there? I mean, just look, he can't even get it *up*, for chrissakes."

(Shelley does this for his manhood.)

They had the big balloon show today. Whoopee.

It's all part of the hoopla to promote the race; I don't know, the Friends of Hot Air Ballooning talked the track into it, I guess.

Anyway, the idea was, they were going to take off a bunch of these big-mother balloons from the track and fly them somewhere. Lot of people came to see the show. Even me.

I was standing there with Joe Floyd, who is the safety director of the track. Floyd wears a vest made out of a checkered flag and he is even funnier than that at times.

Along comes Julene Meyers, who is Miss Panther Valve this year. She gets to wear this nifty panther costume for her sponsor and she rides in the parade and waves at everybody. You know: black net stockings and the long panther tail. And a little panther cap with ears.

"Julene's going to ride in one of the balloons," Floyd says.

Ballooning is not Julene's specialty, I will confess. She *does* have a specialty, though, which she performs in the backs of cars, in motel rooms, in tire trucks. Everywhere.

Floyd nodded. "Yessir," he said. "This is pretty historic. You realize that if she gets into that balloon it will be the first time in her life she ever went *up* on anything."

The best part was where one of the balloons got away.

If I understand this correctly, they didn't get enough hot air up into the big bag. A sudden gust of wind caught the thing as it was filling up and — away it went.

The thing sort of dragged the basket through the bushes and over the fence and there it went, kind of bouncing and half-flying across the infield.

Headed right for the outdoor toilets.

"No," Floyd said. "No. Not that."

Ah, yes. The thing swung right over the outdoor johns and some of the guidelines hanging down caught the toilet roof and — swoosh! — pulled that old outhouse right over on its side.

There was a woman sitting in there, all peaceful, when it

happened. They tell me that it broke her arm and I'm sorry about that part.

My rating on those training films: Two Stars. Goodnight to you from Hollywood.

The post-movie crowd went down to the White Front on Sixteenth Street for a few shooters.

"Look," Lugs had said, "is it all right with you if I leave before the fighting starts tonight? I got a lot to do on the car tomorrow, all right?"

"Fine with me," I said, "but, you know, you can always sit there and *watch*, for chrissakes. You ever think of that?"

"Watch what?"

"Watch the *fights*. Just sit right there with that bottle of beer in your hand and don't get involved. You don't have to hit anybody."

Lugs nodded thoughtfully. "You're right," he said. "You know, you're absolutely right. But look at it this way: I'm working all day on that fucking machine. All *day*. And I can't get the goddam timing to sound just right. Which means that I got to tear it down again tomorrow and retrace all my steps. And I go over and magnaflux a few valves and I discover that this whole shipment — every motherless valve — has a little, teensy crack in the stem. Right? And so now I got to pull those out, too. And then: and *then,* I am relaxing over a nice, quiet beer in the evening with my old pal, Stroker Ace, right? Are you with me? And some son of a bitch at the table next to me hauls off and hits some son of a bitch at the table next to *him*, right?"

"You're right so far."

"Well, then. I mean, look, Ace, don't you follow me? What the hell is a matter with you, you dumb bastard? I mean, *that* is when I jump right out of my chair, see, and I haul this son of a bitch around by the back of his collar and I smash him one in the mouth. Blam! There! 'That's for the fucking valves,' I say. And then his buddy leaps up with murder in his eye and I hit him so hard with the butt of my other hand that the *floor* cracks. Blam! 'That's for the goddam lousy timing,' I say. Now, you understand?"

I nodded. In fact, I *do* understand.

It got pretty frisky, as always.

Bobby Blaney had come in with his gang of guys, plus Jim Luck who works for Firestone. Every single last one of them a very fine fellow. A credit to racing, as we always say. Yessir.

Bobby strolled outside for a moment or two and he got to looking at the four headlights on Luck's company station wagon. And you know how those things go. So he picked up a piece of two-by-four from the parking lot and went: Bash! Bash! Bash! Bash! All four headlights.

Pretty soon Jim strolled out to drive the crew back to the motel. He climbed in, started the engine and turned on the lights. Or so he thought. Bobby piled into the front seat beside him. And Jim looked over at him, blinking.

"Those lights look all right to you?" he said.

"Just a second," Bobby said. He got out of the car and walked around to the front. "Okay," he said. "Hit the brights. Now the dims. Uh-huh." He walked back and got in. "Looks fine to me," he said.

So Jim slammed the wagon into gear and drove right into a parked car.

Beware of Sunday in Indianapolis.

In the Speedway Motel, most every bathtub is filled with ice from the ice machine and beer to get everybody through the day when you can't buy any. After all, you can always take a bath or a shower some other time, right?

And here is Bill Newkirk, who is a public relations man for Goodyear. He has the big Goodyear truck out there in the parking lot behind the motel and he has a couple of cases of beer on ice because it is Sunday and he is *entertaining*.

"You will find," Bill is saying, "that auto racers are among this country's finest citizens. Good citizens. Away from the track they drive sensibly, certainly sanely. They rarely go over the speed limit."

You got that? Now, standing there listening to this, sipping thoughtfully and delicately at their cans of contraband beer, are several top-level executives from Chrysler. They have all come all the way to Indianapolis to rub shoulders with real, live race drivers, and they are all impressed with the fact that racers are such fine citizens.

And at that precise moment:

A new Ford station wagon comes screaming around the corner of the motel driveway about, oh, say, five hundred yards away. It is going full blast — howling along — and it is completely sideways. It is in a full, skidding, drifting, screaming slide. Everybody flinches.

The wagon whips around twice and then spins — perfectly — into a parking space beside the big truck. The door opens and the driver steps out and smiles at everybody there. A really fine smile.

"I just blew off some goddam cop and then chopped his ass off right out there on Sixteenth Street," he said.

It was Tony Hoyle. Race driver and Citizen.

three

Today the suspension did not break. What happened was that everything else broke.

I lost the Indianapolis 500 Mile Sweepstakes today, the goddam Memorial Day Classic. At, oh, say, about 265 miles.

That lousy fucking SHELLEYBURGER SPECIAL got sideways right in front of me coming out of the Number Two Turn and I drove right through him. Right up the middle.

I led the race at the time. Naturally.

Just before we had fired up the car, we were going through that part where everybody — drivers and crews and all the fans — all stand for a minute of silence to honor those racers who have been killed here. It can be a pretty chilling thing if you let it be — I always use the time to stuff the cotton balls into my ears. And then I pull on my driving gloves and buckle them and then punch them hard between the fingers to get them tight.

I do not bow my head for the ceremony. If they're dead, they're dead.

During the Minute of Silence, Lugs edged over to me and talked out of the side of his mouth:

"Now, lissen," he said. "You gotta lot of guys ahead of you and they're a bunch of humpties and they'll be all over the track. So you gotta start slow. Remember, this car is hotter than anything else way back here. You step on it too hard and it'll snap yer head right off, I promise you. So let 'em thin out a little bit and *then* you make your move. All right?"

Lugs Strategist. I nodded at his sage instructions.

"My ass," I said.

Then we had touched it off and the whole field rolled away, with all the fans standing and yelling their heads off.

Pace Lap: I shook it a few times real good to check out the steering. It shook fine.

First Lap: I came off the Number Four Turn and sighted down the line and I could see the race starter jump up and come down with the green flag. I glanced left to where Joey Harkner was just ambling along beside me like a Very Good Rookie.

And then I cranked it over and chopped him off and stood on it in one move — and that sumbitch snapped me back, as promised. And I came firing right down alongside the inside wall, with cars flickering past on my right, all over the track.

Second Lap: off the Number Four Turn again. In fifth place.

Third Lap: off the Number Four Turn again. Leading the race.

I hung it sideways and hung on. At this rate, it was going to be a short, short day.

Understand, now: every single time I came rolling around that motherless track I was piling up Lap Money. The sponsors pay off on lap leaders: I would go howling down the main chute and glance over at Lugs and the scoring pole and mentally tick off another $1,000 or $1,500. Click, click, click.

Once around again and off the Four Turn in heavy traffic, feeling quietly cool inside and chewing away at my gum to keep my mouth moist. The engine was running like heavy cream and purring fatly; for the past several laps I had been stroking it. I had everybody locked. The tires were holding up just right and, occasionally, on the backstretch, I would lean my head back and look up at the sky. And I would crank through another brace of turns and I would think to myself. What I would think to myself was: shit man, this is *racing*.

I ran it right down the groove — perfect — and I glanced sideways over at the pits. Lugs was out there with the chalkboard, crouched down by the wall. He had scrawled on it, in big, smudged white letters:

FEUL?

That dumb son of a bitch. Can't even spell *fuel* right. Ahh, but a hell of a mechanic.

Next time around he had a chalk mark drawn like this:

F/E(U/L ?

Well, hell. Maybe our literate sponsor had gotten to him or something like that. Anyway, I reached down with one hand and switched tanks and got into the Number One and Number Two Turns.

Suddenly: I had a whole lapful of front axle and purple nose cone and radiator and oil and my goddam knees were jackknifed up double under my chin — and I was spinning into the infield with the SHELLEYBURGER SPECIAL hooked on to the front end of my car like it had been welded there. Just like that.

Grover Brampson was pinned inside his car and so was I — but there is not a car that has yet been built that can hold me when there is a chance of it catching on fire. So I climbed out, spewing pieces and chunks on all sides — and I ran over and unhooked Brampson and got one hand under each one of his wet armpits and snaked him up out of there and stood him up. I would have hit him right in the fucking mouth, too, except that he looked already half-dingy and his eyes were way back up inside his head. So I shook him around a lot instead, holding him under the arms.

His eyes finally came back down and he blinked. There was foam coming out around the edges of his mouth.

"I got sideways," he said.

"You prick," I told him. "Couldn't you *see* me behind you? I been on your ass two goddam laps now, trying to get around you. Why didn't you move that son of a bitch *over* and get the fuck out of my way. I'm going to kill you, you little bastard."

"I got sideways," he said.

"Lissen," I yelled at him. "I am LEADING the race. You understand? You're running about *fifteenth,* for God's sake. I already lapped everybody on the whole track a million times, except you."

"I got sideways," he said.

Oh, shit. Forget it.

Same thing with old Tad Hooper. I mean, Hooper is one hell of a steady driver. With me out of the race, he slipped right into the lead.

Man, he was smoking them off.

And something happened: the car came off the corner, all stars and stripes, and it suddenly gave out this beautiful little puffy smudge of black smoke and a tiny belch of fire from the tail pipes behind his head. He shut it down right away and coasted into the pits. And he pulled off his helmet and got out and then he sat there on one of the tires, drinking a Pepsi and staring down at the asphalt.

And up trots Jim Wilson of WISH-TV and he ought to know better right now. But he had been wearing his little earplug and someone had told him to go and get Tad on the air.

Well, Jim Wilson and everybody else in communications has been trying to bring Hooper out for years and it is always the same: Tad just doesn't have a whole lot to say to the press. He likes them, all right, and they love him. But Hooper is what they call taciturn.

Here comes the great interview:

JIM: Tad, we're sorry to see you out of the race. We know that there are many mechanical problems that can force a car out of the race and, since most of the fans are interested in just what would take a car out of such an important race as this one, I know they would all appreciate hearing in your own words just what it was that made you quit.

HOOPER: Engine.

I left the new purple driving suits hanging on the nails in the garage. The other gear I stuffed into the flight bag: dirty Nomex longjohns and socks, the driving shoes I have made in Italy for ninety-five bucks a pair. Some kerchiefs. My regular Bell helmet. The purple helmet they could shove up their asses: I left it on top of the workbench.

"What do you figure?" Lugs said. He was already in his traveling clothes: his Levi's and his hand-tooled cowboy boots and his monster goddam pure solid silver–inlaid belt buckle made in the shape of a midget racecar.

That belt buckle has to run maybe four or five pounds: it has two big rubies in it, one in the exact center of each little wheel on the midget racecar, and the driver's eye is a real chip-diamond. One night at the Mexican Grand Prix, Lugs had been caught in the wrong section of town after dark — right there in a circle of some extremely mean-looking Mexicans. This can happen in the wrong end of any town, which is exactly out by the racetrack, by the way.

The Mexicans had a plan. They were going to (1) kick the

living shit out of Lugs, and (2) get his boots and belt buckle. So old Lugs had whipped off the belt — he does this very fast — and he had wrapped the far end of it around his knuckles a few times and then he had started swinging the buckle around his head. "Pretty soon I was up to my ass in upside-down Messkins," he had said, "and all of them rascals was bleeding from the ears, by God."

Old Lugs could swing that belt buckle and make his way out through a cinder-block wall.

Anyway: "What do you figure?" he said.

"I don't know," I said. "I got the fifty thousand for driving. And maybe I've got twenty-five hundred or so left from the expense money — except that I haven't paid the Speedway Motel yet for all the damages. The shower and the kicked-in television set and whoever it was that threw that easy chair through the front window last night."

"Charlie Heffer," Lugs said. "And it ain't so much throwing the chair out your window. It was just that Joe Crawford was sittin' in the chair at the time."

"Is he all right?"

Lugs shrugged. "Oh, maybe a twelve-stitcher is all. Would have been worse, I suppose, but he was wearing his helmet and —— "

"Now what in hell was he wearing his *helmet* for?"

". . . well, because it matched Shirley's boots, I think was the reason. He was wearing *them,* too. Couldn't get 'em zippered up properly, though."

"I thought Shirley never took her boots off."

"She took 'em off last night. In honor of the race being over and all." He belched, gently. "I drank one of them full of beer. It's okay; I put it on your bill."

"Wonderful. You're going to get clap of the adenoids or something like that, for chrissakes."

"Naw. None of that stuff. We wasn't intimate."

"*In*-timate? *Intimate?* What the hell kind of talk is that?"

He belched again. "I know all the big words, buddy. You think I'm just another pretty mechanic or something? Like I said: we was not *intimate*. Well, not like you think. Oh, maybe a few unnatural acts. But ——— "

". . . but not intimate. Look: don't tell me any more, all right? Now, where was I?"

"The money."

"Mmmmm. Well, let's see. I got the fee and the tire money, of course, and the gas money and . . . uhh, by the way: How do you spell *fuel?*"

"*F* . . . uhh, look: don't dog me around, Ace. You knew what I was talking about. And besides, you never lasted another lap anyway before that asshole cut you off. Besides, fuel is spelled *G A S*."

"Why didn't you say so?"

"Well, there was all those folks in the stands. You know."

"Mmm. Anyway, I got that money and what's our lap money come to? Twenty-five hundred each, I guess, right?"

"Right."

I shrugged. "All right, then. I'm close to sixty-five thousand dollars, give or take an easy chair or two. How about you?"

He bent over and picked up his bag. "Well, I sure got enough to maybe run the speed shop for another year or two back home, and that's if I never get another customer. And, uhhh, well, lissen: I mean, you know. If you figure you need me *any* time, just let me know. I can drop everything and come any time, you know."

"I know. And I appreciate it."

"Any time."

It is always an awkward moment. We both looked around at the empty garage, our bags in our hands. Naked ladies pinned to the wall, the beat-up old Kelvinator refrigerator. The emptied tool benches.

Lugs began clomping out.

"You want a beer?" he said.

I kicked the door shut behind me. "Maybe just one. I've got a four fifty-five flight out of here. Got to go and do my act on television in Los Angeles. But, you know. Maybe just one for the goddam road, right?"

"You mean Hollywood?" He shook his head. "I bet you get laid out there a whole lot. I understand them television folks screw anything that moves."

"Well, now, look, Lugs: just how in hell could they screw any more than they do right here in Indianapolis, for God's sake?"

"It's just that they're prettier out there."

She was waiting over by the tall mesh fence, the one that keeps the fans from eating the drivers alive.

Everybody, all the racers, check out the fence — just to see what the action is. But I would have known that chestline anyplace, in any crowd of ladies.

"Good afternoon," she said. And then I think maybe she blushed. God, I don't know; I haven't seen a girl blush since the year of the blue snow.

"Nurse . . ."

"Polinos," she said. "I'm the one with the needle."

"I didn't think you'd recognize me with my pants up," I said.

She blinked a few times. "Speaking of that sort of thing," she said, "how are you feeling now?"

"I'm cured, if that's what you mean. And I'll never do it again, honest. To anybody."

"I'm sorry about the, well, about the crash."

"That son of a bitch," I said.

". . . but I'm glad you got out alive."

"Uh-huh. Right. Swell. *Alive.* That's the one bright spot in my whole fucking day. That makes me feel good all over."

"Don't be so bitter."

So we looked at each other some more. All over.

"You sure have got a great lower lip," I said.

She nodded, accepting that. "So have you," she said.

Good old suave Stroker Ace. Old Continental. Really smooth: "And you have got maybe the greatest chest I have ever seen anyplace, anytime, anywhere," I said.

"Mmmmm hmmm. You're very direct."

"Look," I said. "Are you *sure* you don't date race drivers?"

"Yes, I'm sure. And if I hadn't been sure a few minutes ago, I'm positive now. Stroker, is that all you ever . . ."

"Yes," I said. "That's all I ever think about. Cars and breasts. Those three things."

It took a little while but then, finally, she smiled just a bit. "All right, it doesn't matter. I've got to go now. I just wanted to come over here and tell you that I was sorry about the crash. I worry about you."

"Why me, for chrissakes?"

She pooched out the lower lip just a little. "Oh, I don't know, really. Some sort of crush, perhaps; it isn't really important. Some girls worry about Paul Newman, I imagine."

"Well, why don't you worry about him? He's a whole lot prettier than me."

"Not all that much."

"You know," I said, "you're absolutely right. Are you really SURE you don't . . . I mean, you wouldn't like to —— "

"No," she said.

"Well, then. When will I see you again?"

She shrugged. "Mmmm, I don't know. Indy next year. The medical tent in the infield."

"Look: I don't have to get another dose or anything like that, do I?"

"I would certainly rather you didn't."

"Uh-huh. Is *that* why you won't go out with me?"

She shook her head back and forth. "No, not at all. It's just that I would rather keep our relationship on this level. Right now, I know you just about as well as I'd care too; that is, considering your life-style. Look: none of this is important. I'll see you next year, all right?"

"Fine. Next year."

And we looked at each other some more. Any closer to the goddam fence and I was going to have a nonskid tread imprinted on my belly.

And then she swung and walked away and I looked through the chain grid at the gentle, easy swing of hips.

"What the hell is a matter with you?" Lugs said. "Ain't you ever seen an ass before? Now, come on. Are we gonna get that beer or ain't we?"

four

Fact of life: southern stock car drivers are mean bastards and they have dirt under their fingernails and chickenshit on the bottoms of their boots. The backs of their necks are red. They race all day and drink all night and screw a little on the side. Plus a lot of interpretive fighting with tire irons. It's their form of ballet.

We had flown down to Daytona to test tires for Goodyear.

The idea behind all this is to rent the empty racetrack and then go charging around it at top speed in racing stock cars to find out what rubber compound and which tread pattern is the best combination for that particular track. And then they announce that Goodyear wins races and you ought to buy Goodyear tires and drive around a hell of a lot safer. You follow me?

I was sitting on the pit wall, stopwatch hanging around my neck and wearing a pair of brand-new alligator boots and watching Joe-Jack Bradley barrel his big damn Mercury around the place. Joe-Jack was a dynamite driver and he was really hanging it out every time he came around. But then, zinging past, he stuck one bare arm out the window and gave his me-

chanic the finger as he came by and — after that — he smoked
it right into the pits sideways to a stop.

He climbed out the window and tugged off his helmet; the
sweat was beaded up in little globs on his oily face.

And there was one of those pleasant conversations we always
hear at trackside:

"Car's not set up right for the tires," Joe-Jack said.

"Shit it ain't," said the mechanic. "It's set up perfect."

"Then you go drive that sumbitch. I'll tell you it ain't set up
no way perfect."

None of that routine for me. I was an outsider, the new hot
rock imported from Indy to run at Daytona. They figured that,
since I didn't know all that much about this track, I could give
them an objective report on how a tire should perform there.

I went over to the beer cooler that one of the college-
educated tire designers had thoughtfully provided, and I
opened a beer and sat down on the grass and stretched out
my legs.

"I don't know the track," I said. "But the fucking conversation sounds familiar."

"Y'mean y'all talk thatta way around them fruity little ole
cars?"

Hoo-Boy. It was one of the big stockers. He was hunkered
down beside me, the flats of both feet on the ground, perched
in that easy pea-picking stance. He spit on the ground between us.

"Careful of the boots," I said.

"Leather is all funny-lookin'," the guy said, looking them
over.

"That's alligator. Comes right off the stomach, right down
by the balls, of baby alligators. Cost one hundred and sixty-
five a pair, tailor-made. For a little more money, they throw in
the balls, too."

He spat again, thoughtfully. "No," he said. "What I was

sayin' was: you-all used to rough talk? I thought you fruity car drivers all talked real dainty and wore silk handkerchiefs around yer noses."

"Oh, we been known to swear a time or two."

"Shee-it," he said. "You Stroker Ace, ain't you." It was a flat statement, not a question.

So I nodded.

He shrugged, faintly, rocking on his heels a bit and shaking his head. "Stroker Ace," he said. "Shee-it. You a big deal up at Indy and Milwaukee and Phoenix and like that. Been winnin' a lot of money, I hear tell."

I nodded back. "A whole lot of money. Every race they fill up my suitcase with it. And if I *finish*, they give me even more."

"How come you ain't been racin' stocks?"

"I've been through all that. When I was a kid. Besides I've been over in Europe a lot. You know: Grand Prix racing. I mean, silk handkerchiefs and fruity cars and, after every race, you get to sleep with a real, honest-to-God European princess, or a hairless, ten-year-old Arabian boy. Whichever you want."

He looked at me for a long, long time. "You a smart-ass, right?" he said.

And I smiled right back at him. "Well, I'll tell you what," I said. "You spit about one more time close to these boots, buddy, and you see this here diamond ring? Well, we get rings like this for winning championships driving fruity little cars. Well, I'm going to take this here diamond ring and I'm going to cut you a new nose with it, shithead."

At last we understood each other. Perfectly. He smiled back at me.

"Shee-it," he said. "They're like little ole power lawn mowers."

"What is?"

"Them little ole Indy cars. They ain't even *real*. You drive one of these big mothers *here* and your ass is suckin' wind, fella."

"Lissen," I said. "If it's got wheels on it I can drive it. In fact, I can outdrive any of you fucking NASCAR humpties any day of the week in any kind of car on any kind of road, any time."

He nodded. "Well. I been waiting for you to say something like that there," he said. "How are you on the highway?"

"Whose highway?"

"Oh, I reckon we got some around here."

"Same goes."

"Uh-huh. Well, how you on a highway at *night?*"

"Devastating."

"Whut's that mean?"

"That means not too bad."

A little thicket of hunkerers had suddenly sprouted up all around us: everybody squatted down on the flats of their feet. Sleeves up. Their arms crossed lazily over their knees. I had never seen so many DEATH BEFORE DISHONOR tattoos in my life, anywhere.

There was a pause.

"Tell you what we gonna do," my new buddy said. "Tell you what. My boy, we gonna bet you some money that you can't even *keep up* with little ole Joe-Jack Bradley here on a highway at night."

"Tell me the part about the money again," I said.

And it started coming out, like salad.

"Well, I got fifty here, to start."

"And I'll put in, oh, forty-three."

"And you can put me down for a hunnert. Shee-it."

"Is he gonna drive in them fancy boots? Chrissakes, gimme two hunnert that he can't even find the brake pedal."

"Wait a minute," I said. "Whose cars do we use?"

My pal shrugged easily. "Who do you like?" he said. "Shee-it, I don't care. Hertz. Avis. National. Hell, *steal* a car; I don't care."

"All right. Hertz," I said. "We just go down and rent two and take them like they come. No bullshit. Just two plain old cars."

"Fine with me. How about you, Joe-Jack?"

"Hell, I reckon."

"All right, then. Where do we race to?"

"Mmmmm. Say between here and Eustis. And back. Them back roads should keep you busy."

We all got up.

"One more thing," my pal said.

"Now what, for chrissakes?"

"You lose, fella, and you got to give me them boots, too."

There comes a time in every man's life — one time — when he feels that perhaps he has shit in his hat.

We had rallied at the Dew Drop Inn Bar and Grill, Country Music on Weekends, in New Smyrna Beach — and we had been drinking Seagram's Seven and Seven, which makes good drivers out of us all. And we had got up all the money and someone had gone downtown and had brought back a pair of Hertz cars that looked harmless enough and had parked them out front. The place was packed and folks kept handing drinks back over the heads at the bar, sloshing them along, and the band was playing "Your Cheatin' Heart" and two or three guys at the bar were all set to fight but there wasn't enough room to draw back and swing.

"Okay," I had said. "Let's go."

And there we were: roaring down that black narrow Florida highway, balls out and belly to the ground, in those Hertz cars with their skinny tires and their mushy suspensions. And right up there in front of me was Joe-Jack, hanging on and going to beat hell. We were nose-to-bumper at top speed, and every now and then he would take one hand off the wheel and hold up one finger in the go-fuck-yourself signal. Then he would honk the horn and I could see him fumble down there on the seat beside him and open a can of beer with one hand. This is very tricky; not too many guys can do it at that speed. Forty miles to Eustis. Forty miles back.

Chrissakes. The heat indicator on the dash panel was hanging right above the boiling mark and the oil indicator idiot-light kept blipping on and off, trying to tell me something. And I could smell the goddam rubber burning right off the tires. And then — just outside Eustis — Joe-Jack did it to me.

The Bootleg Turn.

He screamed that goddam car around and, suddenly, he was going past me in the other direction like Jack the Bear.

So I sucked in all my breath and yanked the wheel as hard left as I could — and I slammed my foot down on the brake. The car actually *twisted* in pain, swinging around, and I could feel bolts popping out in the chassis. But I got that bastard backwards, beautifully.

Seemed like it took forever to get the gears and torque and tires and wheels and engine all going in the same direction again — but then I began burning rubber back toward New Smyrna.

Joe-Jack was running about eight car lengths out front.

But we had a hard left turn coming up. A racing driver gets so he remembers little things like that. You get to memorizing a road as you go along.

Only one thing to do.

I had all the gas going that the car would take and we headed into the turn — and I ducked down inside him, across the double yellow line. Fine. I got my right front fender in there just up beside his left rear fender, and I cranked it even harder to the left.

There was the sound of hundred-dollar-deductible metal

ripping and tearing through the Florida night and we slid right on through the whole fucking turn, welded together.

And there was a hard right turn ahead.

We both took a bead on the thing and, this time, I was slightly on the outside, neck and neck with Joe-Jack. So I wrenched the wheel over and chopped him right off, taking along a layer of his paint with me and all the chrome trim from the side of his car. And there I was: right out front.

We twisted and we weaved. And, occasionally, he would slam me one right in the ass at top speed.

But next turn: I got it into a full four-wheel drift (I am the world's greatest expert in the four-wheel drift. I didn't ask to become the expert. I got that way driving cars out of control as a kid), all side-ass slide so that he couldn't find a spot to duck underneath me — whipping the car straight at the last possible second and running two wheels along the borrow pit on the roadside, showering up a cloud of red-clay spray.

Then up came the lights of the Dew Drop.

Well, always leave them laughing.

So I yanked the wheel left again and hit the brake to beat hell, pumping it a bit — and brought the whole goddam car around again. Then I got off the brake and the gas and *everything* and just sat there — sliding backwards across the finish line.

Face to face with me, Joe-Jack hit his brakes and came sliding by inside an envelope of blue smoke, laughing to beat hell and slapping at the wheel with the butts of his hands.

We finally got the cars stopped and I couldn't get my door open. So I scrooched around in the front seat and kicked out the window. Someone handed me in a Seagram's Seven and Seven, the drink that makes better drivers out of us all.

When Joe-Jack slammed the door on his car, the muffler fell right off that rascal on the roadway.

I climbed out, not spilling my drink.

And there was Charlie Heffer, the Goodyear man, his shirt unbuttoned to the waist and his belly hanging out. He had lipstick marks all over his bare belly and a bottle of beer in each hand. He was looking moodily at the tires on my Rent-a-Racer.

"Hell's fire, man," he said. "Do you know that them fucking tires ain't safe in a *driveway?*"

And my new pal from the track threw one meaty forearm around my shoulders, hugging me in close and tight. He smelled like a boar in heat.

"Lissen, old buddy-boy," he said. "Where kin I get me a pair of them anteater boots like you got?"

"Alligator, *alligator,*" I said. "And, hell, you can have mine."

The operator finally tracked her down. On my end, I was sort of thrown down across the bed with my head and shoulders hanging out over the edge, and the phone was on the floor in front of me.

It only rang twice before she picked it up. Nurses sleep light. "Hello?"

"How do you say *Nursie* in Greek?" I said.

There was a two-beat pause. Then: "Good morning, Mister Ace," she said. "I can only assume that you're drunk."

"Bet your ass I'm drunk. But I won the race. Look: do you have a first name or don't you, for chrissakes?"

"How did you find me?" she said.

"How the hell do I know? All I know is that I got a friendly lady on every switchboard in every motel around the circuit, is all I know. And they found you. Polinos. P-o-l-i-n, uhhhh, well, it's a Greek name."

"I know."

"Why are you calling me at this hour?" I said.

I could hear her sigh across about sixteen states. "What race did you win?"

"Oh. The Great Hertz O'Rooney. Stock sedan class. Small purse, but I blew their goddam doors off."

There was another pause. Finally: "Well?" she said.

"Well, it's like this. I've been out, sort of standing on it see? And then I came walking back into this here motel room and I looked all around, everywhere, and you weren't here. I mean: how the hell do I know why I called you?"

"Are you all right?"

"Nursie, I'm all right. Promise."

"Well, then ..."

I'm pretty sure that's the part where I fell asleep.

I was sitting against the fence the next morning, letting the sun shine down on my hangover.

And there was Clyde Torkle, who got all hunkered down and crossed his forearms over his knees. Peering out from under the rim of his cowboy hat.

"Cigar?" he said.

I squinted out a little bit at him. "No, thanks. What else you got?"

He studied the end of his own cigar. "Money," he said.

"Mmmmmm?"

He nodded. "I hear tell that you are a driving son of a bitch. And I already know what you can do on the championship circuit, all right. You're hot, is what you are. And over in Europe, for God's sake. You really showed them buggers how to do it."

"Mmmmm."

"Yup. You're a real driving son of a bitch. And a touch crazy, I hear tell."

"You got me on all counts," I said.

"Now, then. You know who I am?"

"Chicken," I said.

He nodded, again. "Right. *Mister* Chicken in the South. I got more fucking chickens than you ever seen in your whole lifetime, sonny boy. There ain't a goddam chicken sold here in the South that ain't got my stamp somewhere on its butt end. Rain Tree Farms. I mean: I own this damn market, fella. *Own* it. Started out with one little old chicken-feeding station. Now I own it all."

"You own a few cars, too, I hear."

"Shee-it. I could own every car on this goddam *track* if I wanted to. But I don't want to. I just want to own one. Just one car. But the one I want is —— "

"The winning one."

He snapped the end of the cigar, popping off a perfect ash. "Exactly. Now, is that too much for a man to ask? I mean: you give me a man with balls and talent who can drive a car and that there is the man I want. That's all. Is that too much to ask, now?"

"No."

"Well, then. Can we talk business, fella?"

"Look: I don't have to eat fried chicken for dinner every night or anything like that, do I?"

"Now, lissen here. You shitting me?"

"No, I'm serious. I hate chicken."

"Well, to be perfectly honest, my boy: I hate it myself." He looked around over his shoulder, then looked back and lowered his voice: "Can't really stand the fucking stuff. Give me a good platter of barbecued ribs every time. Hell's fire, I've got to be a secret sparerib eater. I'm like the goddam town drunk. Lissen: I got to pull down the shades in my own house to have a few little old ribs for dinner. But, lissen to me, now ——"

"All right, I might consider it. *If* I had the best car you could get. I mean the best."

"Right. You got it. Just name it. You want a new Merc? Fine. You want to go with Plymouth? I can do it."

"And factory support?"

"Right. You got it."

"And I get to pick my chief mechanic."

"Right."

"Tire contracts?"

"Which one do you want?"

"Well, I got this tie-up on a three-year package that's paying me about eighty thousand and ———"

"Lookie here: I don't care what you put on them wheels."

"Fine. Now: how about my salary? Lissen, forgive me for being so direct. But I've got this terrible fucking hangover and when I'm hung over, being direct is the only way."

"Gotcha, boy. Tell me: what did you get at Indy?"

"This much: first ride, I got twenty-five lousy hundred dollars and expenses. That was the year I finished third. Next time, the price went up to twenty-five thousand, mostly because I finished the season second in point standings. And that was the year ———"

"That was the first year you won that sumbitch. The prettiest piece of driving I ever did see. I was there in the stands."

"With a hamper full of fried chicken?"

"Don't dog me around, boy."

"Well, anyway. After that win, the next year it went to a fifty-thousand flat fee. Plus expenses and transportation, of course. Plus half the prize money."

He thought about it, chewing on his cigar. "Think you can race the NASCAR circuit for me and do real well *and* win the Southern 500? That's important to me. Darlington is right near home and I really want to win that sumbitch."

"Hell, yes."

"Well, tell you what I'm going to do. You win me *that* race. That's all I ask fella. You win me that race in a Rain Tree Farms Special and I'll go sixty thousand. You don't win and it's fifty, your regular Indy fee."

"Plus half the purses."

"Yeah, plus half the purses. Chrissakes, I write all this off anyway."

And that's how Darkies Are Born.

This is how to get rich: don't waste too much time on an apprenticeship.

Two weeks later we raced at Rockingham and I finished second in the Rain Tree Farms Special. The Chicken King was delighted and he added a five-thousand bonus and then turned right around and gave me a chance to put ten thousand into a chicken franchise. "You're going to be old some day," he said. "Too old to drive, buddy-boy. You haven't got anything set aside and you know what they do to you? They make a tire monkey out of you, that's what they do to you."

"Or if you don't get too old," I said, "you get too dead."

He shook his head up and down. "That's entirely possible," he said. "Considering the chances you take, I'd say yes. But you sure are some fancy driver, I'll say that for you. Some plain and fancy driver."

So now I have a damn *chicken* franchise to add to my share in the Goodyear tire dealership out in Los Angeles and the small piece of Lugs Harvey's speed shop. Plus, I own part of a bar in Indianapolis.

I smoke cigars now. And the Chicken King wears alligator boots, handmade, one hundred seventy-five a pair. We're a *team*, man.

Second race, North Wilkesboro, I won. And the third one, this time in Atlanta, and we were really rolling. I don't know where these other superstars get all that newspaper crap about working their way to the top, serving an apprenticeship on the small backwoods tracks and all that. My guess is that they either didn't have it in the first place or maybe they think it will make good reading and bring them in a bunch more fans. Well, fans are not really very high on my list of things to worry about.

Lady fans are something else. Lady fans like to bed down with race drivers. In other sports, the guys have to hide this sort of thing and there is a whole lot of sneaking around. Not in racing. People expect race drivers to live up to the image. God knows, we all try.

Images: here is old Sam Bisby, flying over South Carolina in his twin-engine Aero Commander. And he decides that what he really needs more than anything else in the world is a drink. And down there is Gaffney, which is a little old town.

Bisby comes swooping in and flies that rascal plane right *under* the traffic light suspended over the main street and he lands her gently and expertly. He clicks open the door and steps out, figuring he will stroll over to the liquor store — when he notices that his fancy little landing maneuver has scared a few drivers off into the ditches on each side of the road. And right now one word leaps into Bisby's mind. LICENSE is the word.

If news of this sort of stunt gets around, sure enough, the FAA will take away his license. So Bisby piles back into his plane, fires it up again, and takes off from the main street. Then, craftily, he flies low, about fifty feet above the ground, hedgehopping his way back to Charlotte. He even selects a small airport outside of town so that nobody will recognize him. And he gets on the radio to call in and tell them that he is about to land.

Just so that nobody would know who he was, he mumbled it all into the microphone: "This, uhh, this here is Aero Commander mumph, mumph, mumph, mumph, kilo, approaching runway twenty-seven."

And came back the voice from the control tower:

"It's no use, Sam. They're looking for you all over the South."

Sure enough, they got his license for a while.

But it didn't cost him one fan. Not one single fan. After all, he was a racecar driver.

There is a moral in there somewhere.

Late in the day we were sitting in this Avis car and Ross Farley of Monroe Shocks was driving. The damned air conditioner is broken and the traffic, trying to get out of the infield after the Atlanta race, is worse than the Omaha railyard. Nothing is moving and the temperature has got to be about five thousand degrees. Plus which, somebody had forgot to bring the beer cooler.

"I'm dying, you guys," I said.

Just about that time a gust of hot air filled the car with red dust. We all sat there as it settled down on us in a grainy pink film. Then Farley turned his head and looked over at me.

"Jesus Christ, I can hardly wait for the next race," he said.

This is the way it is: the sun was setting over the motel in Talladega and the air was full of race-driver romance. Which is to say that it was about eight o'clock or so and the sky had turned into a primer-color red over behind the Dairy Queen across the street and the air was a little bit cooler, with a hint of a faint breeze rippling the top of the swimming pool. The guys had all showered by now and had changed into their

Going Out clothes. One by one they were coming out of the doors to their rooms, usually with a can of beer in one hand, and their hair all slicked down. The way a motel is set up, with a sort of courtyard in the middle and all the rooms opening off it around the pool, it makes for a very chummy setup, one of the best moments in racing. You have to experience it.

I was in my red and white checkered golf slacks and this pair of sixty dollar Gucci loafers, and no socks, which is a thing you pick up very quickly by racing at Monaco, where only the hayshakers wear socks at any time of day or night. And I had on this white knit polo shirt and my burnt-orange golf sweater with the very baggy sleeves right around the wrists. All put together it is an extremely sporty costume, just the sort of thing that race drivers are wearing more and more these days.

Also television people, for which, the hell with them.

Well, a guy has got to be comfortable to drink and do the town and the nice thing about an outfit like this is that, maybe at some point in the evening, a stranger is going to turn to you in some bar and say: "Boy, that is a very faggy costume you have got on, there." And you can carefully put your glass down on the bar and say to this stranger: "Ah, *hah*. I take it you think I am wearing a very faggy outfit, right?" And the guy, puzzled, will get a little more belligerent. And he will put down his glass and he will say: "That's what I said, all right. And what's more, I think you are a fucking queer."

And then you can take his head off. We do this a lot.

Towns like Charlotte and Altanta and Daytona are absolutely full of guys who have got up in the morning and looked into their mirrors at big goddam purple lumps over their eyes and cuts just alongside their noses and have made vows right there on the spot never again to criticize anyone's clothes in a bar.

Anyway, we are all coming out of our rooms now and, for

a few moments, the air all around the pool is full of the smell of Aqua Velva and it is very pleasant.

"Where you gonna go for dinner?" someone will say.

"Well," the other guy will say, "what I thought I'd do first is to maybe go over to the bar here and suck up a few beers. Then you know Gordy Landen, right? Well, he says that, last time he was here, that there is this place over there in the colored section that serves maybe the greatest goddam ribs and chicken you ever ate in your life. So I thought I would eat me a whole mess of ribs and —— "

"And maybe change your luck?"

"Well, hell, it couldn't hardly get no worse than it is now, right? You heard the way I was running out there today?"

"Running? Hell, you were in the pits all day."

By now, more and more guys are drifting out of their rooms, all of them slicked up for the evening, and the motel courtyard is starting to look like a cocktail party. Occasionally someone will duck back into his room for another beer, or someone else — particularly those guys who have had a tough day — will come back with a glass of Seven and Seven.

"Hey, Stroker. Them are sure some fancy pants. What did you do with the nigger you stole them off of?"

"Hey, Stroke. You forgot your socks. Lissen: if you're all out of clean socks, you can borrow a pair of mine. I only wore them driving all day and I sure as hell wasn't going fast enough to even sweat them up any, I'll tell you that."

"Damn, I got to get me a clothing sponsor like old Ace here."

"Well, if you do, you also got to get you a guy who tells you what pants to wear with what sweaters and like that. Man, if that old sponsor ever sees old Stroker, he'll come right up and snatch all that stuff right off him. Then he can go out and get himself a really *pretty* guy to wear the stuff. Like me."

"They don't make these pants that big around the gut, Charlie."

"Lissen: you see this here gut?" Pat, pat. "It took me maybe ten years and fifty thousand dollars' worth of beer to build a gut like this."

"How you running, Stroker?"

"Fast as that shitpot engine will allow. And I promise you right now it ain't *near* fast enough."

"Yeah, I saw you sort of loafing around out there today. Sounds like you need a lower gear, maybe."

"They're working on it tonight."

"You going to get some supper?"

"Yeah. I thought maybe I'd try that rib place. You doin' anything?"

"Not special."

"Well, come along. Give the waitresses a real thrill for a change."

"Okay. But no panty-snapping tonight, all right? Chrissakes, the last time — remember, in Atlanta — you damn near got us all killed."

"Well, look: I didn't know her husband was the goddam *bartender*. How was I to know?"

"You see that double-barreled sawed-off he keeps behind the bar?"

"Well, no. I mean: I sort of got a glimpse of it going out the door. But I wasn't all that anxious to stop and admire the hand engraving on the barrels or anything like that."

"Funny thing was: I kind of thought his old lady really sort of *liked* it."

"Well, she *did* sort of back it right up there to me, sort of friendly-like, didn't she?"

"I'll tell you one thing: we'll never know."

"Lissen: let's go over to the bar and get a beer, all right?"

Same night, four hours later.

"I think," says Turbo Ellison, "that what I will do is have

one more beer and then we really got to get out and get something to eat."

Turbo Ellison drinks his beer right from the bottle and always waves off the barmaid when she tries to put down a clean glass. "Lady," he will say, "if God had meant us to drink beer out of *glasses*, then He wouldn't of put it in bottles."

"Another round," says Turbo, drawing a big circle in the air over our table with one forefinger. "Another round, which I am personally going to pay for. I mean, since I personally am going to take all the money out of this here race come Sunday. I feel it's only fair."

Everybody nods thoughtfully.

Except, of course, Hack Downing. Hack simply leans back in his chair and burps loudly. Then he gets the two front legs of the chair back down on the floor and he leans across the table.

"Turbo, my boy," he says, "you had better let me buy this here round and I'll tell you why: the reason why is that, come Sunday, your ass is going to be so broke that you won't be able to buy a sack of Bull Durham."

Everybody nods thoughtfully, passing around the new order of beer.

Now, you have no doubt read in fiction books about where some guy grins *wolfishly*, right? Well, never mind any of that. I promise you that you have never, ever in your whole life read about or heard about or seen a wolfish grin until you have seen Turbo Ellison grin. And he does this right now.

"What's that?" he says, his long eyeteeth showing wetly.

"I *said*," says Hack, "I said: come Sunday, your ass —— "

"I heard you," says Turbo. He tilts the bottle back for a long swallow and then carefully puts it down on the table. "Yes, I heard you, and I got to tell you that it makes my old Mississippi heart sad to hear you say it. You are always, *always*, saying that before a race. And I am *always* beating your ass. Now you know that."

Hack burps again, this time getting in a two-tone effect. He is very good at that.

"Most always," he says, nodding. "But not come *this* Sunday. I'm sorry, old buddy. But not this Sunday."

Old Turbo swings his head around and looks at us, each one in turn. "Does he know something I don't know?" he asks.

I shrugged. "He's running fastest in practice," I say, "and that's got to count for something."

Turbo nods again, digesting this new fact. "I swan," he says. "Fastest in practice. God Almighty. Why I didn't know *that,* Hack, old buddy. I mean, you finally got that shitpot all together, huh?"

Hack blinks modestly. "She's runnin' real good," he admits.

"Well, then," says Turbo, closing the trap. "It's just a by-God good thing that I'm so much better a *driver* than you, ain't it? Damn, you had me scared there for a minute, pal."

This is like the part in King Arthur where the guy tugs off his big iron glove and throws it down. We all sat there, nodding and grinning. Well, except Hack. He was puffing up a little bit.

"Driver?" he said.

Turbo grinned wolfishly. "Driver," he said.

Hack drew his own circle in the air with his finger and got the bar girl's attention. " 'Nother round," he said, "and this one's on me." Then he turned back to Turbo. "You know, old buddy," he said. "You know: for one little old second there I thought you said better *driver.* But, hell. That can't be right, and you got to forgive me for not hearing too well. I mean, after all, everybody knows that I'm not only a better driver than *you,* old pal, but I'm the best driver at this here *table.*" He pauses a moment and half raises from his chair while he looks around the place. "Hell," he says, "I'm the best driver in this whole fucking *bar.*"

We all grinned wolfishly, as best we could. And everybody looked at Turbo.

He was shaking his head, with great sadness. "Shee-it," he said. "Lissen: I can drive a goddam car *backwards* better than you can drive it *any* way."

Hack carefully wiped the top of the new bottle of beer with the flat of his hand — the better to get the germs off it. Then he took a long pull at the bottle and made a declarative statement:

"No fucking way," he said.

Turbo swung out one long arm and pointed.

"Not in my eye," I said.

"Sorry," Turbo said. He corrected his aim just a bit and pointed at the door. "Lissen: I can take that bad-ass Hertz car right out there in the front of my motel room and drive it backward better than you can drive your goddam racecar in any direction."

"When?"

"Right now. Right this very minute."

Hack looks at me. "Whatta you think, Ace?"

I shrugged. "What the hell is so tough about driving backward? That's the way I spend half my time at Indy, for God's sake."

That seemed to decide Hack — and there I go, contributing to the delinquency of race drivers again.

"Okay," he said to Turbo. "What'll it be?"

Turbo thought about it, mapping out a route in his mind. "Airport and back," he said. "Backward."

"Both ways," said Hack.

"Shit, yes, both ways. You think this is a goddam *sports*-car race or something?"

"What kind of car you got?" Hack asked me.

"It's a Hertz-something. Ford LTD, I think. Who knows? The radio doesn't work very well."

"Yeah, well, never mind the radio. How's the *reverse?*"

"Oh, factory-fresh, I would say. I only drive the son of a bitch frontwards, you know."

"Keys?"

I handed them over and we all trooped outside, leaving behind this round table absolutely jammed with beer bottles. Turbo stomped off to get *his* rental car and I instructed Hack.

"Brown metallic hardtop," I said. "It's in front of my room there. If you can't find it, try any one the key fits. Hell, steal one; you're not going to use it all night."

And in a couple of minutes they were both back in the driveway out beside the bar, parked side by side, both in neutral and both zapping their engines. Zap, vroom. Zap.

Sam Bartow stepped off the sidewalk and got out in front of the cars, then he held up both hands. He was weaving just a bit, but not bad. "Gentlemen," he said. "Gentlemen, start your engines."

"They are started, Sam. *Jesus.*" Charlie said.

"Oh. Well, in that case, let me have your attention."

They stopped zapping the engines for a minute and let the cars idle.

"Now, then," Sam said. "Here are the rules. First —— "

Turbo stuck his head out the window of his car. "What fucking rules?" he said.

Sam shook his head like a teacher. "Shhh," he said. "I'm just making them up now. Now don't confuse me. Now when I drop the flag, you guys —— "

"Somebody get him a flag," somebody said.

And pretty soon one of the guys came back with this big goddam red and white checkered tablecloth he had jerked off somebody's table. Plus about twenty-seven diners who wanted to see the official start of the Great Backwards Race.

"Now, then," Sam said. "When I drop this here flag, you

gentlemen are officially racing. Get that? It's backwards to the airport and back. Backwards back, too, I mean. And —— "

"Get the fuck out of the way!" Hack yelled. Three of the diners jumped back inside.

Sam held up the flag and waved it in front of his face. "No, no!" he said. "I don't have to get out of the way, you asshole. Excuse me, there, ladies. Don't forget, you're going *backwards*. This here is the *front* of the cars, where I'm standing. God, you guys are dumb."

Zap, vroom! Zap. Crank. Both racers put their cars into reverse and sat there, riding the brakes and zapping the motors some more.

Then Turbo stuck his head out the window again. "Wait a goddam minute, dummy!" he yelled. "The street is out *that* way. Out there."

Sam turned around and looked over his shoulder at the street. Then he turned back and nodded. "You know, you're right," he said. "But since I am making up these here race rules, that fact appears in your driver's manual under the chapter heading of Tough Shit. You are in the Great Backward Race and you got to get to the street any way you can. Are you ready?"

"Are they ready? They're damn near out of gas, Sam," I said. "Start the race, for chrissakes."

So Sam dropped the flag-tablecloth.

Both Turbo and Hack wheeled in their seats and looked over their right shoulders. And both of them jumped off the brakes and slammed down on the gas. There was a fine, swirling howl of smoke and dust and gravel and off they went — side by side around the motel driveway. Backwards.

Sam got back up on the sidewalk.

"I wouldn't anybody step out there just now," he said. "They're headed for the motel parking lot, see, and soon's they get in there, they're gonna have to turn around somehow.

And then . . . and then they're going to come back by here going to beat hell, headed for the street."

Exactly. We all stood up on the sidewalk and heard the roar of engines back in the parking lot and then — zambo! — here came Hack, holding a slight lead, looking over his shoulder, with Turbo coming on fast. Swoosh . . . and they were by us.

We all stepped out and watched them hit the street with terrible damn bounces and Hack got just a little bit sideways coming around an Allied Van Lines semi-rig that was barreling past. The semi hit the brakes and his rig started to get a little sideways, but the driver wisely got it up on the curbing a little bit and saved it.

And then they were gone.

One of the lady diners shook her head at all of us.

"Race drivers," she said. "Honestly."

Sam stooped and picked up the tablecloth. There was a big, fat tire mark smudged down the middle of it.

"Here's your official souvenir race flag, lady," he said.

"How long do you think they'll take?" Duster Hoffman said.

"Well, let's see. Takes maybe forty-five minutes to make it to the airport from here going frontwards. Oh, I don't know, maybe a couple of hours or so."

"If they don't get picked up."

"Well," said Sam. "Either way, we got time to have another beer, you guys. Come on."

Official Race Report:

Turbo Ellison won it easily, if you count driving time: 112 minutes flat until he walked back into the bar.

But Hack Downing, 162 minutes, more or less, filed a formal protest, which the Race Stewards accepted.

That's because Hack stopped at the airport circle and picked up a couple of girls. Even got out and put their bags in the trunk.

After the Race Committee meeting, there at the round table, Turbo was awarded the trophy (one case of beer) and the Special Grand Award (one of the girls).

Personally, I think he got the worst-looking one.

(It also was decided, for the record, that neither of those bums was anywhere near to being the best race driver at the table.)

five

Welcome to Darlington. The cradle of southern stock car racing. The sport was born near here the first time a U.S. Revenue agent figured that he could catch a moonshiner running along a twisty back road with a carload of booze.

No way.

The women in this part of the country wear magnolia-scented underwear. No charge for this bit of extra information.

Darlington is tradition. First of the big tracks in the Southland, the granddaddy of them all. The land of racing heroes. This is so different from racing Indy-type cars you can't believe it. There are folks who wet their pants every time they hear one of these big bastard NASCAR machines roar to life.

Folks come out of the woods and down from the hills for the Southern 500 at Darlington every Labor Day — and they line up for miles on the approach roads. There is red clay on both sides of the roadway and out across the fields you can see splotches of more red clay. There is South Carolina red clay clinging to the wheels and tires of all the cars and, in each one of them, there sits old big daddy with his big, fucking sunburned knuckles gripping the steering wheel, and blood in his eye. They fill the stands and they're all wearing white shirts open at the throat and tan cotton wash-pants and high-top, lace-up shoes. Every other one has a wooden match in the corner of his mouth and a bottle in a brown paper bag between his feet. They are fine when the race starts — I suppose. By maybe the 250-mile mark they are all liquored up and the safest place to be is upside down out there on the goddam track.

In the infield, there is this cafeteria. Restricted to drivers and crews and press. They put red-eye gravy on everything. Christ, you reach over to get your plate and they'll put red-eye gravy on your goddam thumb if you're not quick enough. In the morning, they put red-eye gravy on the Wheaties and bran flakes.

You ever had to take a crap in the middle of a race?

Any place else in car racing; *any place else,* and the idea is to not bung up your car. Not Darlington. You haven't lived until you have zinged one off the wall at Darlington.

This is the way it works: the track is slightly banked, one and three-eighths miles around. The banking runs about, oh, 26 degrees in the First and Second Turns and Christ knows what it is in the Third and Fourth Turns and anybody with any balls at all can hit 170 miles an hour on the straightaways. And they're only 1,800 feet long. But in order to get a good line on the main straight, the idea is to allow the car to drift over slightly on the Number Three and Four Turns. And just at the apex of the Number Four Turn — just an instant before the car gets itself straightened out — the right rear sort of jiggles over right next to the wall.

The wall is painted white. It is also made out of steel. The cars are painted in all colors. Got that part?

Blam! You come greasing out of that Number Four Turn

with the ass-end sliding, and your right rear fender just *ticks* the wall, and then you go rifling down the old front chute. And sure enough: there is a stripe of white paint along the side of your car, with a shining streak of bared metal showing through in spots. And there on the wall behind you is a spread-out dab of color.

It is a dangerous game, a bit like a carom shot in pool or snooker. Except that you're playing it with a 4,000-pound monster car and if you bank-shot a bit too much you can send yourself rifling down into the infield.

I have got Darlington Stripes on everything but my right buttock.

We take you back to the first day we got here:

It is practice time in Darlington and Speedy Flint comes roaring by in that big motherless Pontiac of his. And by the time most fans have gotten their eyes focused on him the sound of his car is rolling nice and heavy and low back across the red clay innards of the track. Man, he really has his foot right in it. He heads for the Fourth Turn.

And he gets a bit sideways. Just a teensy bit.

Zambo! He bashes the wall a bit and the car bobbles for a moment. But Speedy is still on the gas and he wrenches that big son of a bitch halfway straight again and comes whooping by the pits, still rolling to beat hell. But there is this slight rough spot at the front end of the straightaway and everybody can see that he is right into it.

This time: Slam! He hits the wall and makes one more attempt to get the car around right. And he is *still* hard on the throttle. Now he gets sideways and, this time, the right rear fender catches the wall again. And he comes off the wall with the car spinning the wrong way, naturally. This is the sort of move guaranteed to turn a man's kidneys to stone.

By now, Speedy is flat out of control. The car swings around one more time and smashes head-on into the wall. Then it comes off, spinning again. Into the start of Number Two Turn, where it hits the wall one more time and then flips upside down.

Now the car screams along on its roof, headed right for the infield. When it hits the edge of the grass, it starts to roll over and over, bouncing high up into the air between rolls.

"Oh, shit," everybody says.

The car keeps right on rolling and bouncing, throwing off parts as it goes, wheels and fenders and God knows what all. When it finally stops, it lays there on its right side. A total ruin.

Speedy is just poking his head out through the window when the fire crews and ambulance come wheeling up and the men spill out of their trucks like the Flying Wallendas. Speedy looks up at all of them and he is just a touch glassy-eyed. And he clears his throat and speaks those historic Darlington words, never to be forgotten and maybe never printed before:

"Man," he says, "what a fucking *ride*."

This is the way it was last night: we had been out doing a teensy bit of drinking. Me, for one. Clyde Simpson, for another; he is the race driver out of Texas and very good. Plus three guys from the Goodyear tire engineering crew who had all been to college. College men get as drunk as anybody; possibly drunker.

"I understand," said Simpson, "that there is a hell of a party over at the Highway Hotel. You know? What do you say?"

We all said something appropriate. Like: chrissakes, yet, let's go to the party. That's what we said.

So we all piled into an Avis car.

(Put your fingers in your ears, Mister Avis. This is not for you. Not at all.)

And Simpson has decided that he will drive. Because after all, he had the fastest practice lap today. And we are tooling along at a modest sixty-five miles an hour, through town. And Jim Welty, the Goodyear tire man who had rented the car, is all relaxed in the front seat with a can of beer in one hand when Simpson turned to him.

"You know what I can do?" he said.

"I give up," said Welty. "What can you do?"

"I can get this car into reverse at sixty-five."

Welty shook his head. "No," he said. "No way. Now, look: I know that you're a hot-dog driver and all that. But this is an automatic transmission car, see, and you can't do it. After all, I'm a graduate engineer from MIT and I understand this sort of thing where perhaps you don't. On automatic transmission cars, there are stops built in to prevent that sort of thing, you know."

So Simpson reached down and grabbed the lever and slammed it into reverse at sixty-five miles an hour.

The car filled right up with smoke from the burning tires and there was a certain amount of noise from the transmission underneath. We had to open the doors to let the smoke out.

"See?" said Simpson.

We went back to our own motel to get another rental car. I mean, after all, we couldn't go to a party with no reverse gear, right? This time we got Ed Raymond's station wagon.

Simpson wandered off someplace. He had done his good deed for the evening and had taught a college man his lesson.

"I'll drive," Ed said. "I'll drive because, first, it's my rental car, and second, I'm drunker than anybody else."

Everybody agreed that that made sense: we came hooting out of the driveway and Ed got it half sideways beautifully, thus aiming us roughly in the direction we wanted to go anyway on Main Street.

Only thing was that this constable was parked right across the street and he had been watching us. And, sure enough, he turned on the red bubble-gum machine on top of his car and he took out after us.

Welty spotted the light. Well, for one thing, it was revolving and sending little reddish flashes through the inside of our wagon. A nice effect.

"Hey, Ed," he said. "Somebody back there wants you."

Raymond bobbled the thing just a bit (a good race driver would never have done *that*) and clipped the fender molding right off a parked pickup truck.

"Well, fuck him," Raymond said, making an executive decision right there. "We can outrun him. Right, men?"

"Wrong," I said. "Not in this thing, we can't."

So Bill Wilson reached over and turned off the ignition.

And Raymond sat there, all poised in his position to outrun the law: his hands locked on the wheel, his shoulders all hunched up, a mean look on his face. He tromped down on the gas. Then again.

"Hey, you guys," he said. "The engine stopped."

"Tell you what," Wilson said. "Appearance means everything in dealing with the law. First, you never make him get out of his car and walk up to you. What you do is: *you* get out of your car and then you stroll back casually to him and you lean over and you say something cool. Like: 'May I help you, officer?' "

"Gotcha," Ed said.

And he opened the door and rolled right out onto the pavement. He raised his head and looked up over the door jamb at us. "How'm I doin' so far?" he said.

"I love it so far," I said. "Now, then. You go back and talk to the peace officer, like we said."

Ed pulled himself up, hand over hand, and got on his feet. He did a majestic turn and strolled casually back as far as the rear fender. Then he leaned against the car. That was because the constable was already there. Ed raised one hand and waggled all his fingers at the lawman.

"Hi, sweetie," he said.

"Where are you going?" the cop asked.

Ed straightened, then pitched into the cop's arms. He spoke roughly into the guy's shirt collar. "We're going to a big party," he said.

"Wrong," the cop said. "I'll tell you where you're going. First, one of you guys is going to drive this wagon back to your motel there. And then you're *all* going to stay there. And I am going to park outside all night long, if necessary. And if I see any one of you so much as *walk* out of the motel, you're all in jail for at least a month."

We missed the party.

But what we did is this: we joined the rest of the racers, who were sitting around the swimming pool drinking Seven and Seven. We talked about driving. We always talk about driving.

A guy can learn a lot in such seminars.

Like Sam Bisby's Law: It is useless to step on the brakes when your car is upside down.

Things like that. And finally Killer Harris looked thoughtfully at the swimming pool for a long time, sipping moodily at his drink, and made his announcement.

Announcement: "You know," he said. "I think it just could be done. Of course, it would take a pretty fair country-boy driver to do it."

"Do what?"

"Put a car in this here swimming pool."

We all looked around with our Expert Eyes. A few guys got up from the lounges and walked around, taking imaginary sightings along the fence and the driveway. Then we all sat down again, shaking our heads. "No way," we said.

Killer (this is not his real name. His real name is something

like Shirley. Or Francis. But he claims he killed the last guy
who called him by his real name), Killer shook his head. "No,"
he said. "I don't know about you *fruits*. But I could get a car
into this here swimming pool right here."

Charlie Heffer, the Goodyear man, stood up and looked at
the motel driveway again. He shook his head back and forth.
"No fucking way," he said. "In fact, I'll tell you what I'm going
to do. I gotta bottle of Jack Daniels in my suitcase. You get a
car into this here swimming pool here and I'll give it to you."

This was the layout: first, there wasn't enough room to get
a car up to any sort of speed, which we figured would be necessary. To get from the parking lot to the pool, there were two
90-degree turns to negotiate in the driveway, sort of a narrow
passageway between the two motel units. Then there was the
main building to deal with, which stuck out a bit too much.
Which meant that, after the two 90-degree turns, a guy would
have to bank slightly off the main building to get a line on
the pool. And, finally, there were those steps leading up to the
pool.

So Killer got up and stomped away and we all sat back down
on the lounges and poured another round of Seven and Seven.

Charlie held up his glass. "Here's to" he said.

And we could hear that goddam Avis car coming around
the driveway, tires screaming.

"Jesus Christ!" everybody yelled. "He's going to do it!"

We all scrambled out of the chairs and dove into the bushes.

And here came Killer, slamming that car through the two
tight turns. Then he zinged the back end off the building wall
and got a perfect line on the pool. Whap! Right up the three
steps and into the pool. Perfect. The water sprayed up and the
car just sat there and sank slowly, the headlights on and the
horn blowing.

We waited, sipping at our drinks.

Pretty soon Killer surfaced, like Lloyd Bridges in *Sea Hunt*. And he dog-paddled over to the side of the pool.

"All right, you sons of bitches," he said. "Where's my fucking bottle?"

That was last night.

What happened today was this: I won the Southern 500. I beat Clyde Simpson out by half a car length at the finish. The Chicken King may not sober up until the end of the season.

In fact, the last time I saw him, he was with Killer, sitting in the car — fully clothed — at the bottom of the swimming pool. They were drinking Seagram's Seven Crown and chlorinated water — that makes it a might weak — but they didn't know the difference. They had cut up the lawn sprinkler hose and were using pieces of it as breathing tubes.

Which is all right. I promise you. It's not every day Torkle has a winner at Darlington.

six

Eight-thirty a.m. Eight-thirty in the *morning*.

And Shirley nudged me. "There's somebody at the door," she said.

"Impossible."

"No, really. Hear that? Somebody's knocking."

I eased one edge of the pillow up so I could hear. The room was still nice and soft and velvety black inside. So I lay there and blinked for a few minutes until I had it pretty well figured out where my arm was in relation to the rest of my body, and I wriggled it out and looked at my watch.

Eight-thirty, all right.

"Go see who it is," I said. "And then, soon as you find out who it is, tell them either to go to hell or to bring us around some coffee and sweet rolls."

For some damn reason she decided to whisper: "Lissen. I can't. I'm *naked*." When she said "naked," it ruffled the hair around my left ear.

"S'all right. Go give 'em a thrill."

"Have you got a bathrobe?"

"Have I got a *what*?"

"You know: a dressing gown or something like that. A *robe*. You know."

"Have I ever had one?"

"Ummm. No."

"Well, then. Go and answer the goddam door."

The untangling took a little time: Shirley had our legs locked and both arms around me. Sleeping with Shirley is a lot like sleeping with a silk boa constrictor. And she finally flumped out of the bed and stood up. She turned on the lamp and then she stretched.

Hot damn. Watching Shirley stretch in the morning is a reward you get for winning races. She is all nice and tawny all over, like a puma, and all bouncy, and when she raises her arms up over her head, everything stands right up and *quivers* — and her nipples get right up and say good morning. Shirley has a flat tummy rolling down into what has got to be America's Last Great Pubic Arch — she is furry and pink in all matching shades — and her bucket is made up of two perfectly matched scale-model world globes.

Still: the knocking at the door kept on.

"Naked?" she said.

"Why not? Hell, *everybody* can't be dressed at eight-thirty in the morning."

"Well . . . maybe a towel." So she padded into the bathroom and came black out holding a little teeny hand towel in front of her. It left an awful lot of top showing and just a little of bottom, sort of a miniature triangle. "How's this?"

"That's great. A washcloth would be a little better, but that's fine. Now answer the door, I'm starting to get a headache."

She opened it and stood there in a fuzzy silhouette.

It was another woman.

And they both stood there, looking at each other for a long, long time.

"Excuse me," the woman said. "I must have the wrong room."

"Well, what room did you want?" Shirley said.

"Five twenty-two."

Shirley leaned forward, the little bitty towel flapping out, and checked the number of the outside of the door. "Well, this is five twenty-two," she said.

"So it is."

"Uh-huh."

And they both just stood there and looked at each other for another long time.

Finally: "I'm looking for Stroker Ace," the woman said.

"Isn't everybody," Shirley said.

"On business," the woman said.

"I'll *bet*," said Shirley.

"Well, is he . . . is he in?"

Shirley shrugged. "Could you come back in a few minutes? I'm really not *dressed*."

"So I see."

Shirley shrugged again and closed the door. Then she swung around, the towel arcing out like a little bullfighter's cape. "It was another *woman*."

"Do tell."

She flounced over to the bed. "What the hell are you *doing*? Keeping office hours or something?"

"Look, Shirley. It's eight-thirty in the *morning*, for chrissakes. Come on back to bed."

"While another WOMAN is waiting *outside*? Never!" And she wadded up the towel and threw it at my head. "I'm *leaving*. You know what I'm going to do? I'm going to LEAVE. That's what I'm going to do. And you know what *else* I'm going to do? I'm never going to speak to you again, that's what else I'm going to do. The very idea." And she paused at the bathroom door, looking like the girl in the Springmaid Sheets advertisement. "May I use your *shower*?"

"Why not? It comes with the room."

"Well, how would I know? Maybe you want to save it for your fancy WOMAN out there. How do *I* know?"

"Look, Shirley: if you don't go get in that shower, I'm going to get up and drag you back into bed. Now, take your choice."

So she scampered into the bathroom and slammed the door. And I rolled over and pulled the pillow back over my head. Eight forty-five in the morning, for God's sake.

When she came back out she was wearing her Miss Fire Injection costume, switching the long tail around like it was real. Every time she breathed, it made the sequins sparkle in a soft rise and fall of glitter.

"I'm *going*."

"I can tell. Lissen: how do you make that tail twitch around like that?"

"I'm not speaking to you, *Mister* Ace."

"You used to call me Strokie."

"Humph!" And she bounced right out, damn near slamming the door on her tail.

There was some sort of muffled conversation just outside the closed door and then it popped open again.

"Mister Ace?"

Oh, for chrissakes.

"Mister Ace. May I come in?"

I lifted up just a little, tiny corner of the pillow. "Well, first tell me who you are, all right?"

"I . . . am . . . Miss . . . *Feeny*." And while she was saying it, she was yanking the drapes open and, suddenly, the whole place was flooded with bright damn sunshine. "I am . . . Miss Feeny, and I am . . . here . . . on business. There, now! Isn't that a lot better?"

"Well, no."

"Rain Tree Farms," she said, still standing there, looking down at me. "I am the public relations director of Rain Tree Farms."

"You got a fried chicken on you?"

"Mister Ace. Will you please get up and look at me? We

have a lot to do here and it's already eight-fifty. Now, that's a good boy. Up we go now."

Good boy: that part figured. Miss Feeny was wearing a sort of tweedy suit, pants and all, fly front and all, and when I sat all the way up I could see that she had on brown shoes with *laces*. There was no way to tell if there was any kind of lady inside the suit or not. So I grabbed Shirley's towel and held it in front of me and got out of bed.

"My, my," she said. "Do we always sleep this late?"

"Mmmm. We sure do. Ever' goddam chance we *get*, we do."

Then she moved my pants and shirt and underwear out of the chair and held them up with her fingertips as though they were packed full up with the Black Plague, and she dropped them on top of the television set. And she sat down, sort of pigeon-toed, and put her purse on her lap. "Well, I'm sorry, but we're early starters at Rain Tree Farms. Go, go, go, all the time, that's us." Then she looked me over. "My, my," she said. "We certainly do have a lot of nasty *scars* all over our body, don't we?"

"We sure do. You want to see the other side?"

She held on to the purse a little bit tighter. "No, no. That won't be at all necessary. Now, then. Shall we start?"

"What is it you got in mind? I'm pretty tired already."

She looked over at the bed. A quick look, then away; then a quick look back again. "I can imagine. Yes, indeed. Which, uhh, which brings me to a pertinent point. I'm not quite sure how I should bring this up. But, well . . . but we try to maintain a certain, well, a certain public image in our business. You understand."

"Mmmmmm."

"Well, then. Now, believe me, we certainly don't expect to exercise any control over the, uhh . . . over the morals of our contract drivers. Certainly not. My, no. Still . . ." She clicked open the purse and reached in there and got out a cigarette.

Then she lit it and started talking again while huffing out quick little bursts of smoke. "Still, I wonder if it might not be more appropriate — in the future — if you arranged for your overnight guests to, uhh, to leave while it was still dark. I'm sure you understand: we at Rain Tree Farms deal with the public constantly — families with children buy our fried chicken. And, well, I'm not sure that it would do to have some — shall we say — some wench, slipping out of your room in broad daylight. You understand, of course." She puffed in some more, looking at me again. "You know," she said, "you are a lot more *lean* than you appear in your pictures. Without any clothes on, I mean."

"Uh-huh. That's because nobody lets me get enough sleep, for chrissakes. And now you want me to get up in the middle of the night and shag some lady out of my room."

She nodded. "Well, look at it this way: Mister Torkle has seen fit to sign you as our Number One driver and to lavish money on you. Now, of course I understand that race drivers as a breed have the morals of mink. But I'm afraid that, where Rain Tree Farms is concerned, you'll have to make some concessions for the sake of image. We must be discreet, mustn't we?"

Oh, balls. It was too early in the morning. No coffee and now my goddam head was starting to hurt. "When do I get to talk?" I said.

She held up one hand, palm out toward me. "In just one little minute. Now, then. Once we understand the role expected of us, why I'm just sure we'll all get along just so nicely. Now, I have dealt with a great many race drivers in my time and —— "

"Mizz Feeny. I'm waiting."

She stamped out the cigarette. "All right, now. What is it we have to say?"

"Just this. In just about two seconds here, *we're* going to throw down this here little towel so that *we* have both hands free. And then, we're going to throw your ass right out of here. In broad daylight, Mizz Feeny."

She blinked a lot.

"And then. And then I'm going to call Clyde Torkle the Chicken King and I'm gonna tell him to shove his sponsorship right up his ass. *Sideways*. Same goes for all his fucking chickens, Mizz Feeny, and all the families that buy them, and all the dumb-ass children, too."

She was still blinking. And breathing through her mouth.

"And if Clyde Torkle wants me to drive for *him*, we got to have an understanding about Public Image, like you said. One: my image is *my* image and not Torkle's. Two: all you got to do is lavish money on me and sit back in the goddam stands and take the championship when I WIN IT for you. Which none of Torkle's other fucking humpty hayshaking drivers have ever been able to do. Morals or not. You with me, Mizz Feeny?"

She nodded, fast.

"Now, then. As for keeping 'wenches' in my room overnight: I'll run a goddam *bear* in here if I feel like it — and I'll march her out at goddam high *noon* if I feel like it. Lissen: that *wench* just happened to be Miss Fire Injection, who is a pretty famous lady around racing. And Fire Injection Carburetor Systems also happens to be a sponsor of mine. And *they* pay me damn near as much as Rain Tree Farms. And *they* don't give me any bullshit about *image*. What they want is the goddam TITLE, is what they want. Are we right, Miss Feeny?"

She was still nodding, hands locked together over her purse.

"And one more thing. It just came to me. If Miss Fire Injection represents her firm all that well, why maybe *you* ought to give it some thought, Mizz Feeny. Why, hell, we could put you into a little chicken-suit and get some net stockings and a little feathered tailpiece and you could shake it all around at all the nice folks. And you could ride in all the parades on the

Rain Tree float. And if you get real lucky, why, some nice race driver would drag you back to his motel room and——"

"All right, all *right*," she said. She was holding one hand up against her throat.

"Well?"

"All right: I'm sorry." She was running her words in together, speaking fast. "I'm truly sorry. I can see that you are, well, different, from most drivers I have to deal with. Mister Torkle warned me about it, but I see now that I didn't fully understand."

"You going to be a good girl now?"

She nodded, up and down.

"All right, then. Can I go and take a goddam shower now?"

She nodded some more.

When I came back out, she was lugging things into the room from the car outside. She kept on carrying in things while I got into my Jockey shorts and some fresh pants and shirt.

Things: a set of luggage, real leather, with *Stroker Ace* stamped on each piece in gold. A canvas racing bag with RAIN TREE FARMS RACING TEAM printed on it. Plus the symbol: a cartoon of a chicken wearing a crash helmet and goggles. A blue blazer and a red blazer with the Rain Tree Farms patch over the pockets. A pile of driving uniforms, bright red, with the lettering in white across the shoulders. Rain Tree Farms garment bags, with *Stroker Ace* woven right into the fabric. Two new Bell helmets with the chicken cartoon right over the earpieces. A red cowboy hat with a white band and S.A. stamped on the band. And a silk bathrobe with little teeny chickens all over it, all wearing crash helmets. And a black notebook, which she threw down on the bed.

"What about the goddam underwear?" I said. "You mean to tell me that I don't get chicken-underwear with Stroker Ace printed on the fly front?"

She was panting, carrying in an armload of racing warm-up jackets, all printed up.

"Better not mention underwear," she said, "or Mister Torkle will have that printed up, too. Where shall I put all this? Oh, I almost forgot. The car is yours too."

"What car?"

"Out here in front."

Just as I figured: it was a bright-red new Dodge and guess what was printed on the door?

"All right, Mizz Feeny. Knock it off, for chrissakes."

"Look at the notebook," she said.

I sat down on the bed and began turning the pages.

"Now, these are our designs for the new racing vans," she said. "See here? They will have Rain Tree Farms painted on the sides — with the little racing chicken, of course. And the name STROKER ACE in gigantic letters right over here, as the illustration shows. And, finally, in the space indicated here, we will print WORLD CHAMPION. That is, when we win the title."

"Ummm hmmm. And what's this?"

"These are the new billboards that will go up around the country. See there? With your picture on them. And over here on this page . . . right here, are the designs for our newest fried-chicken promotion. We plan to call it the *Stroker Ace Special Fast Pack — The Pole-Position Chicken.* You like that? And each box will carry your picture on it, like this. And the napkins inside will say *Stroker's Pole Pack.* Isn't that nice?"

"Mmmm. What's this?"

"Oh, yes. And this is a sample entry blank for our new nationwide contest. Guess Stroker Ace's qualifying speed for the Charlotte 500 and win a one-year supply of Rain Tree Farms fried chicken for the entire family. You get one entry blank with each box of Stroker Ace's Fast Pack, the super-speed chicken dinner. And, over here, on *this* page is —— "

"What the hell is it?"

"This is the *Color Stroker Ace* contest for children. Isn't this super? Each franchise will have your picture like this, see? All blank. And the children can color it in any way they'd like — and the winner gets: A Day with Stroker Ace."

"A what?"

"A Day with Stroker Ace. A ride in your racing car. Dinner, ice cream, everything."

"Do I have to get the kid laid, too?"

"Now, now. I'm serious. We have a great deal of money tied into this campaign. How do you like it so far?"

"It's your money. Except that the car out there has got to go. What the hell does Torkle think I'm doing: running a fast-order delivery service or something?"

She blinked at me. "But he had the car prepared just for you. A crew worked all night on it. Surely you ——"

"No, Mizz Feeny. No car."

"Well, Mister Torkle is going to be upset."

"Fuck him."

"Well, you're certainly direct, I'll say that for you." Mizz Feeny shook her head at me.

I was actually starting to *like* her.

"Now, then," she said. "Let's get on with it."

"Mizz Feeny, there isn't any more goddam room in here for more stuff."

"No, no. I mean, I've got to get the official Stroker Ace biography ready for our releases. The Stroker Ace life story. In brief, of course."

"Lissen: you leave out the dirty parts and it gets to be pretty brief, all right."

She sat back down again, knees together again, and took a small Nikon and flash attachment out of her purse. "I'm going to take your portrait," she said, "and we'll have them run off today to go with the press releases."

"You want me to take my clothes back off and get the towel again?"

"Mister Ace, will you please get serious? Honestly. Now, here, read this. I've gotten some material from your official United States Auto Club biography. There isn't much of it there, I must say, but I think it will do. And I've taken the liberty of quoting you in a manner I'm sure you will approve."

And she handed over the release.

RAIN TREE FARMS
The World's Finest Fastest Fried Chicken

TO: Southern Motorsports Press Assn.

FOR IMMEDIATE RELEASE

Clyde Torkle, known throughout America's Dixie as the Chicken King, announced today the signing of Driving Superstar Stroker Ace to head up the Rain Tree Farms Racing Team for this season's assault on the NASCAR Championship.

Ace, the record-setting winner of the famed Indianapolis 500-Mile Race and the foremost champion car pilot of all time, will drive the speedy new *Rain Tree Dodge* in at least four of the Super-Speedway 500-Mile classics and as many other major races as his busy schedule permits in his effort to become a champion in both racing worlds.

"We are proud and honored to have Stroker Ace on our team," said Mr. Torkle, "and this contract marks the new campaign to make Rain Tree Farms as fast on the racetracks as our delicious fried chicken is on its way to the kitchen tables of this great country."

As for the talented Mr. Ace, "I am certainly delighted with this new association," he said, "for, as we all know, the Rain Tree name stands for quality as well as speed. And we shall make every effort to bring home the Trophy."

Stroker Ace should be the man to do just that. Already a legend at just 31 years of age, he has boldly carved his mark on the sport by starting in those buzzing midget racers at such places as the famed Ascot Speedway in Los Angeles and Soldier's Field in Chicago, and then advancing to drive Sprint cars on some of the world's great half-mile dirt tracks, "the cradle of racing," as they say. Stroker also spent two winning seasons as a stock car racer before moving on to the Indy-type cars and stirring hearts and turning heads alike as he roared to victory after victory against the Knights of the Roaring Road, soon earning the sobriquet of Mister Pole Position among his friendly adversaries.

How did it all begin?

"I was born to the sound of a racing engine," Stroker recalls. "Our family always had several sports cars around, Allards and Jaguars, and I longed to drive them from the time I was a wee tot. My father often sat me on his lap while driving his lively Aston-Martin and he let me handle the wheel as we drove the twisting, tree-lined roads around our Newport, Rhode Island, home. He taught me early the finesse and delicate touch it takes to handle a spirited machine."

Stroker was presented with a "Birdcage" Maserati for his 15th birthday and soon learned to drive it like the wind in SCCA events in the Cape Cod area, winning several trophies and establishing early the mark of fine sportsmanship that he later carried with him into the racing game as both a professional and a gentleman driver.

But tragedy was to play its role in the career of this young charger. Stroker Ace's parents were killed many years ago in the tragic crash of their private plane en route to the Kentucky Derby, leaving their bereaved son, their only child, to mourn them alone, and to carry on the family banner as his sportsman-father would have wished it.

"I vowed many years ago to carry on the family banner as my sportsman-father would have wished it," Stroker Ace said. "And I want to bring into the game of professional racing some small touch of the grace and gentlemanliness my late father would have wanted me to. I know that, somewhere up there, he is proud of me today and he knows that I continue to race, as he would have done, not for the money or the glory, but for the benefit of the game and good sportsmanship, and any safety improvements that it might lend to the greater world of safe civilian driving."

Prepared by Pembrook Feeny. Pictures Attached.
Please Credit Rain Tree Farms Photo.

She was watching me, breathing through her mouth again. "How do you like it?" she said.

"You write this all by yourself?"

"Well, of course. I *told* you I was the Public Relations Director of Rain Tree Farms. I write press releases all the time, really. Now, this one goes out to all the papers today. You like it?"

"It sure is nice. Huh. Let's see, here. Your first name is . . . uhhh, *Pembrook?*"

"Well, what's wrong with that?"

"Well, nothing, I suppose. It sounds like a stationery store in Salt Lake City, that's all."

She flounced around just a little bit. "Humph. Well, I must say, it's certainly a more sedate name than, uhhh, than, Miss *Ram* Injection. The point is: is everything true in there?"

"In where?"

"In the press release. I mean: is it all accurate and is your life story correct and that sort of thing? This goes out to newspapers and radio and television stations, you know."

"I know. Uh-huh, it's exactly correct. You captured the real me."

She paused for a minute, looking at me. "Well, may I say something?"

"Fire away, Pembrookie-babe."

"Well, what I want to say is . . . you don't seem to exactly fit that background and I must apologize if I offended you earlier. When I came in, I mean. It's just that you seem like all the other —— "

"It's me, all right. Racing has just *hardened* me. There's no dear, sweet little boy left, driving that fucking Aston-Martin on his daddy's lap, that's all."

"Well, I'm not sure your late father would have approved of Miss *Ram* Injection."

"It's *Fire* Injection, for chrissakes." I managed to get her by the elbow and lead her to the door. "But we'll never know, will we?"

seven

Well, all right. So much for the real me.

None of it is true, of course. I mean, the part about the Aston-Martin and those twisting, tree-shaded roads around Newport, Rhode Island — although they could easily have roads like that, for all I know.

No Birdcage Maserati.

No SCCA events: the Sports Car Club of America would never have touched me with a ten-foot Ferrari.

No dear Mom and Dad killed in a tragic plane crash.

And fuck sportsmanship.

Look, everybody has a secret life; I mean, the real one. And the life they let out for publication, or just the life they talk about to other people, is always touched up here and there with some fancy needlework embroidery. Nobody is what they seem.

Look, again: people polish up their image because it suits them, and everybody would like to look just a little bit better than anybody else. They always leave out the parts where they go to the bathroom, for chrissakes, or where they pick their noses.

Everybody is jacking-off life to a certain extent.

Consider my true story. The Secret Life of Stroker Ace:

My old man wears Hoover collars. They *detach* from his shirt, for chrissakes. He wears J. C. Penney black serge suits and when he walks down the street, he carries his hands folded behind his back and he hunches forward and looks down, as though he is maybe hunting for something he lost on an earlier trip.

My mother is built like a two-bedroom brick bungalow and she wears Coty's Emeraude perfume. I can still close my eyes and smell it now. Her idea of a terrific treat is a New England boiled dinner and when I left home the whole fucking upstairs still smelled like parsnips.

The downstairs smelled like calla lillies and iris. That's because the downstairs of the house was the family mortuary. Workshop in the basement, separate entrance.

It was to have been Ace and Sons, Funeral Directors and Embalmers.

It now is: Ace and *Son*. They carry a small ad in *Sunnyside and Casket*.

I still get the feeling that my father's first words to me were: "Don't do that, son, it isn't becoming for our family for you to do that."

Don't run around upstairs when there is a service going on downstairs.

Don't play out in the yard when there is a viewing going on downstairs.

Don't mess around in the coffin-display room. It isn't funny, how many times do I have to tell you that?

Don't rev the engine on the hearse; it has to last us a long time.

Don't think you can get away with wearing that red shirt. What would people think?

Stroker, what are we going to do with you?

I used to stand in front of the mirror in the bathroom and practice my Funeral Look. It took months to perfect it: I would get everything set on the outside of my face to where I looked very somber and practice the look until nothing could change it.

Once I was serving as an attendant at a service downstairs (I did that a lot. Mother played the organ; you save money wherever you can) when Dock Seegle suddenly popped up in the coffin-display room off to one side. Dock Seegle was my best friend. The coffin-display room sits at an angle to the main room; everybody was facing my father and I was the only one who could see Dock.

And he looked at me until he was sure he had my attention.

Right away I snapped into my Funeral Face.

". . . was a good woman," my father was saying. "Her good works with the Garden Club and the Ladies Literary League are well known to all of us here today. And —— "

Everybody was listening to my old man. And looking occasionally to where the good woman he was talking about was lying in a $69.75 coffin with the top part open.

I glanced sideways at Dock Seegle again.

He slowly undid his belt buckle, very slowly.

". . . and all of us here today," my father said, "must look to the state of his own mortality and look to the state of his soul as —— "

By now, Dock had his pants unbuttoned. And he let them drop to his knees.

Then he started on his undershorts.

I let my eyes slide back to the center of the room. This was my father's Number One funeral oration and people were dabbing at their eyes and some of the bigger ladies were snuffling openly. Bigger ladies always do that.

My head muscles ached. But I stood there, my hands folded in front of me. And, finally, a little teeny bit at a time, I moved my eyes back to where I could see Dock Seegle.

He had his shorts down around his knees now.

Funeral Face. Tighten it up.

". . . but there is a message for all of us in this dear woman's life," my father was saying. "A message that we all might heed. And that is —— "

Flash back to the mourners. Still snuffling and blowing noses.

Then, slowly again, I eased my eyes back to the side room.

Dock looked right into my eyes. And he carefully turned around and put one hand on each cheek of his backside.

Oh, God. No.

My father was just getting to his punch line when Dock Seegle bent right over and pulled his cheeks apart and flashed me a *GOTCHA!*

I blinked. Several times, hard.

But I held the Face. But, later, when I was driving the hearse back alone from the cemetery, I howled and cried and pounded the steering wheel with both hands.

"I thought you did a little better today," my brother said to me when I got home. He had been the head usher and had been standing at the back of the room, near the doors, looking right at me. "You might amount to something yet."

My brother was always saying things like that. My brother wore high-top shoes and drove a dark gray Hudson Terraplane and went with a girl who parted her hair in the middle and gathered it up in a bun in back and who was so fucking lumpy she looked like maybe she had three breasts.

She loved New England boiled dinners.

One time I asked him if they ever done anything together.

"Done what?"

"Aww, you know."

"I'll have you know that Myrtle is a *good girl*," he said. "What's the matter with you? She is saving herself."

"For what?"

"For our Wedding Night, of course."

"Lissen: you get her out of that corset and you'll think you're being beaten to death by giant marshmallows or something."

"Stroker, what are we going to *do* with you? In the first place, this is not a proper subject even for men to discuss. In the second place, you would do well to cultivate some good people yourself. And while we're on *that* subject, I must say I certainly do not consider Dock Seegle a very good ―――"

They all hated Dock Seegle.

Dock Seegle lived over in Troublesome Valley, which is maybe the one spot in West Virginia that everybody took at absolute face value. The trees grew close to the road going up there and it twisted and turned and dipped and practically dropped out of sight in a few spots, and it was dark there even on a sunny day. Up at the end of the valley there was a clutch of dog-ass farms with the buildings all falling down and a few skinny cows with their ribs hanging right out.

The school bus wouldn't go up there. No way.

Every morning, we would stop at the mouth of the road where it turned off into the dark and here would come old Dock, leading a bad-ass, raggedy gang of kids and every last fucking one of them had pinkeye.

Dock would climb on the bus and he would always walk back to the seat where I was sitting and, if there was somebody sitting by me ― even a girl ― he would simply take them up by the collar and throw their ass right out in the aisle. And then he would plunk down beside me and usually say the very same thing.

DOCK: "You got anything in that lunch I can eat? I ain't had no breakfast."

When the Troublesome Valley kids got on the school bus, the whole damn thing would take on a different smell, maybe a rich blend of mud and horseshit and dirty underwear, with occasional flashes of wet corncrib.

But Dock and I were a team.

ꜱ We had been friends ever since we had met.

Understand, now, there was none of that Tom Sawyer bull-shit. That is, we didn't meet in the schoolyard and then get into a fight and bloody each other's noses and then get up and shake hands and become fast friends for life. None of that.

I liked Dock because he was free and easy. He was the only kid I ever knew who was the *pure stuff*, all etched out there perfectly with no mean shadings underneath.

TEACHER: "Now, Dock Seegle, what is the capital of Alabama?"

DOCK: "Now how in hell would I know?"

And Dock liked *me* because I lived in a house and slept right upstairs with a couple of dead people down in the basement on stone worktables.

"God *damn*," he would say. "It would scare me spitless. I mean: what if one of them suddenly got up in the middle of the night and started walking around the house? Or, what if you got up to go and take a leak, see, and you opened your bedroom door and there was one of them, sort of standing there like *this*, see, and you —— "

"Hell, Dock, I been doing that all my life. Chrissakes, I was *raised* with dead folks down in the basement. Ain't none of them got up to my room yet. Maybe as far as the kitchen, but never —— "

And Dock would shake his head at me in wonder.

I had Dock over to the house a couple of times for supper — over my old man's and my brother's protests — and he didn't like the New England boiled dinner any better than I did, but he sure liked the feeling it gave him to sit there in the kitchen and eat, knowing there was maybe a stiff downstairs in the basement.

"You got any *dead* ones down there, Mister Ace?" he would ask my father.

"I don't see that it is any concern of yours, young man," my dad would say. And then, somewhere during dinner, he would always work in the Lecture aimed at me.

"Funeral direction is an honorable calling," my father would say. "It offers both steady employment — no mean thing in these uncertain times — and it offers the opportunity for community service. And all this" — he would wave his hand around in a circle, indicating the house and the parlor — ". . . and all this will be *yours* some day. You and your brother. As you know, the moment you graduate from undertaking school, I intend to change the name outside to Ace and *Sons*. And then, one day, your mother and I will retire and you two can —— "

"You're not eating your dinner," my mother would say.

And I would sit there, full of parsnips, and wonder if this was the whole thing.

Up at Dock's house everything was different. I mean, the house was pretty poor-ass on the outside but it was warm and cozy inside and everybody moved real easy and they all laughed a whole lot at each other and they ate chicken and roasts and big chunks of some sort of meat and Dock's mother would stand at the stove all through dinner, bringing more hot food to everybody. And Dock's old man would lean back every now and then, slap her on the ass with a nice loud *thwack!* and then turn back to Dock and me and nod solemnly.

"The old lady's still got all the moves," he would say.

Or, he would say to me, just as I had a mouthful of fried chicken:

"Hey, Stroker. You gettin' any strange stuff?"

And everybody at the table would laugh at me while I choked to death.

And then came the signal.

Hell, everybody gets a signal.

The thing is: you have to be listening when it comes.

Lissen: a journalist or maybe a big-time editor gets a signal when he is a kid and he writes a paper called "What I Did on My Summer Vacation," and the teacher says, "Why, *Roger*, this is really *good*. You certainly have a way with words."

Sold: one writer for life.

It happens to jocks. Let a kid score one touchdown and the coach slaps him on the bare butt in the locker room and says, "Lissen, kid, you get a few more pounds on you and yer gonna be just *fine.*" And the kid goes right out and chews up turf for miles around and comes out the other end as Roman Gabriel or somebody.

Understand, it is not always like being hit by lightning or anything. But it happens to everybody.

It happened to me at eight o'clock one night.

Eight o'clock.

Lissen: this is etched and burned into my mind like color film and I can play it back any time, complete with wide screen and music if I want.

Old man Seegle pushed his chair back from the table after dinner and he reached into his shirt pocket and fished out a dirty wooden match and began to pick his teeth with it, looking right at Dock. Finally, he said:

"Dock, you gotta drive tonight."

And old Dock just nodded, spooning in rhubarb pie.

"Grampa ain't feeling any better?" he said.

"Is Grampa sick?" I said.

Dock's father looked at me for a long time. "If you call having an ass-end full of bird shot *sick*, why then he sure as hell is sick," he said.

"Kin Stroker come along?" Dock said.

Everybody left at the table looked at each other. Over at the kitchen stove, Missus Seegle paused with a spoon halfway to her mouth. The place got awful quiet for a minute there and all I could hear was the dog breathing heavy under the table.

"Stroker is *fine,*" Dock said.

And finally his father nodded a little bit. "I suspect so," he said. "You wouldn't be running around with no candy-ass."

The pickup truck was parked out in the yard, loaded with

hay bales. The right front fender was gone and the hood was wired down with baling wire and the whole thing looked like it had been attacked by midgets swinging ball peen hammers. And when we climbed into it the thing creaked and groaned.

"Look out for that broken spring there," Dock said. "You sit wrong on this here seat and you get a rusty spring right up yer ass."

Dock's father came around to the driver's side and stuck his head in.

"I reckon cousin Ned will be waiting for you over a-hint the depot in town," he said. "Soon's you unload, you hightail it right back here."

Dock nodded at him and reached for the ignition. It wasn't a key; it was two wires. He gathered them up in his hand and got ready to touch them together.

"Shitfire, you think we can *make it* down to the depot?" I said.

Dock looked over sideways at me for a minute and then he gave me a strange sort of smile.

Strange: it was like being stabbed in the groin with an icicle.

And then he touched the tips of the wires together.

Jee-*zuz*.

The engine came on with a deep, smooth, bubbling sort of *ba-roooom* and then it just ran like heavy dairy cream, very deep, and the truck didn't even shake a bit. Somewhere down under the frame of the truck I could hear the thick music coming out of some hidden twin pipes and the whole thing sounded like nothing I had ever heard before. The pitch of it was matched exactly to the tuning fork just at the junction of my ribs and it vibrated me right along in perfect time.

"Whut in hell have you got *in* there?" I said.

"Well, it ain't exactly a nineteen thirty-five Ford block," Dock said. "Hell, the fucking carburetors cost more than our whole house." And he reached down and popped it into low with the butt of his hand and we wheeled out of the yard.

Lights out.

"You can't run down this here road in the *dark*," I said.

"Can, too."

It was like going down a long tube of pitch night and being born all over again.

The truck came howling out of the valley road and onto the county road and Dock had the wheel cranked hard left. He was hunched over, peering through the windshield. It is a tight, absolute left-hand turn, right where the school bus always stopped, and then Dock did a couple of nifty things.

One: he got the whole fucking truck sliding flat sideways, coming out of the canyon road.

Two: he flashed the wheel around right as far as it would go and then he gave it more gas.

It was like being hit by lightning: the goddam truck shuddered all over and then suddenly the tires got a bite and it snapped around just as the right wheels were on the edge of the borrow pit — and there we were: blasting down the county road, flying into the dark behind that throbbing sound.

And at that point I *knew it*.

Ahhh, dear God. This is LIVING.

The road was full of tightening turns — each way — and deep dips and long uphill and downhill stretches. On each turn, Dock would drift it a little, sliding way over on the other side, always on the gas, never once touching the brake.

Occasionally, we would look at each other and laugh to beat hell.

Then it happened.

Really tight, left-hand corner, a West Virginia hairpin. Followed by an uphill right-hander, just as tight.

Dock swung the pickup over into the left-hand lane and took

the corner tight and just as we got into the middle of it he cranked her back a bit.

And there was another car — headlights on — zinging along in the same direction we were. And he wasn't exactly lolly-gagging around; he was really on it.

We came right in under him. And at that moment, both lanes of the two-lane road were now exactly full of vehicles all going in the same direction. Except that we were still drifting a bit.

There was a dandy *ting* of metal and we slid right over and rubbed our right fender up against his doorhandle. Not far from where the big STATE POLICE sign was painted on his front door.

"Police," I yelled.

"Shit!" Dock said. "What'll I do now?"

We were already cranking back into the right-hander when his siren came on.

"You better *drive* this sumbitch, that's what you better do."

Dock just nodded, getting back hard on the gas, and we hauled it down a long straightaway so fast that we practically bottomed that rascal when we started up the other side. Now we were really zinging and the goddam truck was all gathered up into itself and you could hear the lovely roar all the way to Steubenville.

"Hang on," Dock said.

Dirt side road coming up.

He zapped the throttle twice and actually got that bugger down two gears and then let out the clutch and got off the gas and tapped the brake all in several blinding moves with his hands and feet, like Ethel Smith playing the organ, and the engine didn't protest one lick. And then he swung it wide and cranked it toward the dirt road.

Ahhh. Hot DAMN.

The pickup hunkered down and slammed flat sideways for

at least fifty yards, spewing up pure black smoke from the tires.

For just a few seconds there nothing was happening.

Well, not exactly nothing: Dock and I were both floating just about an inch off the seat, all so full of G forces that our shirt collars were afloat. I was hanging onto the door handle on my side and the only thing that kept Dock inside the truck was the fact that he had both hands on the steering wheel.

But he had his arms completely crossed over, so that the forearms rested against each other.

And then, just about up to the dirt road entryway, he spun the wheel around again and the goddam truck caught hold.

And we came howling into the road, clipping off three RFD mailboxes on one side like matchsticks and fishtailing to hell and back, churning up a mushroom of pure sand. There was a long straightaway down to a farmhouse ahead of us.

Dock shook his head, blinking.

"First time I ever done that," he said.

"Lissen: it wasn't too bad."

"Lissen: my old man would kill me if he ever saw how sloppy I done that turn. He don't put up with sloppy driving at all."

I twisted around and looked out the back window.

The patrol car had come barreling around the last corner on the country road and he had seen us turn too late. And now he was all brake lights and skidding to beat hell and his car was fishtailing something awful trying to come to a full stop.

"Well, the po-*lice*-man didn't make it at all."

"He ain't got half our horses," Dock said.

The farmer had one of those fancy over-the-road entryways just at the end of the straightaway: split logs nicely leaned together and, in the middle, hanging over the road, was a swinging wooden sign: Meadow Dairy Farms.

He also had the gate swung closed.

Blam! We went right through the gate with about the nicest cracking noise I have ever heard, and Dock swung a soft left turn around the main cow barn.

There was a hog wallow around on the other side, with another little bitty fence around it, and we snapped right through that rascal and did a full slew-around in the mud — about three full whipping turns until we could get some traction.

Dock downshifted again and we eased around the back side of the barn and nosed up to where there was a big tractor parked under a tarp.

And, sure enough: here came the headlights down the dirt road, bobbing to beat hell, and the police car came yipping into the yard with all its brakes locked. It slid right up to the front porch and hit it and then rocked back and forth a bit. Then the door popped open and the patrolman jumped out, half-crouched and looking all over the yard.

"About now," I said.

And Dock revved it up full, sitting on the brake for just a second, and then let it go.

We came screaming out from around the other side of the barn. And we did a half-slide through the front yard and we were back on the dirt road just about the time the cop's jaw was dropping.

We did the turn better getting back onto the pavement — mostly because we started the drift further back down the road — and we went howling into town with no trouble at all.

And finally, we idled up behind the train depot, right up to where there was a new black Buick parked with its lights out.

My blood was singing, charging first down to the bottom of my feet and then sort of zinging up through my head, and I was so goddam full of hoo-hah that I damn near glowed in the dark.

"Hurry up," Cousin Ned said. He was an average-looking guy in bib overalls.

So we got out and moved the hay bales and there — just as I had figured — were several old cardboard Oxydol boxes. And each box was full of blue quart-size Mason jars. And each jar was full of liquid about the color of kerosene. Cousin Ned and someone else loaded the boxes into the trunk of the Buick.

"Here," Cousin Ned said. He seemed to be a man of few words. He handed Dock a great big roll of bills, with a rubber band wrapped around them, and Dock simply put them into his back pocket. And Cousin Ned took one long look at me and then he got into the Buick and drove off into town.

"Well," Dock said.

"Well, my ass. Where'd you learn to drive like that?"

He shrugged. "Pa taught me. Soon as my feet could reach the pedals."

"How fast were we going, you reckon?"

"Don't rightly know," he said. "We got everything unhooked on the dashboard. I just lissen to the engine and sort of guess at the rest of it."

"I'll bet we were prolly doing a hundred."

"Nawww," he said. "Mmm, well maybe down that dirt road for a piece when I was trying to get us gathered up there."

"Well, that was the best part."

"I know."

"I mean: well, I mean . . . this is *it*, right?"

"Right." We shook hands. I think maybe it's the first time in my life I had ever shaken hands.

"Think your old man can teach me how to drive?" I said.

"Don't see why not. And he's the best."

I was fifteen years old.

Papa Seegle slapped me on the backside.

"Cousin Ned tells me yer a wild-eyed sumbitch," he said.

"He says that he can tell; hell, he can spot 'em a mile away. He tells me he took one look at you down there behind the depot and he knew right away you'd grow up to be a regular piss-cutter."

"What'd he mean by that?"

"Well, I just *tole* you. I guess you town kids just don't understand good old West Virginia English. What he meant was that yer gonna grow up into a regular kiss-my-ass, mean bugger. Some kids got it in their eye when they're young. You got it, that's all."

"Is that good?"

He looked at me for a long time.

"Wall, it's a hull lot better than sucking all the blood out of *dead* folks. Somehow, I don't just rightly see you as an under-taker."

"Well . . . tell me the part about driving into the turns again," I said.

We were standing by the car down at the end of Trouble-some Valley Road again. I had been driving up and down that road every chance I had for five weeks now — and my times were getting better with every run.

"Can't take you out on the county road," Dock's father had told me, "because I'm what they call a two-timer. That is: I get caught out there one more time with a load of stuff and they haul my ass away to jail for *good*. I done lost two times now. The third one is it."

But the Troublesome Valley Road was plenty. Chrissakes, it had more dipsy-doo turns in it and switchbacks and wet spots and high-humped turns than anything anyone had ever seen.

"Well, here's what you got to do," he said. "Now, lookee here: a car is just like a horse. It's a mean-headed, ornery sum-bitch and if you don't watch it every minute it'll get right skittish on you and throw your ass out into the bullrushes alongside the road. Now, when you come up on a turn real fast, it is plumb natural to want to back off the gas a little bit. Maybe even reach for the brake — though I got to confess I ain't seen you go for a brake pedal yet, which is a good sign. Now, then: if you do back off, the car is in control and you *ain't*. So you got to *drive* her into the turn as far as she'll go without skittering. And then . . . just at the moment she bucks a little bit, why you ease off just a bit and let the momentum carry you on right to the peak of the turn. Go ahead and let her slide a little bit, if you have to — though you got to remember yer wasting time just ass-sliding. And you get to the very peak of the turn —— "

"And you get back on the gas," I said.

"Right! And then the car gets all gathered up and it really comes rifling right out of there. Now, you want to try her again?"

"Yessir."

The car was a 1936 Ford sedan, all rusted, with the side windows all cracked and the back seat torn out right on into the trunk so that it would hold a whole load of the Mason jars. But it sat lower than any 1936 Ford sedan anybody had ever seen, and coming out from under the body on each side just ahead of the rear wheels were some velocity pipes.

Old man Seegle had shown me the engine, although he had warned me never to let anybody ever look at any car engine of mine. "Tell 'em to kiss yer ass," he said, and it was dull burnished aluminum on the heads, with two downdraft carburetors.

So we climbed in and I fired it up.

"Not yet," the old man said. "Run her up a little first before you get off that brake. Okay. Now."

And we rifled off into that dark tunnel of trees, going to beat hell with everything hanging out.

"Balls out and belly to the ground," he said. "Only way to go."

I was staring into my bowl of boiled dinner and trying to spoon my way around the parsnips when my father spoke.

"I see where young Dock Seegle finally got caught," he said.

"Caught?"

"Yes," my father said. "He was driving a truck without lights after dark on the county road. I understand the lawmen have been lying in wait for him for weeks now. He ran directly into a roadblock and was arrested."

"As I have always predicted," my brother said.

"Lissen," I said. "Was he going *to* or was he coming *from* Troublesome Valley?"

"I believe he was going *to* the valley," my father said, "although I can't for the life of me see what possible difference that makes. He was speeding all the same. And driving without lights."

"Well, where is he now?"

"He's in jail, of course," Dad said.

I got up to the farmhouse at about eleven o'clock, all panting and out of breath. And just as I was crossing the yard past the privy, there was a small rustle.

And someone put the barrel end of a thirty-thirty rifle right up against the side of my neck, just under my right ear.

"It's me, for chrissakes!"

"Oh." And the barrel pulled away. And Grampa Seegle put one arm around me. "Can't be too careful," he said. "You oughtn't to come crashing up here like this after dark, son. A body could get hisself all shot full of holes that way."

"Is Mister Seegle in?"

"He's in the house. Come on."

I handed over the big roll of money while Dock's mother poured out some hot coffee.

"Dock hid it in his boot," I said. "So I went by the jailhouse and saw him and he gave me this and said to tell you he was all right but that the truck was plumb smashed all to hell. He got a small cut underneath his eye, right about here."

Mister Seegle shook his head. "Too bad," he said. "Dock's a fine boy but he's a sloppy driver. I done *tole* him that a hunnert times."

"What'll happen to him now?"

The old man looked up. "Reform school, I reckon. They keep a regular room up there permanent for the Seegles. We usually got one kid going in and one or two coming out most of the time." He sighed. "Makes them appreciate home more when they get back."

"Well. Lissen, I got to get home."

He stood up and stretched, the kitchen match in the middle of his mouth. "Well, I'll run you back down to the road. Looks like I got to go all the way tonight. Here Dock's in jail and Grampa's ass is still shot up and —— "

"But you said you were a two-time loser and —— "

"I know, I know. But this is the high-grade stuff and it goes all the way to *Clarksburg*. And I got to take the chance, just for tonight. Too much money tied up in this for anybody not to go."

"Take me along."

"No way."

"Come *on*, Mister Seegle."

"My ass," he said. Then he turned at the door. "Come on. I'll drop you off at the end of the valley road, and you kin hike on home from there. Let's go."

We came firing down the road absolutely belly to the ground and, suddenly, the old man hunkered up his shoulders. And he barked out three fast sentences:

One: "Aww, shit!"

Two: "It's the law!"

Three: "I can't stop to let you out now — get down!"

At the end of the road there was a highway patrol car waiting, pointing uphill, its lights dimmed and carrying four men. I got a quick flash of it, and the two men in the back seat were wearing peaked hats and carrying shotguns.

Seegle double-clutched the Ford and swung it right out into the bushes off the road and then rammed down on the gas and flicked on the lights.

The high beams raked across the patrol car when we came roaring out of the high grass, cutting right to beat hell, four-wheel drifting right up onto the road — headed downhill. And then I could hear the gears change again and the force of it pushed me back in the seat and my goddam eyeballs went around a couple of times and — we were off.

"Hang on," he said.

God*dam*. I had never seen anything like it: the old man swung it into corners absolute full-bore and the force of it was pushing me back and forth on the seat and, couple of times there, he would get the left or right front wheel right up off the pavement.

We came rocketing around where there was a sheer drop-off going down into the quarry and old man Seegle simply clamped down on the pedal and let the rear end swing right around on the loose gravel until my side of the car was riding out over the edge and I could look down into the endless blackness. Then we got the bite.

And by the time I could swallow, we were around two more turns.

Two snaky turns and then a long, long straightaway into town.

We careened off the last one and got it all straightened out and there they were:

Roadblock.

There were two cars parked nose-to-nose, blocking the road. And there were a few men walking around, carrying shotguns. And then they threw spotlights on us.

Deadsville.

Wrong: the old man popped the clutch again and dragged it down a gear. Then he hunkered up his shoulders a bit and said:

"Hang on."

I watched him and the roadblock at the same time.

Seegle revved it and got it all straight in the middle of the road and then — suddenly — he slammed down on the brake with his right foot and cranked the wheel all the way around hard left, far as it would go.

With his left hand he reached down and whipped back hard on the emergency brake.

There was the most beautiful howl I have ever heard in my *life*: it started right at the pit of my stomach and it took me a flash to find out that it was the sound of the tires. And the ass-end of the car snapped around to the right, whipping my head around. And the second the car got totally backward, the old man got off the brake, pumped the hand brake back in and straightened out the wheel.

And got back on the gas. Hard.

We were flat sliding backward and I looked over my shoulder. We were aimed right at the roadblock.

Wrong again.

Suddenly the tires caught hold and we changed direction so fast my tongue pasted itself to the roof of my mouth. And before I could blink we were back up the hill and into the snaking turns again.

The old man slapped at the wheel with both hands. He was *laughing*, for chrissakes.

"That there, my boy," he said, "was a bootleg turn. That

there was about the best fucking bootleg turn you'll ever see in your whole life."

We swung it around past the quarry again, screaming.

More patrol cars.

This time they were going in the same direction and, in a second, they were right on our ass, all lighted up.

"Sorry 'bout this," the old man said. "But we seem to be up to our goddam ass in policemen. Keep hanging on. I think maybe I kin outrun these bastids right a-hint us, but I figger there's got to be another block up ahead."

And then it hit me.

"Hey," I said. "The quarry road!"

"What about it?"

"Look: you got to get back to the quarry road. It's pretty goddam steep going down there, all right, but you can cut around behind the quarry and come out on a little dirt road the trucks use. And you follow it down and go through the garbage dump, see, and —— "

"Look: I *know* the road," he said. "Shitfire, I know every road in this goddam state. But all that does is get us into town and if you think there's a lot of cops *here*, why . . ."

They were losing ground on us now. Couple more turns and we'd be back at the Troublesome Valley roadblock.

"No. I got an *idea*. You roll it into town, see, and cut left on Orchard Road. And we go to *my* place, see?"

He didn't bother to glance at me, but I could tell he was thinking.

Besides, he had both forearms crossed over and we were drifting flat sideways around a tight one.

"And after we get to your place?"

I was so full of the idea that I could hardly hold it in.

"The hearse!" I said. "The fucking *hearse*, man!"

He nodded.

"You know," he said, "Cousin Ned was right. Yer going to grow up to be a real ass-buster."

And here came the roadblock.

And here came another bootleg turn.

We rolled up quietly, lights out, ambling down the alley behind our house.

"Here," I said.

He boosted me up until I could open the back window on the garage. Then I stepped down on the workbench and came down on the floor beside the hearse and opened the main garage door. He was there.

"Help me load the stuff," he whispered.

It took six trips each. The back of the hearse was all lined with crinkle-velvet and the Mason jars went in very quietly. Then the old man leaned over with his mouth right next to my ear.

"What'll we cover the jars with?" he said.

"Flowers. They're right over here in the greenhouse. Come on."

"Whut about the casket?"

"Don't worry about the casket. It's always in there, see. Just pile the flowers on each side here."

"I really hate calla lilies," he said. "And iris."

"Me, too. Come on, get some more."

It came out real well: the banks of flowers fit on each side of the casket, covering the jars. And then the old man climbed in back and huddled down in the little space just ahead of the casket and just behind the front seat.

"How's this?"

"Can you get your head down a little bit more?"

"Them fucking flowers," he said.

"Come *on*."

"All right, all right."

And I opened the garage door as quietly as I could.

Roadblock. Awwww, shit.

"There's another roadblock up here," I said, talking over my shoulder. I was driving very slowly now and the engine on the old Buick hearse was meshing along without a sound.

"Well, keep on driving. No way yer gonna do a bootleg turn in *this* big sumbitch."

"Lemme try, will you? I think I got the hang of it."

"No way. Lissen: you get *this* goddam sled sideways and yer gonna be picking lilies out of yer ass for months."

Too late anyway. I could see them flashing the lights up ahead and, off to each side were the men with shotguns, all wearing pointy peaked hats and breeches and puttees.

So I let it ease up gently. And then I rolled down the window.

"Yessir?" I said.

The patrolman leaned in and shined the flashlight into my face for a second. Then he straightened up and talked to someone over his shoulder while I was still blinking away those little bubbles of light dancing around my eyes.

"It's Milton Ace's boy," he said. "You know. The one from over at the funeral parlor." Then he leaned back in at me. "Where you going, son?"

"Clarksburg, sir."

"Whut for?"

I blinked and eased into my Funeral Face. "I'm delivering the remains of someone, sir. The last rites are the first thing in the morning."

He straightened and then pulled off his peaked hat and held it over his heart. And he shook his head.

"Terrible business for a boy yer age to be mixed up in," he said. "But, go on. And be careful, you hear?"

"Yessir." And I eased it into gear.

Ahead, they were backing away one of the patrol cars so that I could go through.

Wrong.

"Wait just a goddam minute!"

It was a very fat man in a rumpled tan chino suit, and the points on his shirt collar were starting to roll up. He was sweating and he was madder than hell. "Who tole you to let this here ve-*hicle* through?" he growled.

The cop was just a little bit flustered.

"It's Milton Ace's boy," he said. "The undertaker. And he's goin' off to Clarksburg with a bod — with the RE-mains of a . . . uhhh, body, to deliver to a *fun*-eral. Uhh, sir."

"My ass," the man said. And he bustled over to me and shined his own flashlight into my Funeral Face. I held it tight until my jaw muscles hurt.

"Who you?" he said.

"Stroker Ace, sir," I said. "Milton Ace is my father, and he's the funeral director. Like the officer said. Sir."

The fat man straightened up again and talked to somebody else.

"I'll tell you one thing," he said. "This fucking town is FULL of moonshine, you *understand* me? *Full.* I mean: this goddam, miserable-ass town is up to HERE with illegal booze and they got to be getting it through some*how*. I'm tired of being assed around by these fucking hillbillies. You underSTAND me?"

There was a pause while, presumably, everybody nodded yes.

"And when I say nobody gets through without being fucking searched, I mean no-BODY." He bent down again and flashed the light into me again. I was getting pretty tired of that routine. But I held the face. "Get out of the car, kid," he said.

"Yessir." So I climbed out and stood there.

"Now SEARCH it!" And the fat man turned and walked back into the shadows, wiping at his face with a handkerchief.

"Sorry about this," the officer said. He still had his hat off.

He looked at it for a minute and then plopped it back on top of his head. "Really sorry."

"You know what they say about violating the dead, sir," I said.

He groaned a little at that. "I know. Well, come on. Let's look in there."

So I opened the rear door.

"Watch out for the flowers," I said.

"I won't touch the flowers. I just wanta see *in* there." And he shined the flashlight in, quickly, and snapped it out again.

From out of the darkness where the other men were huddled came the voice of the fat man.

"Look in the *coffin*, you idiot," it said.

The cop and I looked at each other for a long, long minute.

"You do it," he said, and handed me the flashlight.

"No, *sir*. Not me. This is your search, sir." And I handed it back to him. Then I turned back to the casket. "Now, see, the casket rolls out here on these little rollers like . . . like this. Let me get this here latch undone. There. Now, you ease it back like this and then you can open it up." And I stepped back.

He took his hat off again and held it over his heart, and then he put it back on his head again. And then he shifted the flashlight from one hand to the other.

"Look, kid: would you do it? I mean, just open her up a little crack there so I can shine this light in there just a second. The inspector over there'll never shut up until I do."

"No, sir. You do it. Not me."

I unlatched the top part for him.

And he reached over and lifted it up just a crack.

And he shined the light in.

I sort of sidled over and looked in, too.

And there was Mister Seegle: hands folded up across his

chest. The shadow of the coffin lid fell across his face when the flashlight shined in. And the cop quickly turned away.

"Close it, for chrissakes," he said.

I closed the lid and wiped the palms of my hands on the seat of my pants.

And he sort of leaned against the side of the hearse. He took off his hat one more time. "Lordy," he said. "Lordy *me*. Whatever did he die *of*, for God's sake?"

I gave him the full Funeral Face. "Please," I said.

He shook his head some more. "Yer sure it's all right? I mean, my lifting the coffin lid and all?"

"Well, you know what they say about desecrating the dead."

"Oh, God, kid. Look: just get the hell out of here, all right? Come on. Just *go*, for chrissakes."

I was about five miles out of town, driving along at a pretty smooth clip, too, when the lid lifted up on the casket just behind my head.

"God *damn*," Mister Seegle said, "but I sure do hate the smell of calla lilies."

Childhood always ends at a roadblock.

I took my share of the big Clarksburg haul and kept right on going.

I drove the hearse all the way to Georgia, where I saw the sign just outside a small county racetrack. A half-mile dirt track.

The sign said:

DEMOLITION DERBY
SUNDAY

And I eased into the parking lot and went up to the house trailer that served as the office.

"Sign me up," I said.

"Whut you got?"

I shrugged. "A pretty new Buick hearse."

The guy looked over the top of his glasses at me. "Let me ask you just one thing, kid," he said, "and I'm not gonna ask you anything else. Okay?"

"Fine."

"Can you drive pretty good?"

I looked at him with my Funeral Face.

"Let me put it this way," I said. "Does a black bear shit in the woods?"

Uneasy Rests the Head
That Wears the Crown.
—*Anonymous*

That's Horseshit.
—*Stroker Ace*

came whipping into the pits at ninety-seven miles an hour with all my brakes gone. This little move is absolutely, flat guaranteed to give everybody a little thrill right down the line — and I could see all the other crews hopping right up on top of the pit wall as I came past, with the car doing wide, sweeping fishtails. And when I figured I had it slowed down just enough, I double-clutched the balls out of it and popped that rascal right into reverse. And I came sliding right up against Lugs Harvey's belly button.

He shook his head and then ran around to the driver side and stuck his big, sweaty face right into the window at me.

I yanked down my mask.

"Brakes," I said. "No fucking brakes."

He nodded and pulled his head out just as the whole right side of the car went up into the air: the crew had jacked it up and was snatching off the wheels. Behind me, they began dumping in the gas and, in front, Limpy Clawson came hopping up with that crablike gait of his. He had a cloth rag in his left hand and a paper cup full of cold Dr Pepper in his right hand. He stuck the cup in through the window at me, hitting the doorsill with the butt of his hand and spilling most of it right down into my lap. I drank what little there was left of it and tugged my mask back up, contemplating the prospect of finishing the race with sticky balls. Then Limpy swabbed off the window with his rag and stepped back just as the car came banging back down on all four.

Poised over by the right fender, Lugs waved to get my attention. Then he drew a small circle in the air with his left hand; he was holding his thumb and forefinger together. And then he held both hands out in front of him and motioned downward with the palms. And then he jerked his right thumb back toward the track.

I hit the throttle and got the hell out of there.

Lugs had just told me a lot. This is what Lugs had told me with his hands:

Mister Ace, it sore grieves me to tell you that your brakes seem to be hopelessly shot. Ruined. There is no goddam drum left, as you can see from the position of my thumb and forefinger. However, in my experienced mechanical judgment, you should be able to finish the race if you will only take it easy, as I am indicating by holding my palms down. And while you are mulling over these fearsome prospects, may I respectfully suggest that you get your ass back into the race, since we don't have that much time left. It sure was nice seeing you again here in the pits, but now you gotta go.

All this took 16.7 seconds. Dr Pepper and all.

Everybody does this, though maybe nobody in the world does it as well as Lugs Harvey, who can make a fast pit stop look like he is directing the Mormon Tabernacle Choir through a tricky section of Handel's *Messiah* or something like that.

We talk to each other this way for damn good reasons: (1) I have got cotton stuffed into both ears and (2) I have got my

Bell helmet over that with its big, padded earpieces, and (3) who the hell wants to listen to Lugs Harvey talk about brakes in the middle of a race, anyway?

I wound that son of a bitch up as high as it would go in second gear and while doing that I looked all around through all the other cars for Turbo Ellison and Hack Downing.

When last I left the two of them buggers they were slamming around the track in that order, front bumper against back bumper, as if they were welded together. Turbo was leading the race. Hack was second. I am third.

Take it easy, my ass.

I cranked into the Number Four Turn and came howling back down the main straightaway — and out of the quick-corner of my eye I could see Lugs standing at the pit wall with the two stopwatches on his clipboard. In a couple of seconds, when he got my time calculated, he was going to have something of a mechanical fit.

And *there* was Hack Downing, that bastard. Turbo was smack in front of him and, going through the One-Two Turn, they looked all blurry and stretched out like the longest racecar in the whole goddam world.

Understand now, everybody knows that Hack Downing is a Drafting Son of a Bitch: he is know all over the South for it.

Here is the way it goes: at top speed a car churns up a whole lot of air turbulence behind it, and if you are riding a bit off to one side, it can suck the fillings right out of your teeth. But at the same time, just behind the same car — right smack behind it — there is this little, narrow envelope of quiet air. People who know all about Physics have a proper term for this, I think. But race drivers around the South all know it just naturally and most of them don't know what Physics means. Besides, they couldn't pronounce it if they saw it, let alone spell it. Hellfire, most of them would have a tough fucking time making the letter *P*.

They all call it drafting.

Any race driver with any balls at all knows that, if he can ease his car right up behind, that he can ride along inside this little breather-space. Right away a couple of great things happen. One: he can back off just a little bit on his own gas because the car in front of him is pushing all the air and doing most of the work. Two: he is actually conserving fuel, a factor that could just win the race for him if it is close. Three: if you *really* pin down that Physics bullshit, there are times when he is actually going just a little, teeny bit faster than the car in front. Thus, four: if his timing is really good, then he can pull off what is known as the slingshot. Now, I don't know what in Christ's name Einstein called the slingshot, but consider this: when the car directly in front of him slows down just a touch for a hard corner — well, then, just for that split second there, the back car is still going faster, see? So, if a driver is good enough, that is the precise second when he will whip his own car around and pass the front car — slingshotting out in front.

Item five: drafting also drives the front driver goofy. I mean, every time he glances into his rear-vision mirror he sees nothing but windshield and radiator behind him and the only thing he can do is trust the other driver a whole awful lot and pray to beat hell that nothing goes wrong on the track out there in front of him. Any front-running driver who would hit his brakes at a time like that knows goddam well that he will absolutely, promptly end up with a 4,000-pound stock car right up his ass.

And there was Turbo: screaming down the back straight, steady as could be. With Hack Downing right on his tail pipes.

I touched my brakes going into the turn and got just about what I expected. Nothing. So I just stayed on the gas. I mean, what the hell, right?

The force of the curve without any brakes was twisting the car on its frame and just about pulling me out of the seat toward the right-side door, and my damn heart and spleen and bowels and everything sloughed over to the right side of my damn stomach and hung there like tapioca pudding, shaking. Tires howling to beat hell, I came up alongside J. R. Hoffman in his Olsen Garages Mercury and we rubbed door handles there for a fast second or two. Old J.R. always races with an unlit, dead contraband Cuban cigar clamped right in the middle of his mouth and when I nicked him I also glanced over at him: he bit the fucking cigar smack through and it fell away from his face somewhere into the inside of his car.

Well, screw you, Hoffman. If you can't race that sumbitch, you had best park it.

And now you, Hack, my boy. And I snuck right up behind him. At, oh, say, about 198 miles an hour.

We all came off the Number Four like a damn three-car, close-order parade and I could look up ahead and see old Hack hunch up his shoulders and hunker down his head when he suddenly saw me in his mirror. That's not all I could see: just out of the edge of my left eyeball I could see Lugs Harvey holding up a pit sign that had "E-Z" smeared on it in giant chalk letters. And then he was gone. And then came the end of the straightaway, just like that.

Easy, my ass. As we say in racing.

Just ahead, Hack dropped his left shoulder just a teeny bit and hunched his head down ever further. I knew what it meant.

It meant that he was about to slingshot Turbo, that's what it meant.

And, sure enough, he hauled right out to the left and rifled up alongside Turbo. The space between them was thinner than a goddam infield concession-stand hamburger.

Good for Hack.

Bad for Turbo. That's because I was tail-piping Hack and what neither one of them bastards knew was that *I* was the only one who didn't have any brakes. And that's the way we got into the middle of the turn, right up there on the banking. Chrissakes, I think maybe I hunkered down my own shoulders there for just a little bit.

Turbo wasn't having any of that old bullshit, not a second of it. He had more power left than either one of us in his monster goddam Plymouth and he was a dead, immortal cinch to outdrag both of us down the straights. So he put his foot right into it. And, as we came off the turn, he inched up ahead of Hack again and he drew a goddam bead on the curve.

Hot damn. Drew a bead. That means that Turbo came diving down to his left, going to beat hell, and he chopped Hack off right there. Good for Turbo.

Bad for me.

Naturally, Hack hit his brakes right now. Well, hell, fans, it was either hit his brakes or let Turbo rip off the whole right side of the car. Which certainly makes a lot of sense. Except that I was right there on Hack's tail. Drafting, remember?

Oh, shit, Ace.

This sort of thing makes for what they call Great Moments in Stock Car Racing.

I cranked that son of a bitch left as quick as I could and got out of Hack's air pocket and out into the turbulent world on my own. And there we were: three abreast on the back straightaway, all three cars fishtailing an awful lot, puffing up smoke from the tires. With Turbo on the outside, poor old Hack in the middle. And Stroker Ace — no goddam brakes — roughly on the rail.

They tell me the crowd went wild.

There was no way we were going to make it through the turn in that sort of lineup. No fucking way.

Well, hell. Somebody simply had to give it up. I stayed on the throttle and I ran all the prospects through my mind like a very quick Public Opinion poll:

QUESTION: Mister Racer-man, has Turbo Ellison ever been known to back off in a race?

ANSWER: Turbo Ellison? Are you crazy?

QUESTION: Well, how about Hack Downing?

ANSWER: How about that?

So long, Hack.

We came boiling out of the turn in the world's most dangerous game of Chicken and there was just one split flash there where I could glance to my right and see two sets of radiators and hoods glaring at me. And that's exactly when Hack Downing's bowels froze right up. He eased off and let us through.

And then it got worse. *Worse.*

For one thing, I was already into the turn too damned fast for a guy who couldn't tap his brakes and that meant that there was probably only one thing to do. So I did it: I cranked the wheel hard left and let that sumbitch drift right around.

Well, you got to know how to do it and I hadn't spent all my wasted youth in cars for nothing: I once got a brand-new Nash Rambler into a four-wheel drift coming around that big turn near Wendover, Utah, and drifted the damn thing all the way to Lily's whorehouse in Ely, for chrissakes. And Ely is in Nevada.

So I stayed right on the gas and listened to the car do strange things and twist and pop and I was so full of torque that my damn eyes began to water and my tongue was squashed flat over against all my right-side teeth and I could feel the rough texture of all my fillings and that one gold cap that I have back there on the Third Upper Right Molar.

Then there was a clean sort of *snap!* and the right side of the windshield suddenly turned into a spiderweb of little, radiating cracked lines from the strain. And the gearshift began acting like it was going to jump clean out the right-side door, so I tore one hand loose from the wheel and held the shift-lever down with the butt of my hand. And I looked along the nose and drew a bead on the main straight.

And I stayed on the gas.

Turbo must have been right out of his gourd. There he was, hammering along nicely, right beside a car that was flat fucking sideways. Turbo was going frontwards, right enough, giving it all he had — and here was this damn car going just as fast *sideways,* for God's sake, with the damn front stretch coming up.

And you think that dumb bastard would choke up just a little bit?

No way.

Then we snapped right out of the turn and there was only one small comfort. Small comfort: I was in the groove and Turbo was on the outside. Probably madder than hell, I would venture to say.

We rocketed down the straight and, this time, Lugs was just a despairing blur. *Smudge,* and he was gone.

Down at the end of the straight, Race Starter Dollar Bill Handley had the white flag out: one more lap. Except that he wasn't waving the flag in that very flashy manner of his that is something of a tradition all over the South. He was just standing there with his poor goddam mouth open, watching the two of us come right at him. About two full seconds after we had gone by he jumped out of the way.

Question-and-answer time again:

QUESTION: Let's see, now. About one more of them dumb fucking dipsy-doo turns and you'll have no more windshield. Is that right, Mister Ace?

ANSWER: One more. Right.

QUESTION: Or any chassis. Is that correct, Ace?

ANSWER: Correct, yes. No chassis. Not to even mention nuts,

bolts, doors and roll bars. And pretty soon that gearshift is going to boogaloo right over where I can't even reach it, for chrissakes.

QUESTION: But what the hell, Ace. You do want to win this race, don't you?

ANSWER: Well, yes. Matter of fact, I do. I do.

Okay, then, Let's try it one more time. Jesus Christ, there's only this one more lap to go. You do this and you've done it all.

Two hands, this time: I wheeled left and jammed my foot down on the pedal until my toes hurt inside my seventy-five-dollar, handmade Italian leather driving shoes. And I yanked it back hard to the right and clenched my teeth. I also clenched my: armpits, kneecaps, elbows, thigh bones and testicles (which were already pretty well clenched anyway from that spilled Dr Pepper). And around we went.

CRACK! The goddam windshield sort of *imploded* when the frame twisted and for a few seconds the inside of the car was full of gently floating, drifting little pieces of glass, like the pictures you see of a spaceship at Zero Gravity. Then the gearshift just sort of jiggled right out of the damn socket and lay on its side, kicking and quivering. And then the glass shattered on the tachometer and sprinkled itself down on top of my right knee like bright, shining crystal rock candy.

Still, there was the goddam backstraight. And I eased the wheel left again and let the car snap back around.

And there I was: ahead of Turbo Ellison. I glanced at my rear-vision mirror and discovered that there wasn't any rear-vision mirror.

But I knew he was back there, all right. That's because he came powering right along and gave me a sharp *whap!* on the rear bumper.

Uh-huh. Well, at least it was nice to know that the rear bumper was still there.

So I took my right hand off the wheel for just a second and I flashed old Turbo a half a peace sign and then I got set to crank into the last turn.

I'm not sure where Turbo was just then. Except that he sure as hell didn't have enough room to come around me and I was just too busy to check and see.

Down the main straight — and by this time I had my foot locked into the gas. And two things happened:

Thing One: Just as I rolled past Lugs Harvey, the whole fucking transmission blew apart.

Thing Two: and just after that, I got the checkered flag. The winner and the new NASCAR Champion.

I took my feet off everything and let the car roll and roll. And then I shook my head around a little bit to try and unlock my neck muscles.

And I sort of drummed my fingertips on the steering wheel and I hummed a few bars of "Stick It in Your Ear, Missus Murphy."

The car coasted and coasted and coasted. Right through the Number One and Number Two Turn, and I let the rest of the drivers come on around me, including Turbo Ellison. You recall Turbo Ellison. He's Number Two, that fucking meatball.

Finally, just as I was reaching over to turn it off, the engine just gave an apologetic kind of little cough and died. Little wisps of blue smoke started curling up from around the hood edges.

And then the steering wheel came right off in my hands.

I sat there, parked alongside the infield, until the fire truck came up. Lugs was perched on the front fender, still carrying the clipboard with the two stopwatches attached. He hopped off before the truck even stopped and came running up.

Lugs gave me his usual cheery post-race greeting:

"You dumb bast —— "

"Hey, Lugs. How you doing? Here — " I handed him the

steering wheel out of the window " — here is a special award from all the gang at Rain Tree Farms. I want you to take this here award and give it to old Turbo. Tell him he knows where he can hang it."

Lugs snatched the wheel away and threw it down and kicked it halfway across the infield, just missing a few spectators who were running up. "Come *on*," he said. "Goddammit, now, Stroker, come *on*. Chrissakes, you crazy goddam —— "

"And one more thing," I said. "I'd like this front windshield replaced and maybe check the oil and check on the transmission. It squeaks just a bit there on the turns. You know. Probably nothing serious. Oh, yeah. The brakes need just a little work. Think maybe you can have it ready for me by, say, five o'clock?"

Lugs threw down his clipboard and stamped it right in half under his heel. When he gets real worried he always sputters just a little bit.

"F-f-f-f-for chrissakes," he said. "Y-y-y-y-you scared me half to d-d-d-death, you crazy son of a b-b-b, uhhh, you son of a b-b-b-b, ummm . . ."

"Bitch," I said. Then I unhooked the master release on all my safety harnesses and shrugged them off. "Look out there just for a second." I sort of squinched around in the front seat and put the bottoms of both my feet against the door. Sure enough, it fell right off. "I thought that might happen."

Lugs kicked the door, too. Then he danced around a little bit, holding on to his toe with one hand.

"You could have been k-k-k-k-killed," he said, full of reproach. "I tole you to take it easy. God's sake, I even wrote it on the fucking chalkboard. *E-Z*. No brakes, for God's sake. And you had to go out there and take off after Turbo Ellison. You coulda been killed out there."

"Uh-huh. Lissen: how'd I look on those turns?"

Lugs thought about it for a long minute. Then he grinned.

"Never seen nothing like it, ever," he said. "I mean, *ever*. Shit, this whole place was nothing but eyeballs and elbows and teeth for them last two laps. I mean: you was absolutely flat fucking *sideways*, you crazy bastard. And that Turbo was squinched right up against the wall. Why, shit, he —— "

"Come on, you guys," the fire chief said. "Your goddam adoring public is waiting."

"Shall we?" I said to Lugs.

He bowed. It was not really all that bad a bow for a guy with his size stomach. "Leave us," he said.

And we took our victory parade lap standing up in the back of the fire truck.

Lugs waved at everybody just as much as I did. Hell, a couple of times there, I caught him blowing kisses to the crowd.

This time, the operator found her in the hospital. She was quite a little while in getting to the phone.

"Yes?" she said.

"I hope I didn't take you away from a tonsillectomy or anything," I said.

"Stroker! Are you all right?"

"Bet your ass," I said. "I just won it all. All of it, the whole thing. But what counts, what really counts with all of us here at Atlanta, is how are *you*, Nursie?"

"Oh, I'm so glad for you. You didn't get hurt or anything?"

"I'm fine. The car is a little sick, but I'm fine."

"And you just called to tell me that . . ."

"That's all I called to tell you. And now, if you'll excuse me, I'm going to go and have a little shooter. Maybe two shooters, all right?"

"Of course it's all right. Have a lot of shooters. And congratulations again. Tell me . . ."

"Mmmm?"

". . . tell me: why did you call me, of all people?"

"Nursie," I said, "it beats the hell out of me."

"This here," said Clyde Torkle, the Chicken King, "is *imported* champagne. I mean, the real stuff. See here, right on this here label? It says right here: Napa Valley."

Lugs leaned over and looked at it. Lugs moves his lips when he reads things. "Well, Napa Valley is in Cali*forn*ia, for chrissakes," he said.

Torkle shrugged. "Exactly. They're all a bunch of gahdam foreigners back there anyways. Here, have some more."

Lugs made a face. "Shit, doesn't anybody have any *beer* around here?" he said. "Cham-PAGNE, for God's sake."

We were sitting in the Goodyear tire van, the two big back doors open and the tailgate down. I had my shoes off and my driving uniform unzippered down to my belly. I also had lipstick all over my neck and a check for $26,890.64 in my pocket.

The crowd had gone home and, outside, the slanting sun was turning the track into a sort of shimmery gold. There were just a few trucks and campers left, and one or two lonely drunks throwing up in the infield, and the air had cooled down real quickly like it does in the South. And, maybe if a man breathed in deeply enough, he could smell honeysuckle. This is the best time around a racetrack.

We were sitting on stacks of tires wrapped in brown paper and there was a galvanized iron washtub full of ice and bottles in front of us.

Clyde Torkle had his cowboy hat pushed back and his forehead was sweaty. He had started drinking, I suspect, just about the first time he saw me get his brand-new car sideways on the track. And now his face had a really sort of fine, shiny glow to it. Matched the tip of his cigar.

"I can't believe it," he said. "I *got* the champeenship. Honest to God, I can't believe it."

"You better believe it," Lugs said. He burped, gently. "This here" — he waved one of his greasy hands at me — "this here is the greatest fucking race driver ever to get a-hint the wheel of a racecar. I mean: did you see that finish?"

"Shitfire, I *seen* it. I don't believe it, but I sure seen it."

"Sideways," Lugs said, nodding.

"And going faster than Turbo. Sideways."

"Never mind that," I said. "More champagne here."

Lugs leaned over and pulled a fresh bottle out of the washtub. He closed one big, massive hand around the cork — the fancy aluminum foil, those little tiny wires and all — and he simply snatched the whole thing right off in one smooth pull. The wine sprayed up and down across his stomach. Then he leaned back and yelled out loud.

"CHARLIE!" he yelled.

And Charlie Heffer stuck his head up at the back doors. "I'm countin' tires," he said.

"How many you got?"

"I got, uhhhh . . . I got, mmm . . . shit, Lugs, you made me lose count." And his head disappeared.

"That there," Lugs said solemnly, "that there is the greatest fucking tire buster in the whole world. I mean: Charlie is the greatest. You understand me? Ain't a thing that Charlie don't know about tire compounds. Always saves the best tires for Ace here. Hell, Charlie tells *me* what tires to put on and when to change 'em. Shee-it. Imagine that. He tells ME. You understand?"

"Mister Harvey?"

It was the track maintenance man, his head appearing at eye level at the back tailgate. "Mister Harvey?"

"Have some champagne, my good man," Lugs said. "I'm awful sorry, fella, but we don't have any beer."

"Thank you. Just a drop. There, that's fine. Uhh, well, congratulations on the champeenship, Mister Ace."

"You can call him Stroker," Torkle said. Then he thought about it for a minute. "Well, for today only."

"Mister Harvey?"

"Mmmmmm?" Lugs said.

"Mister Harvey, what do you want done with the car?"

Lugs looked blank. "Whut car?"

"The *race*car. The one you all won the race in. It's still a-sittin' out there by the backstretch."

Lugs swung his head around and looked at Clyde.

And Torkle thought about it, shaking his head. "Well, now," he said. "Uh-huh. The car. The *car*, right?" He looked at all of us. "You know now, that there is the car that won the champeenship. I mean: that there is a *historic* car, you dumb pecker-heads. You realize that we just won the gahdam title in that very car? I mean: you can't just let it sit out there."

"Sure can't," the maintenance man said.

"I didn't ask you," Clyde said.

"Excuse me, sir."

"Can you drive it back to the garage in town?" Clyde asked Lugs.

Lugs leaned back and yelled again.

"CHARLIE!" he yelled.

And Charlie Heffer stuck his head up over the tailgate again. "Now what?"

"The man wants to know kin we drive that car back to the garage in town."

"Mister Torkle," Charlie said, "everybody knows that when Lugs builds a car, he builds it to run five hunnert miles. Five hunnert miles. And that's all."

Lugs burped again. "And then the little fucker self-destructs," he said.

"And that ain't all," Charlie said. "When Ace here gets through with a car, the goddam frame is bent all out of shape and the chassis is sprung and the doors is all off and the windows is often bust right out."

Torkle nodded, blinking. Then he sniffed deeply and a perfect tear came out of each eye and rolled halfway down each jowl. "Lissen," he said. "Think of Goshen, New York. I mean: that's all I ask." And he sniffed again.

"Goshen?"

"Well, *sure*, Goshen, you dumb bastards. I mean: ole Messenger, the world's most famous trotting horse, right? I mean: one day ole Messenger just up and *died* right there in harness. I mean, he just fell right in his traces and by-God *died*. And, by God . . ." Torkle snuffled again, heavily. ". . . and, by Jesus, they buried him right there on the spot. And today, to this very *day*, there is a little ole, teensy white picket fence around his very grave there in the infield at Averell Harriman's racetrack. And there's a little printed sign that says: 'Here Lies Ole Messenger, Greatest Fucking Harness Horse That Ever Drew a Breath!' "

Then he really started crying.

Lugs stood up and put one big hand over his chest.

"By damn," he said, "we'll dig a hole and —— "

Torkle looked up. ". . . and we'll *bury* that car right there in the infield. And I'll have a monument made out of real, solid Georgia Sea Wall marble and —— "

The maintenance man blinked. "I don't think we're allowed to do that, sir," he said.

"Who asked you? Here, have some more champagne."

"Excuse me, sir. Uhhh, yes. Just a drop there. But, no, I don't think you can just up and bury —— "

"Tell you what," said Lugs. "You got a truck, fella?"

"Yessir, I have. This here is sure good champagne."

"Imported," Torkle said.

Lugs poured some more all around. "Now you take your truck," he said, "and . . . you know where Hobbs Corners is at?"

"Yessir, I do."

"It's imported from Napa Valley," Torkle said. "Them fucking foreigners."

"Well," Lugs said. "You just load up that racecar in your truck. Now, don't forget to pick up the steering wheel in the infield there. And then you drive the whole thing over to Hobbs Corners. You got that part?"

Charlie stuck his head up. "Take the tires and all," he said. He turned to me. "You know, Ace, you flat *rooned* them tires on the turns? I mean: going sideways at the speeds you was going. Hot damn. Talk about flat spots."

"Sorry."

He nodded. "S'nothing. Goodyear got plenty more."

"More wine, Charlie?" Torkle got up again, a little bit unsteady.

"You made me lose count again," Charlie said. "But, yup. Just pour her right in there."

"Well, anyway," Lugs said to the maintenance man. "You get to Hobbs Corners and you come to the stoplight. And you turn left there and you go on past the hardware store. And you go on down the road a section and you come to a sort of fawn-colored house. Got that?"

"Uh-huh. Yessir."

"Well, then. On the mailbox, you'll see painted there: *Turbo Ellison, R.F.D.* And you take that racecar and you dump it right in the middle of the driveway. Best if you do it at night."

"Well, sir. All this will cost . . ."

Torkle jammed his hand down deep into his pocket. And he came up with a fistful of big bills. He bent over at the tailgate and peeled a few off.

"Here," he said. "This'll cover it, won't it?"

"Sure will. Golly dog, yessir. Uh-huh."

"Remember now," Lugs said. "Turbo Ellison. Dump it right there in the fucking driveway."

"So much for that," Torkle said. "Now, then."

Lugs snatched the top off another bottle. "Cups!" he yelled.

We all held ours out. Charlie Heffer popped up at the tailgate. "Me, too," he said. "Son of a bitch, but, I swear: a few more of these here and I may start to *like* this stuff."

"I propose a toast," Torkle said.

"And I accept," said Lugs.

"Not you, asshole. No. I propose a toast to the new NASCAR Champeen. And to the greatest fucking feat of stock car driving ever done on any racetrack at any time, any*where*."

We all stood up to drink the toast.

And Charlie looked up over the tailgate at me.

"Stroker," he said. "Kin I ask you something?"

"Hmmmm?"

"Did you piss in your pants out there during the race?"

"No, why?"

"Well, look there."

I looked down at my crotch. It was all suspiciously yellow-stained.

"You are not going to believe this," I said. "But that is Dr Pepper."

Torkle burped. "That Dr Pepper. Another fucking foreigner," he said.

nine

He bellied right up to the Avis counter and leaned his face over close, and he used his air-cooled Franklin voice:

"Hey, baby, how's about you and me checking in over there at the Ramada Inn for a month or two?"

"Hi, Charlie," the girl said — without even looking up from the contract she was filling out. Another customer was standing there. He was wearing horn-rimmed glasses and looking a whole lot like a ladies' underwear salesman.

Charlie put his elbows up on the counter. "How'd you know it was me, Nancy?"

"Easy. I don't really get too many opening lines like that in Salt Lake City, Charlie."

"Well, then. You had better get your cute little tail out of this hick burg and get transferred to Atlanta or someplace like that where they know how to treat a lady." And Charlie plopped his package of Goodyear tire specs right down on top of the contract she was filling out.

The salesman huffed up just a little bit and looked at Charlie like he was really considering perhaps popping him one.

"I think you've made this nice gentleman mad," I said.

Charlie leaned over to the guy: "Don't hit me, mister," he whispered. "I'm wearing contact lenses."

The guy looked in there at Heffer's eyes real close to see if maybe this was true. And if he didn't see any lenses, he saw something that changed his mind. "You go right ahead, sir," he said. "Please."

Charlie turned back to the girl. "Now, then," he said. "I wanna rent a racer."

"Charlie, for heaven's sake. You can't keep coming in here like this every time and chasing our customers away. It's not nice."

"Lissen: it's all right, Nancy. I chase a lot of Hertz customers away, too."

"He does," I said. "He really does. It balances out."

"Oh, yeah. I almost forgot. Nancy, this here is Stroker Ace." He waved one hand, casually. "He . . . uhh, he races cars or whatever. I forget."

"Stroker Ace," she said. "Stroker Ace."

I nodded. "Uh-huh. Lissen: how's about you and me checking in over there at the Ramada Inn for a month or two?"

"You get the room and I'll be there at five-oh-five," she said.

Charlie turned back to the salesman. "All right, then," he said, "what are *you* doin' tonight, sweetie?"

The trip from Salt Lake City to Wendover, Utah, goes like this: you set the rental car at 105 (which is not really 105, no way), and you hold it there for 120 miles or so. No need to look right or left, or up or down. It sometimes helps to have a few cans of cold beer along.

About five miles or so out of Wendover, we came flying past the side road that leads off across the salt desert to the Bonneville Salt Flats. There is a billboard there with a picture of old Ab Jenkins and his Mormon Meteor, or something, and the sign says something about the world's fastest speedway. I must confess that I've never really read it that close, because every time I come by the damn thing we're going so fast that it blurs a bit.

"More beer," I said. "Lissen: what time does the Ford stuff get here?"

Charlie popped open another can. "I dunno. Sometime today, I think. They said they'd have the car set up maybe tomorrow morning if you're ready to run it. Tire truck prolly got here yestiddy from the coast. You wanna run in the morning?"

"Why not? There sure as hell isn't anything else to do out here."

"Well, yer ass. What about the ladies at the Western Cafe, buddy?"

"They're all yours."

He rolled down the window and threw out the empty beer can. "Yeah, well you can scoff if you want. But maybe they got a new one or two there now. Lissen: you remember that Indian lady who was here three . . . maybe four years ago? You know, when you ran the stuff for, mmmm, Champeen Spark Plugs? Well, that's the one who did everything but scalp you when you got her in bed, buddy."

"Mmmmmmmm."

I slid it into the parking lot at the Wendover Motel and shut it down. We were pulling our gear bags out of the back seat when someone came over and goosed me.

Fergie Lattimer.

You've seen him. Well, you may not know it but you've seen him: Furgison Oliver Lattimer III looks like the guy doing a Jack Oakie imitation at a party. Sometimes he will put a lampshade on his head and jump out into the middle of the room and say:

"Hey! Let's get the kids together and put on a Broadway show!"

Otherwise, Fergie Lattimer is (1) a racing mechanic and (2) insane — sort of a Lugs Harvey with a real college degree from MIT or someplace — and (3) *respected in the industry* — which means he can walk into the Ford Design Studios in Detroit and slap secretaries on the ass and not get thrown out.

Fergie designed the over-and-under, free-breathing double-thin cam or same goddam thing, who knows?

Still: Ford had sent him all the way out here with a big vanload of brand-new Mach I's, with instructions to get them all set up for me so that I could go out on the Salt Flats and break a bunch of speed records.

Motor companies do this. And, Lord knows, plenty of world speed records are available, if you have a taste for being bored while scaring yourself to death. The thing is, you must slam a car absolutely balls-out around a ten-mile circular track or down a straightaway: Two Hours, Four Hours, Twenty-four Hours, Forty-eight Hours, Night into Day; Kilometers and Furlongs. You are allowed to leap out and piss on the salt while your car is being refueled, but not much else.

And the more bored you get, the more danger you are in.

Last time I did this I set the world record for dozing and three international records for blinking my eyes at 165.45 miles an hour. Please do not tell USAC or the Fédération Internationale d'Automobile about this. Once, about four o'clock in the morning, I damn near drove through the tent where five mechanics were sleeping.

And the motorcar companies pay an awful lot of money for this, so that they can advertise on television that their car is hot stuff.

And now: Fergie grabbed my hand and started right out without saying hello:

"New talent. New talent in town," he said.

"Uh-huh. Swell."

"Where?" Charlie said. "Cafe?" He dropped his gear bag on my foot and started over there.

Western Cafe: it sits not far from the Wendover Motel right on the main drag.

The main drag also is U.S. Highway 40 where it goes right through town and, all around the clock, in both directions, the road is full of big semi-rigs and cars and everybody pulling in off the desert to get some sort of break from the monotony.

That's it: Wendover is a half-dozen gas stations along each side of the road, a couple of motels, a general store, and up at one end of town is the State Line Casino with a big statue-sign of a cowboy waving at you. (The Utah-Nevada state line really does run right through this place; they got drinking and gambling on one side of the casino and a restaurant on the other side where they got a fry cook who should be taken out in back of the place and beat to death with a tire iron.) There also is the beat-up remains of what used to be a town during the war, next to what used to be an air base during the war.

And all of this just sort of hunkers there, huddled up against the mountains, looking down on the Salt Flats.

Nothing had changed: the room had linoleum floors with sort of smaller rugs scattered around, and both beds sagged in the middle. I threw down the bags and Fergie and I crunched back along the gravel to the Western.

This is some cafe. A long counter and several booths and a jukebox and a rack with picture postcards.

Charlie was at the counter, leaning over on his elbows and hustling a waitress who looked like a Pontiac hood ornament.

"Promise her a set of tires," Fergie said. "Never mind the Arpège."

We sat down with the rest of the crew that Ford had sent out: Cannonball Elliott and Wimpy Logan.

"Fat goddam chance I got of getting any records with you clowns working on a car," I said.

Fergie nodded at them. "Repeat after me," he said, "I will

not touch Mister Lattimer's carburetor. I will not touch Mister Lattimer's linkage system. I will not ——— "

"Never mind that," Cannonball said. "I already got the car ready to go; it's out under the tent now. What really counts is: soon as we get cleaned up here, we're gonna go over to *Wells*. You wanna come along?"

Fergie handed me a menu. "Ahhh, yes," he said. "Wells, Wells, passion pit of Nevada. What visions of carnal pleasures dance through my head when you say that name. Yes, I think it's safe to say that my esteemed friend here, Mister Ace, and I, will join you in Sin City. That's what I said about the new talent. What's for dinner, Stroke?"

"What has the lowest goddam danger level here this year? You ever try to set a world land speed record when you got diarrhea?"

The waitress stood there, chewing gum and looking over our heads out the window, watching the big trucks roll by.

Fergie looked up at her, blinking. And then he slapped his forehead with his hand. "Perfect," he said. "She is per . . . fect!"

She looked down, at last. "Well?" she said.

"No," Fergie said. "Don't move!" He eased out of the booth and took her by the arms. "Don't move! Let me just drink in your beauty. Let me remember you always like this. Just you . . . silhouetted against the milk dispenser. My God." He turned back to me. "She's perfect, Ace. Tell me: who do you see when you see this lady? Tell me."

"Pontiac hood ornament?" I said.

"No! You fool, you *fool*. Why, this is MELISSA in our new movie. She's perfect ——— "

"You awreddy said that," the waitress said.

He turned to her again: "Would you . . . could you, play the part of Melissa, that poor, wronged wretch, ravaged by her lustful father and brutalized by a pack of purebred English

bulldogs before she was *three?* That poor lass who, despite
fate's bludgeonings, rises through life to become, to become ——— "

"Don't shit me, fella," she said. "Whaddya want to eat?"

He slumped back into the booth. "Remember," he said,
"you're going out into the kitchen just a miserable waitress. But
you're coming back a STAR!"

"We got chicken-fried steak," she said.

Fergie was looking at me now, all despair. "She would have
been just right for the part, too," he said. And then he brightened. "You remember that British guy who was in here the
last time we were here? He was from FIA or something. A
timer, I think. Remember him ordering?" And he turned back
to the waitress and spoke in a clipped British accent: "My
deah, I'll have a steak and one of those, oh, what do you call
them, one of those elephant testicles wrapped in al-yu-
min-ium."

She turned and looked over her shoulder. "Chicken fry and
a baked 'tato," she yelled.

She turned back to me. "And you? Don't shit me, now."

"I'll have the same, Melissa."

"Name's Gert. Besides, that fella over at the counter, Charlie
there, he tole me not to speak to you. He said you was one of
them sex fiends, a *pre*-vert."

"That's true," Fergie said, "but we prefer not to discuss it in
mixed company. After all, it's Mister Ace's cross to bear; he is
the one who must slog through life's stormy path, knowing all
the while that he's hopelessly hooked on *oral relations*." He half
raised in the booth and looked all around to make sure everybody could hear.

They could.

"And remember," Fergie told her, "*I* like to make love *straight*.
Face-to-face, the way God intended us to. And besides, I can

get you into the movies. Melissa of the Salt Flats, in the *Perils of Bonneville.*"

She nodded, writing down the order. "Well, can you get me a new set of tires for the car?" she said.

I was staring down at the big chunk of steak when the door opened. The gravy had congealed into oily puddles and, under it, the steak was slowly curling up on the edges, like something alive.

"You better hurry," Fergie said, patting his face all over with a paper napkin. "About the next time you reach over, that steak is going to eat you."

But then: the smell.

It wasn't *bad*, understand. It was just that I happened to breathe in deeply and, suddenly, it was there: I could smell sweat and dirty socks and wet *corncrib* and the instant flash of a school bus jammed into my mind. I'll be damned.

Dock Seegle.

I looked up and there he was. And then he swung his hip in a little and shoved me over. And he sat down and picked up a knife and fork and started to eat my steak. He sawed off an enormous chunk, struggling to beat hell, and popped it into his mouth. Then he worked it over to one side of his cheek, poofing it all out, and looked at me.

"Hey, Stroke," he said.

"Well, kiss my ass. How you, Dock?"

"Tol'able," he said. "God *damn*, this is awful steak."

"What are you doing here?"

He swallowed. "I'm running the big car. I saw yer crew out there today. You running tomorrow, right?"

"Uh-huh. Lissen: I haven't seen you in, what? Three years? Four?"

He shrugged. And attacked the steak again.

"How're you doing?"

"Well," he said. "I'll tell you. I got me maybe the biggest Eldorado convertible parked out there you ever seen, and I swear, that son of a bitch is bright *red*. And I got me a new sponsor, and the rocket car is out there on the Flats, and to-morrow morning I'm gonna get the record back. And I got me one ole wife and one new girlfriend and, let's see, eight kids, four of them from the first time I was married; one from the second marriage and one more from the one after *that* and . . . how many does that make?"

"Six. Damn, you're some stud."

"And two from this here *new* marriage." He reached over and drank the rest of my beer. "Chrissakes, I got to go and run the rocket car just to get away from the *house*."

"How's your pop? Grampa?"

"Pop gets out in two more years, I think it is. Grampa died two, three years ago. Never did get all the number three bird shot out of his ass. Your dad buried him. Free."

"Uh-huh."

"You ever go home?" he said.

"Not so far. What's the use?"

"Well, where do you live?"

"All over."

He accepted that, nodding. And then he leaned over and pat-ted Gert on the ass as she came by. "Gert, drop everything and bring me some coffee, hear?"

"You betcha, Dock," she said. And then she looked at the rest of us in the booth.

"Now, them rocket-car drivers is real *men*," she said.

"Never make *oral love*," Fergie said, "like those men who drive little bitty cars."

"I oughta warsh yer mouth out with soap for saying that," she said.

Dock shrugged. "Just bring him some of the coffee, Gert. It's all the same."

Little known fact: the real world land speed records are not always set on the Bonneville Salt Flats. Mostly they are set between Wendover, Utah, and Wells, Nevada. The world record for the 59-mile run through the mountains on those narrow, twisty roads is thirty-nine minutes flat. Think about that.

There is a whorehouse in Wells.

Anyone who is at all interested in American history knows that the world record was set by Slick Williams, all alone in a full-race Ford coupe. This was the evening of the very day that Slick had broken the world land speed mark at 500 miles an hour and he was in a hurry to get over to Wells and tell the girls.

And here we were: undulating along in Dock's Eldorado, all floor-boarded and nicely set up on the corners and dips.

"Just like West Virginia," he said.

"Yeah," I said. "And you still haven't learned to drive any better."

Fergie popped up in back and said, "I say, chaps, could you hurry it up just a bit? That's a good fellow. I do believe . . . wait a moment here, let me check . . . yes! I do believe I feel just the first faint stirrings, just the slightest flutter of an erection. Yes, by George. My ardor is waxing!"

Dock looked at me. "What'd he say?"

"He's horny."

"Oh."

Right at the edge of Ida's parking lot, Dock crossed it up and hit the brake hard. And we slewed right around and came in backwards, thunking to a stop against a row of telephone poles that had been set in there to keep folks from making a drive-in out of the place.

"Now I ask you," Dock said. "Is there anybody else in the whole world who kin *bootleg park* a car?"

"Nobody else would try."

Cannonball pushed the buzzer and Ida answered.

Ida could play the part in the movies: she looks like a madam and smells like a madam, which is sort of violet perfume, and she wears all the right beads and she has a bunch of bracelets and rings and her dress is cut just right in front and she wears a rose right there.

Everybody went whooping in.

"Hey, baby," I said. "How's about you and me making it tonight?"

And she drew back and peered over the tops of her little half-glasses. And then she yelled: "Stroker! Is that you, honey-babe?"

And then she picked me up and hugged me a lot, crushing up the smell of violet perfume.

Homecoming: I had been a customer at Ida's ever since the place first opened years ago. In fact, there are just a handful of us guys in this whole country who got personal invitations from the sheriff (who owns the place) to come to the grand opening night party.

You have to understand that part: Wells is a tradition to racers. Anyone who has ever raced on the Bonneville Salt Flats has to go to Ida's in Wells whether they want to or not. (Mostly they want to. Anybody who doesn't want to can't be serious about automobile racing and the hell with them.)

The place is perfect for untying all a man's knots that he got by risking his ass all day at very high speed. A man and his pals can sit there and drink Seven and Seven, and just simply work out all the problems of the world. And a guy can do some pretty serious talking with a whore — you can tell a whore things you wouldn't tell anybody else, and she will listen.

And she will understand you. Whores do that.

My secrets — your secrets — are safe with a whore.

I don't know what it is. Maybe our lives are pretty much the same: sometimes I feel like I am selling my *self* to give a lot of people some kicks. In fact, sometimes when I haven't crashed or gone up in flames or gone slashing through some other car, I feel like maybe I have *cheated* those folks up in the stands. I'm whoring for them, in a funny kind of way. Maybe I'm wrong.

But a hooker has seen it all, too. She has had it *done* to her, and I'm not talking about sex. But she can look into a racer's eyes and understand what drives him.

There have been many nights, I promise you, when I have spent hours at Ida's just drinking and talking. And every once in a while, regularly, you will lose your companion while she has to go upstairs with a cowpoke or some other customer who has come in.

There are rules, just like in any game: when a new customer or a gang of guys come in, the girls all have to get up and go stand in front of the bar in their shortie pajamas. And if a cowboy picks your lady, well, you just order another round of drinks and you wait for a half-hour or so and she will be right back and sit down.

"Now, then," she will say. "You were telling me about that time at Indy when . . ."

Ida's is an old house, really. There are maybe twelve-foot ceilings with frescoes going around and those fine old combination gas and electric light fixtures. To the right of the entrance hall is what was once a living room. There is a bar in there now and eight or nine stools, and there are maybe a half-dozen tables, each with four chairs.

There is a fire in the fireplace. This is better than any home.

"I'll get you some drinks," Ida said, and she sat me down near the fireplace.

"Fine."

And Fergie did a very quick wheel-around, coming right up with a chunky sort of girl who had eyes like a basset hound.

They started right for the front staircase, hand in hand, and they took two steps at a time. And he turned at the door.

"You understand," he said, "that I've got the pole position."

Charlie was walking up and down the line like he was running a USAC tech inspection, and every now and then he would stop and bend down and sight along a line of bosom. He looked like he needed a template. Cannonball was moving behind, feeling bottoms. And Wimpy was whispering to a girl who looked like she was carrying around a matched set of volley balls under her pajama top.

Nothing much had changed.

"Hey, Dock," Ida said. "How's your rocket car?"

He leaned back and put one boot up on top of the table. It had *DOCK* all hand-punched into the leather, reading sideways up and down the boot. "Fine," he said. "I'm all set to go for it tomorrow morning, first thing."

"That's a good boy. Lissen: you get the record, honey, and the house'll buy you a drink tomorrow night, all right?"

"Jus' one drink?"

Ida nodded. "No way you're ever gonna get that car to go fast enough for me to buy you *two* drinks," she said. "But you be sure and come over and tell us the news."

"Uh-huh."

We drank to that. And I held up my fingers to Ida for two more and turned back to Dock. "So, all right. Tell me what's been going on."

"Uhh, well. Let's see. I been running pretty good. I mean: I'm winning enough purses and supporting myself, you know. I got a lot of kids to feed."

"Well, that's your fault. But when are you coming up to run the big ones?"

"Lissen: I'd be running them now if I had your sponsors. Hell, I've *told* everybody that I can beat your old ass any day of the week. All I need is a good car."

"Uh-huh. So?"

And he brightened: "Well, anyway, *anyway*: now I done it, see? Lissen: I got Goodyear on this rocket car, see? And a whole passel of others; hell, spark plugs, ignition systems, aircraft folks, *everybody*. All right, then. Now, I had the land speed record a couple of years ago, right?"

"Right. Twice, in fact."

"Right. But those bastards from the West Coast keep coming along and pushing it up. So I got this big mother together and I put a system into it you won't believe, ever. And I took it all around and showed everybody and got up the money. And now I'm gonna put that fucking mark right off the board. Easy."

We drank to that. "And then?"

He grinned at me. "And *then*, first thing I do is, I let Goodyear send me and the car to the Paris Auto Show, where I just stand around and get my picture taken with it. And then I *keep* the sponsors, see, and I buy myself a good Grand National car and I campaign it. Beating your ass for the champeenship, naturally. And then, I don't know, I may just sit around and maybe count all my money. You know."

"I know. And what about me?"

He ordered up more drinks. "Well, I'll tell you what. If you behave yourself I'll let you work on my car. If yer in town."

"Well, goddam, Dock, that's the first job offer I've had all day. Just for that, I'm going to buy you a small shooter. Ida!"

I was pretty far down on the base of my spine, feet out toward the middle of the floor.

Dock was upstairs.

Cannonball was back downstairs. But getting ready to go back up.

Charlie had just come back downstairs.

Fergie Lattimer was doing *The Sound of Music* for the girls, singing all the Trapp family parts.

Wimpy was sleeping, his head on the table.

Is that everybody?

And that's roughly when the girl said hello.

"Hello, Stroker Ace," she said.

Focus: she was tall, running to maybe five-ten, and she had long, silvery-platinum hair that spilled down around her shoulders. She was wearing paisley shortie pajamas and she had two very long legs.

She leaned over me: "Are you in there? I'm Laurie."

So I made the big effort and got a little more straight up on the chair. "Well, that's enough of this casual chitchat," I said. "Let's go screw."

She got me headed in the general direction of the stairs. "I know you."

"Who am I?"

And she ticked them off on her fingers. "Indy. And Riverside. And Atlanta. And —— "

"Is that *me*?"

"What's bugging you, baby?"

"You want to go on the race circuit with me, uhhh, mmm . . ."

"Laurie."

"Right. You want to come along?"

"Yes. But where'll you keep me?"

"In my helmet bag."

"No, really. Why would you want to take a hooker along with you? You can have any girl you want, really."

So I explained it to her: "All the others: they're just *girls*."

"Well, something's bothering you. Ooops. Look out for the bottom stair here. Do you want to talk about it?"

"Absolutely."

And then I turned and looked back into the living room. At Cannonball. At Charlie. At Fergie. All my friends.

Laurie tugged at my arm, watching me.

"You race drivers have all the fun," she said.

Five a.m. I was lying there, the Nevada champion, waiting for someone to bring me the gold medals. I weighed seven pounds.

"Good morning, lover," Laurie said. "Can I go downstairs and get you some coffee? You've got to run today, don't you?"

"Uh-huh. Coffee sounds fine. And tell them to put two teaspoons of plasma in it, okay?"

And then came a sort of heavy thumping around in the hallway. Someone was going down the line, pounding on the doors.

It was Ida.

"ALL RIGHT," she yelled. "It's five o'clock. Everybody out for the world land speed record!"

ten

The mornings are the worst part: the Flats are cold, colder than anything ought to be, and no parka, no long underwear or boots can keep it away from biting you. The Flats are this way every morning winter or summer and the figures of men shuffling along all have their shoulders hunched up. Mechanics drop wrenches and swear at each other; two sips from a cup of coffee in a waxed-paper cup and it turns cold on you.

So I stood there inside my big, down-filled Ford parka and stared at the car. I am getting very goddam tired of standing somewhere in the morning staring at cars.

Out there: the Bonneville Salt Flats go on until the very edge of the world in all directions. Perfectly flat, with a faint rim of mountains at the far end. The salt is crunchy under your feet, all pulverized, and it is cracked and broken into millions of tiny spider-webby black lines through all the whiteness. In the sunshine it shimmers and you can't look at it.

Out near the edge, the mountains float in the daytime.

All this was once the bottom of the ocean (I'm not fooling, you could look it up somewhere). And when the ocean went away, the salt stayed. And it sure as hell didn't take long after cars came along to discover that this was a hell of a place to drive fast.

Finally, Fergie came over, wiping his hands on a paper towel. It was still not quite full daylight, but anybody could tell from any distance that his eyes were one hell of a fine shade of pink and red.

"Ready," he said. "You all set?"

"Mmmmmm."

The bucket seat on the car is always cold and the whole inside of the thing gives off more chills and I pulled in my elbows and hunkered up my shoulders. Everything about running on the Salt Flats in the morning is a giant pain in the ass.

But you have got to do it.

Reason: there is no wind early in the morning or late in the afternoon. In the middle of the day, it usually blows too hard against your car and slows you down. A cross-wind could blow you to Ketchum, Idaho.

Fergie checked my straps. "Do me about an hour at 6,500 RPMs," he said. "Here, set the timer. And then come in and let me look at it for a minute. Now, an hour of this will get us a few of the smaller speed marks, and then I'm going to put in a higher gear and we're going to pick up the speed to about 170 and go for all the others. Okay?"

"Mmmmmm."

"One more thing," he said. "The damn road department was supposed to grade us a more or less *circle,* but what we seem to have instead is a ten-mile oval. It'll wear you out a little faster, I suppose, but they tell me there's some soft salt out at the far end and this is the only way they could do it. Okay?"

"Mmmmmm."

"You're sure as hell the cheery one this morning."

"Look: can I go now?"

He nodded and pulled his head out of the car and backed away.

And then Dock came over. In a long raccoon coat.

"Take me back to Ida's," he said. And then he took hold of

the roof of the car and rocked it back and forth. "Man, this sumbitch *creaks*."

"Dock, will you go the hell away so I can run?"

"Man, you sure don't look good."

"Dock, for chrissakes, will —— "

"Real bad. Lissen: the only reason I run that big car is so I can get on the *oxygen*. And lissen: I'm almost ready; how long you gonna run this here shitpot?"

"An hour. If you'll kindly get the hell away."

"Well, hurry it up, sunshine. I'll be ready when you get back, hear? And then I'll show you what a real car runs like."

And then they all backed off and looked at the car some more.

So I fired it up and trundled it out. It *did* creak, at that.

The ten-mile oval is not much to look at. It is a graded area about, say, fifteen or twenty feet wide, and there is a black line painted down the middle of the salt. The only reason the black line is there is to give you some connection with life. Otherwise, you'd drive off somewhere and nobody would ever find you.

And I brought it up to 140 right off and settled down on the cold seat, both cheeks frosty. And I got the wheel into a turn and held it there. Five miles. Eight. Ten.

Sure enough, there was a soft spot where the salt was mushing up like oatmeal. And the ass-end would slew around, trying to break loose, and I had to fight it back.

It took roughly a year to run that hour. Hell, I thought maybe the goddam timer was broke.

But then I pulled in and unhooked everything.

Dock was all strapped into his silver suit: knee straps and crotch straps and American flags all over everything and silver boots. And a really big-mother racing helmet with this big picture window going all around the front of it and red, white and blue rockets over each earpiece.

"Isn't he pretty?" Fergie said.

"You like this?" Dock did a slow turn-around. "It's this here stuff them astronauts wear. Here, feel it."

"Not me," Fergie said. "I don't want to get emotionally *involved*, cutie."

"You look like you're sponsored by the fucking Tinkerbell racing team," I said.

The car was right out of Captain Go Fast:

First, it was polished silver and second, it was *38 goddam feet long*. There was a fourteen-foot-high vertical tailfin at the back end and the front end — at the cockpit — was only forty-eight inches high. Behind the cockpit, buttoned into all that polished metal, was a lunar-descent engine or a lunar-takeoff engine, one of those, and it didn't seem to matter much. There were flag decals and rocket pictures all over it and *DOCK SEEGLE* painted on the sides with that streaky paint that made the name look like it was going about fifteen hundred miles an hour all by itself.

They had to lift him in, for God's sake.

And Dock started squinching around, getting all comfy, and hooking up all those straps, shoulders and balls. "Ain't a roadblock in the world can stop me now," he said.

Fergie shook his head, looking at the rocket part. "Be sure to send us a card from Pennsylvania when you pass through," he said.

"Well, come *on*," Dock said.

"Come on, what? Are you waiting for a kiss or something?"

"No. Push me out there. Come on. Now, don't get any fucking fingerprints on the car, all right? Let's go."

Well: everybody races, everybody works.

So we rolled that big tube out to the course and then backed and straightened it and got it pointed roughly due east. And then we all backed off a bit and looked at it some more.

Due east: the world land speed record course is not really all that glamorous. It is a straight black line painted down the salt, going thataway. The line is painted far enough so that a car can run through a five-mile buildup for speed before it hits the first electric-eye clock. And then there is a measured mile and measured kilo, where there is another electric-eye speed trap. Then there is a five-mile runout where the guy shuts everything off and pops his drag chute and wishes he could go to the bathroom.

The idea is to straddle the line. The sensation is a little bit like having a ribbon running right up your ass at blinding speeds. Some sensation.

Thing is: you got to run both ways to get the official record, once down, once back, within an hour.

They pulled up the service truck and Fergie and I walked back over to help him get his damn bay window and oxygen mask on.

"Lookee here," Dock said. "Silver gloves, too."

"You set the record," Fergie said, "and I think I can get you two weeks at the Palace, lovie. *Dock Seegle and his trained car.*"

"What'd he say?" Dock said.

"He's horny again."

"Oh."

And they fired him up: there was this really dandy roar, with wavy air coming out of the big pipe in back. From underneath the canopy and inside his big helmet and from behind his oxygen mask and big faceplate, Dock looked over at us and nodded.

We wheeled and ran over to Dock's Caddie and jumped in it and cranked down the course.

And here he came: the rocket was in full roar and the wheels were spewing up the highest goddam rooster tail of salt anyone had ever seen and then — swooooosh! — he was through the clocks and had become just a black speck up against the horizon.

And about a split second later the sound came along behind him and rattled all the windows on the Eldorado and shook all my teeth.

He was out of the car when we got down to Mile Zero, standing there with his silver uniform unzipped and whizzing in the salt, kicking up a tiny little fountain of steam in the cold.

"I think I got it," he said.

"The clap?"

"Your ass. You see how fast I was going? I think I got the goddam *record*, man."

So we all stood there and whizzed to that: it was very companionable, all standing there in a sort of half-circle in the chill. And then we zipped up and backed and turned the rocket around again and pointed it west.

And we waited for Joe Pirelli to come motoring down from the timing shack. We could see his car taking shape downcourse, wavering in the light, and finally he pulled it up and shut it off and climbed out.

He was smiling. That's a good sign.

And he walked over to Dock and showed him the little piece of paper torn out of a spiral notebook.

"Lookee here," Dock said.

It said: 637.336.

The record, all right.

So we got him all buckled up again and put a sort of fireman's hold on him and crammed him back into the cockpit.

"Now, here's what you do," I said. "You get down at the end, see, and you crank a soft left — you can turn this sumbitch a little bit, can't you? — and you crank this soft left and you head it right for Wells. All right? And we'll join you over at Ida's."

He nodded. "I'm gonna get me *laid* right in this here silver suit."

"Lissen: this car ain't *that* fast," I said. "The way I figure it is, about the time we get there, you'll be standing in Ida's driveway taking a leak, for chrissakes."

"Well, you gotta remember that going this fast just shakes it right out of you."

So we squinched his helmet on again and then got back into the Caddie and headed back up the course.

This time the rocket came by under a thirty-foot spume of salt and there was this really pretty trail of fire following it along. And the rolling thundercrack of sound came jazzing along behind it.

Perfect.

"Look," Fergie said.

The twinkle of fire went out for just a second and then came on again.

"One of the nozzles must have plugged up," Fergie said. "Shit. There goes his rec ——— "

And then there was a puff. Just a *puff* on the horizon like a tiny little burst of box lightning, and it stung our eyes for a quick flash.

And that was all.

So I swung the Caddie right as hard as I could and got that sumbitch right on the floor and we aimed it at where the puff had come. Behind us and slightly to the right, the service truck was booming along with its lights on and horn going.

And off from the left the county sheriff's ambulance took shape against the salt, the red light going. He was slewing back and forth, hunting for traction on the salt.

We all came roaring toward the spot like arrows converging on a target. Then the black line of the measured mile flashed right under the Caddie, diagonally.

"He was off the course," Fergie said.

"Mmmmm."

It took forever to get there.

First: there were little bits of polished metal lying here and there. None of them seemed to be any bigger than a dinner plate. And then we ran across a ragged piece of silk parachute.

And, finally, I slammed the brake down and let the Caddie come around. It did two three-sixty turns in the salt, leaning hard, and coasted sideways to a stop.

"Jesus," Fergie said.

The rest of them came howling up, fishtailing to beat hell.

Nothing. *God damn fucking, flat-ass* NOTHING.

There was a stretched-out oily stain across the salt for several yards. Maybe fifty or so. A gouge or two. And on all sides of the oily spot, fanned out in a radius, like a circle, there were little pieces of things.

Little pieces.

I walked all around the edge of the circle.

Nothing.

Not a piece of silver. Not a helmet buckle. Not a piece of faceplate. No American flag decals.

Just oil and scratches in the sand.

I did everything very slowly. First: I got out a pack of Camels and I looked at all the labels on the package. And then I carefully opened the pack and got out a cigarette and put it in my mouth. And then I reached into my parka pocket and I took out my Rain Tree Farms lighter with the little racing chicken picture on it, and I lit the cigarette.

I walked over and stood beside the Eldorado.

And then I turned around and I hit the goddam car in the window with my fist and I smashed it all to hell, with little spider-webbing lines radiating out.

A few feet away, like in a goddam ballet, Fergie slowly turned and looked at me. And the sheriff turned and looked at me. And Cannonball and Wimpy. And Charlie Heffer.

And then they all looked down, on cue, and looked at the sudden little puddle of blood that was dripping off the front side of my pants and down onto the salt.

Finally Charlie looked up again.

He shrugged a little. It is exactly the oldest shrug in racing. Men do it a lot.

"Stroke," he said. "Uhh, Stroke . . ."

I walked around and got into the Caddie and fired it up. They were all standing there, watching me.

And then I let it go, right across the oily stain in the salt, hanging a big, loopy left turn.

They all sidestepped out of the way as I came by.

I was doing pretty well over one hundred going through Wendover and I kept right on going.

At Wells, it took quite a while for someone to answer the door.

Namely Ida. And she blinked at me a lot.

"Stroker, honey," she said. "What —— "

"Let me in, Ida."

"Sure, sugar. We don't usually get any customers at this time of day."

And then she sort of leaned over my shoulder and looked out at the lot. "Where are the boys?"

"Mmmmm."

"Where's Dock? Did he get the record this morning? You gonna start celebrating early?"

"Dock couldn't make it."

"You're bleeding, honey," she said.

"Mmmmm." And then I sat down at the bar. And I looked all around the room.

Nothing had changed. Nothing ever changes in a whorehouse, really.

"Let me fix your hand, honey."

I finally got her in full focus. "No. What I want is, I want a bottle of Seagram's Seven Crown. Have you got that?"

"A whole bottle?"

"Goddam, Ida, do I *lisp* when I talk? A whole bottle."

"All right," she said. And she plunked it down.

"And get me Laurie."

"She's asleep and . . ." But she looked at me again and nodded. "I'll get her right away, honey."

I was looking over the rim of the glass at the stairway when she came down. "Hi," she said.

"Hi, yerself."

"What's wrong, Stroke? You don't look good."

"Mmmm hmmm."

"And your *hand*. Honey, your hand is all . . ."

I poured some more and held the glass up to the light and looked through it at Laurie. "Stay with me," I said.

"Of course."

"I've got a lot of money here. I mean: really a lot."

She shook her head. "I don't want the money. You don't have to pay me to take care of you when something's wrong."

"It's not for taking . . . look. Look: just stay with me. All right?"

"All right," she said. It was a very small voice.

We walked up the stairs and I carried the Seven Crown in my good hand. And when we got to her room I got right into bed: driving uniform, driving shoes, long underwear, socks, goose-down parka and all. And the bottle.

"Now, then," I said. "Tell me the part again about where race drivers have all the fun."

eleven

We were sitting in the motel restaurant, memorizing the menu and waiting for the coffee to come.

And finally the waitress flipped over the top few pages on her order book and tucked them under, pulled a pencil out of her beehive hairdo and moistened it with the tip of her tongue.

"What'll it be?" she said.

"Well now, little lady," said Lee Roy Harber, "ah'll just have me a short stack and a mess of hash browns and a pile of toast about this high and, mmmm, four eggs."

She took it all down.

"How do you like your eggs?" she said.

He thought about it for a second.

"Well, now that you ask," he said, "I *really* like them little buggers."

You all remember Lee Roy Harber. He's the one who got belly-up in the very first lap of last year's race here and smashed his car flatter than a goddam sled. And he came walking back through the infield with his whole ass hanging out and carrying his helmet in one hand and kicking up great big chunks of grass.

And one of them two-man TV crews came running up, all

excited, one fat guy huffing along, carrying the camera and battery backpack and the other guy with the microphone. And they stopped Lee Roy.

"What happened, Lee Roy?" the announcer said. "You blow a tire or something?"

And Lee Roy looked at him and looked at the microphone for a long time. Finally he said:

"No. Ah just fucking crashed. It *is* possible to crash out there, you know."

Later on that night Charlie Heffer had tried on Lee Roy's helmet and then finally tugged it back off.

"Shit, I know what your problem is, Lee Roy," he said. "This here helmet would give a squirrel a headache."

But there was more: that was the same night that Lee Roy got all full of Southern Comfort at the Goodyear Tower and had come wheeling down the stairs and into his car. Lee Roy had a big new, sort of violet-colored Olds 88 at the time and he just sat there and cranked her up in the parking lot about as high as it would go, until the leaves started falling off trees on all sides — and then he let it loose and spun rubber on that big rascal all the way down through the infield tunnel and out into the street, where he hung a big, sliding turn roughly in the direction of Columbus, Ohio, and then he really stood on it.

Well, these things happen, you know: there was a cop out there directing traffic and this 88 came zinging right by and just about snicked off the policeman's gunbelt, for chrissakes, and he did a small half-turn and ran for his cycle.

And the cop shagged old Lee Roy all over northern Florida until they were both blasting down this little two-laner some-where out near East Frostproof or some place like that, when Lee Roy finally lost it on a real tight left-handed turn. At maybe 120 miles an hour or so.

And, sure as hell, he got the Olds upside down, too.

And that damn car took out one whole grove full of young orange trees, snapping them like matchsticks, and then hopped up over a ditch and went end-over-end in the air and came down astraddle a chicken coop and came out the other end carrying about six chickens and spewing feathers in all directions. And then it clipped right through a three-strand barbed-wire fence and, by now, Lee Roy had finally figured out where the brake pedal was and he braked that bugger and sure enough, flipped it right over on its side. And the 88 did a couple of full circles and slammed right into an irrigation pond.

And rolled over upside down again.

And the cop carefully picked his way through all this, just idling his cycle along because he knew for sure the driver had to be very dead. And he shut her down, got off, and waded into the pond up to his boot tops. And bent over and peered into the car.

The wheels on the 88 were still going around, slowly.

And there was old Lee Roy, hanging by his seat belt, trying to light a cigar with a wet match.

The cop was stunned. And then, still hunched over, he began to sniff around. Every cop in all Florida knows what Southern Comfort smells like. It's part of their regulations.

"Why, you're *drunk!*" yelled the cop. "That's what you are. You're drunk."

And Lee Roy turned his head and looked at him.

"Well, of *course* I'm drunk," he said. "What the hell do you think I am — a fucking STUNT car driver?"

These people are my friends.

Hell, good old Orville Hammer used to BE a real stunt car driver and worked for several seasons in a traveling thrill show before he got into racing. And even then, he came up the hard way.

Understand now, Orville is the sort of a driver who fills right up with the sound of applause and is just liable to climb right up on the roof of his car and take a bow in the middle of a damn race. And for a while there, before the sponsors found out how good he really was, Orville had to be content with driving in demolition derbies. Man, those humpties and hay-shakers all over the South just love demolition derbies and they sit up there in the stands and just get wet to the knees watching those big cars crash.

And Orville wasn't exactly turned *off* by the action.

First thing, he went out and bought an old Packard and beefed that son of a bitch right up to where he could have driven it smack through a Brontosaurus, for chrissakes, and then he whipped it out on the course and began to knock people silly with it.

This one event: he methodically smashed every car in the main event and then cranked the old Packard around the track in a victory lap. And, somewhere along there, he heard the roar of the crowd.

Well, hell.

So he snaked it back and forth a few times for effect and then he rolled it right over in front of the main stands and let it slide right into the wall. Ka-boom!

And the crowd was silent for just a second there until they saw old Orville come wriggling out of the Packard and then they really went wild again. And he heard the applause.

And, behind him, the old car was on its side with its bare belly showing and oil pan ripped out and there was a big rupture in the fuel tank and a little stream of gasoline was running down across the track.

And here was the crowd, cheering like mad while Orville doffed his helmet and took bow after bow.

Well, hell. Only one thing to do, right?

So he lit a cigarette and casually turned away from the wreck and started to walk away.

And threw the match over his shoulder.

Ka-*boom!* For a split second there, you could see all the way to *Houston.*

Lugs insists that they don't make men like that any more.

"Lissen," he says. "Them were the good old days. I mean, when men were men and smelled like horses."

If Lugs could, he would probably bring back the days when racecars went something like fifty miles an hour flat out on those skinny little tires. And the drivers all wore shirts and ties and put their caps on backward like, say, Barney Oldfield.

". . . and they had real *riding* mechanics," he says, shaking his head for the days gone by. "Imagine. I mean: I could climb right up there beside you and ride right along in the *races.* And if anything was to go wrong with our car — you know — why, hell, I could climb right down there and fix it right on the spot."

Hoo-Boy. That's all I need, for chrissakes, is a riding mechanic.

Have a true fact from the inside world of racing, never before told:

If Lugs was to climb into my new car with the idea of going along as a riding mechanic, he would *break* that sumbitch.

Well, at least un*balance* it, which is worse.

He just finished my new car and my backup car at his shop last week and he put them into this big-mother van that says RAIN TREE FARMS on its side — with the picture of a chicken wearing a crash helmet and goggles — and he trundled the cars down here for the shakedown runs to get them properly set up.

And he got a bunch of guys together and they unhooked the tailgate and they carefully rolled the No. 2 car down backwards onto the track apron. Then Lugs walked quickly back up the ramp and closed the big doors on the van so nobody could see the No. 1 car sitting in there.

Still, there are always a few racers around a track, some of them shaking out their own equipment for the new season — and some of them because they haven't got a single thing to do anyway and want to get out of the house for a few days. So there was Lee Roy Harber, smoking his cigar, and he nodded at Lugs who was coming back down the ramp. And then old Lee Roy walked all around the new car, shaking his head wisely and huffing out blue clouds of smoke. And finally he stopped and stood next to Lugs and both of them stood there, nobody saying a thing, with their hands stuck down into the back pockets of their Levi's. And then Lee Roy turned to Lugs and held out one hand to shake.

"I'll say this for it," he said. "It sure as hell looks like a *real* car."

"DON'T TOUCH IT," Lugs said.

"Well, shit, I'm not gonna *touch* it, you know that. I just wanted to say you're a cheatin' son of a bitch. And I *mean* that. *Honest.*"

Lugs nodded, never changing his expression. "Thanks," he said.

Understand now: that was a *compliment* from a competitor. And there just isn't any higher praise from people inside racing.

Whenever Lugs Harvey unveils a new car it's a goddam *event* around a racetrack. Hell, sometimes the *waitresses* come out of the infield cafeteria to look at it.

"What is it?" they'll say.

"Stroker Ace's new Dodge. The one he's gonna run this season."

"Lordy, it sure is pretty."

It is all of that: the thing looks just like someone drove it right to the track from a Dodge showroom floor. This one is bright, spanking Electric Red. There are no signs or stickers or decals or numbers on it yet. The chrome looks like *real* chrome and, sitting there in the cold sunlight, the car looks as though it has its nose down just a tiny bit. But then, from another angle, it doesn't. No, the nose is right. Maybe it seems just a bit, mmm, *wider*. But, no. From another angle, it looks perfect. The car is wearing fat, black Goodyear Blue Streaks and written neatly on the sidewall of each tire in yellow chalk is a tiny little message that says: "Heffer's Own Tires. Do Not Touch."

And Lee Roy threw down his cigar. Then he walked all around the car one more time and came back to stand next to Lugs. Finally he leaned over and said: "All right. How'd you do it?"

Lugs just looked back at him and then did his own Wolfish Grin, the one where all his eyeteeth show.

And then he shrugged.

What Lugs Harvey has done is this: he has just done a work of art, a sculpture; one of those paintings that changes every time you look at it. He has just built a monument to a 1973 Dodge. It looks *real*. It should not be raced, maybe. It should be put on a revolving velvet turntable and exhibited at art galleries across the country.

This thing goes back to the earliest days of stock car racing. When men were men and smelled like horses. And when stock cars were stock.

Consider this: in 1950 at the first Southern race in Darlington, good old Johnny Mantz bought a Plymouth right off a dealer's lot and then went out and raced it. And won.

Hell, time was when a couple of moonshiners were passing by the track and heard the commotion and went inside to look around. They watched the cars for a couple of laps and then went back out into the lot and got their own car and drove back in there and blew the goddam doors off everybody there. And that's with a trunk full of Mason jars full of hooch, for chrissakes.

No more.

After all, a stock car is one thing — but everybody knows that there are ways to make it go just a little bit faster. Well, hell.

The reason that stock car racing caught on so much in the first place was that the grandstands were full of folks who had those very same stock cars parked right outside. And old Dad would sit there and see this stock Ford whomp the shit out of every other car on the track — and the Ford folks could just as well have had salesmen outside with order blanks to sell more cars. People *identified.* "Hellfire," the old man would say, "that there car parked out there by the chicken coop is the same model as the one that won Darlington t'other day. *Same car.*"

There were Tech Inspections right from the start.

That is: NASCAR would permit certain modifications to the car, but not many. And they would send around a man with a clipboard and he would go over the car, checking things off, and then he would take out his pliers and clip an *official seal* on the engine and here and there. And that was that; he went away.

"Lissen," Lugs says, "give me about four hours and I can jack up a car — any car — and remove everything but that fucking seal and put a *whole 'nother car* under the seal and nobody would know."

The rest of it started slowly and more sneakily. First, the good old boys started changing little things — like maybe the shocks or a suspension part. Then they graduated into tricked-up valves and real machine-shop stuff. Some of them started to pull off factory bumpers and build them over again out of Bondo, which is sort of like fiber glass, and then use chrome tape to make them look real.

It was great. From the stands the cars looked *stock*, sure enough. And there was no question that they were running to beat hell on the track. But you get up close and Helen Keller could tell the difference.

Hot damn: the doors weren't even *doors*, and how's that for a ballsy touch?

Lee Roy Harber was one. It didn't take him long to figure out that if he had to bring in the car at, say, 4,000 pounds, the best thing was to put all the goddam weight in the frame and engine and the hell with the body. So he poured himself a whole car out of fiber glass and then took a stylus and drew in the doors and all. And he took a real door handle and just stuck it right on the side: pop. The trunk had a little etched-in part around it to make it look just like a trunk. And since he had saved himself several hundred pounds — guess where he put it?

Answer: engine.

And then one day NASCAR pulled a surprise rule: they sent to Detroit, to the manufacturers, and they got a bunch of templates of real stock cars. And they hauled them down to Atlanta.

"Now, then, fellers," they said. "Your car has to fit this here template perfectly or you don't race. Now, who is gonna be first? How about you, Jiggs Findlay?"

And Jiggs said: "Who, me?"

They popped it over his car. Well, hell, he could have slid *sideways* through the whole goddam template and not touched one little part of it. What Jiggs had done was to build himself a goddam perfect little three-quarter scale model of a Plymouth.

What he also had done was to cut down his frontal area wind resistance by maybe 25 percent — and he still had that big engine sitting in there that all the real big Plymouths had.

"Out," they said.

Another time, folks couldn't help but notice that old Max Finster seemed to be running long after everybody else had pitted for fuel. Hell, here he was, racing his goddam head off and getting about the same mileage as a Volkswagen. And since NASCAR had limited the size of the fuel tanks to twenty-four gallons — and the average stock car was getting about three miles to the gallon — it figured that something was wrong.

So they sprang a surprise check on Max.

Surprise: he had put in hollow roll-bars and he had them full of fuel. And he had a couple of secret little fuel-bags hidden inside his frame. Maybe even in his helmet and shoes, for chrissakes.

Look at Lugs.

Lugs Harvey runs maybe the greatest speed shop anywhere in the world and sometimes even the Euro*peans* come around to look at it.

"Don't touch anything," he says.

When Clyde Torkle ordered my two new cars, the factory called Lugs.

"We're sending you our good, unit-body frames," they said. "Something new this year and it ties in with our advertising. Plus, of course, the undercoating, the predipped chassis and all."

"Swell," Lugs said, dryly.

And first thing: he jacked up the whole goddam body and filed it away with all the others in one corner of the shop. Then he threw out the frame. And he built one of his own that looked just exactly like it — except that *his* had more of what he calls *flex*. And then he hooked that up to his own chassis and his own suspension system.

Naked, sitting there, the skeleton looked fine.

But the Lugs Harvey Magic Suspension System works like this: it has two positions which Lugs can fix practically by *breathing* on that bugger.

One: it rises up so that the finished car will fit under the factory template.

Two: it squats back down where Lugs sets it.

Which means, naturally, that the car has its nose down in a race a little bit lower than the other noses, and it has less frontal resistance.

Tech inspectors have been known to go crazy over this sort of thing.

"All right, Harvey," they will say. "Let me under this fucking car."

And Lugs will nod, brightly. "Sure," he will say. "Limpy get a crawler over here so this man can get under the car."

And everybody will stand around the car, looking at this guy's feet hanging out, and nudging one another. And, finally the guy will come scooting out and he will lay there and look up at Lugs. And Lugs will bend down and hand the guy a clean rag so that he can wipe his hands.

"I'm an engin*eer*," the guy says.

"Do tell," says Lugs.

"Lissen: I'm an engineer, and I'm a son of a bitch if I — or anybody at Carnegie *Tech* — can figure out how you do it."

"You want to look at the motor now?" Lugs says.

And the guy shrugs. "Jesus Christ, I suppose so. What the hell you got in it *this* year?"

Lugs raises the hood.

"Dodge," he says. "1973 Dodge. Take a look."

Not long after Lugs unloaded the monster at the track, Torkle came around with a gang of his chicken franchisers; he likes to take them around to these things and play Big Daddy. And they all stood in a circle around the car, wearing their crew cuts and Robert Hall suits and nodding approvingly while Torkle talked.

"This here is the stock car that's gonna win this here *race*," he said. And he slapped it on the hood.

"JESUS CHRIST!" Lugs said. "Don't touch it!"

But the car went under the template perfectly. Folks came from all around to look at it.

"A real, clean stock car," said the inspector.

"Sure," Lugs said.

Moral: If you're gonna be a goddam race driver, go on out and get yourself a good car.

Not everybody knows about good cars. But it doesn't always make that much difference.

I take you back now to, oh, about 1964. Back in those days when NASCAR was really catching on and folks were finding new glamour in stock car racing and everybody began to get into the racing act.

Like movies: there was *Redline 7,000*, which was very big on the drive-in circuits, and there was *Thunder over Carolina*, which I would personally give maybe *one star* just for the guts it took to release it.

And along came Sam Noon, who had done a short subject or two and figured that maybe it was time for him to do a Big Epic on Stock Car Racing. He settled right away on the Charlotte race. Gritty stuff with a real easy plot so as not to confuse racing fans, but with stock cars and drivers and crowds and a cast of thousands. Which is not bad for a guy who has a rented camera and one shirt and not enough money for lunch at the Ramada Inn Northwest.

But Noon knew a few producing tricks: you go to a race supplier, like, say, Goodyear or Firestone. And you get the loan of free tires. The idea is that you promise, several times during the picture, a scene will take place in the pits, and the camera will dwell lovingly on the *tires* there with the big brand name. (You also got to promise that, if your hero crashes, that it sure as hell wasn't his tires that did it to him.) Same routine goes for cars. As for casting, old, broken-down race drivers could be hired for a few bucks and the promise of free beer between takes.

The crowds came free with the official speedway film. Splice 'em in, for chrissakes.

The star almost always turned out to be Elvis Presley, who never went near the track, but did his numbers in a studio somewhere near Memphis, surrounded by girls who danced and jiggled a lot.

Anyway, this time, Goodyear went for the tire deal and sent a vanload of racing tires down to the track. But nobody would provide the cars. No-body. And Producer Noon and Goodyear PR guy Bill Manly were sitting there one day in absolute despair when Manly suddenly looked up and snapped his fingers.

"Hertz!" he said.

"Avis!" said Noon.

"National!" they chorused.

Well, that's roughly the way the dialogue went — which, I promise you, is a whole lot better than most of the lines in Noon's script — and, next thing, Manly had rented a couple of Hertz cars and had gotten them out to the track.

They pulled out all the seats and the carpets and the dashboards. They pulled out the roof liners. They taped over the headlights. Then they took some black plastic heater hose and built real-looking roll bars for the inside. And then they painted racing numbers on the sides with water paints and lightly stuck on a bunch of sponsor decals.

For the next several days they raced the hell out of the rental cars; whooping around at top speed for the closeup shots, scenes where the camera comes in tight on the drivers wrestling with the wheel, all goggled and sweaty and tensed. For the faraway shots, Noon planned to splice in actual racing footage, which he planned to steal.

Then one day Manly got a call from Goodyear headquarters in Akron.

"Lissen, I gotta go," he told Noon. "I can just make the eleven o'clock flight if I hurry." And he jumped into one of the cars and wheeled off to the airport.

At the Hertz counter, he dashed by on a dead run and tossed the car keys at the girl. "Car's out in the lot," he said. "Mail me the bill."

"Thank you, sir," the girl chirped. And then she said: "Uhhh, sir. Sir? Where did you park it?"

"Can't miss it," yelled Manly. "It's the one with the big number six on the door."

Flash forward again: I have just come back from playing racecar.

In my old backup car: it has been put back together with great big pieces of silver tape and Double Mint. The *new* car is hidden back inside the van, with the doors locked.

We're making a movie all our own. Lordy, it ain't easy, being a sex goddess.

What we're really doing is making a promotional movie for Goodyear to show around the country. And there will be a whole lot of real, live footage in it showing me winning the National Championship sliding sideways on Goodyear tires. The rest of it — the parts about the pit stops and all — we are re-creating here at the track.

When I took off my helmet today, a guy came over and rumpled up my hair — and then sprayed it with some perfumed stuff. And then he took one thumb and put this little smear of grease down my cheekbone. And he stepped back and looked at me.

"Perfect," he said.

"What are you doing after the show?" I said to him. And then, while he was sort of laughing and holding on to my arm, right at the bicep, I said a little something else:

"Take off that fucking grease spot," I said, "or I will pinch your goddam head off."

So he took off the grease spot and scurried back behind the pit wall again and complained to the producer that I was so uncooperative.

"If I was you," the producer said, "I would leave him alone."

So I re-rumpled my hair the way I wanted it and stood there while a guy came out and held a light meter up against the car.

"Don't touch the fucking car," Lugs warned him.

The guy looked puzzled. "I thought this was *last* year's car," he said.

Lugs nodded. "I know. But you touch that sumbitch and it is going to fall apart into a bunch of little old pieces right here on the track. Besides, nobody touches Lugs Harvey's cars on general principles."

"Well, I was wondering: could we shine up the metal on the hood here a little bit? I want a nice highlight."

"First place," said Lugs, "that ain't metal."

"Oh? What is it?"

"It's hard to explain," Lugs said. "But let's put it like this: Just keep the fuck AWAY FROM THE CAR. UNDERSTAND?"

"Gotcha," the man said.

Lugs started to act like a Love Goddess himself just about

the time they told him that *he* would have a bit part in the movie, too.

Mister Pit Stop. Jesus.

All afternoon he had been sort of dancing lightly around the front of the car, waving his arms and doing things with his fingers and kind of *pirouetting* around and giving me pit signals no man has ever seen before.

Finally I had to threaten to run over him to get him out of the way.

Hell, Charlie Heffer has a part in the movie.

They both think they are Robert Redford.

Lugs had spent all morning downtown casting T-shirts. And he came back and tried on a few of them for me, turning in all directions in front of the mirror.

"How do you like this here little number?" he said. "It really is *me*, ain't it? I mean: shit, you know."

"Lugs, for God's sake, you never wore that kind of a T-shirt in your whole goddam life. You always wear a dirty white one with holes and grease all over it and those big stains under the arms."

"Come *on*," he said. "This here is a *movie*."

"But a *purple* T-shirt?"

"Purple, my ass. It's *vi*-let."

"It's what?"

"Wait a minute," he said. "Maybe this here is the *moove* one. The lady told me herself that it brings out the blue in my eyes, see?"

And Charlie Heffer had come in by kicking open the door. That's because he had a can of beer in each hand. He also had lumps and bandages all over his head. He hovered there on the doorstep.

"What's that?" he said.

"That's old Lugs Blue Eyes, Big Movie Star, for God's sake. But never mind. What the hell happened to you?"

Charlie looked thoughtfully at the beer in each hand. Finally he made an Executive Decision and took a long drink out of the left one. "I got here last night," he said.

"Uh-huh," Lugs said. "That explains everything."

"I'm not sure," Charlie said. "But I think I got into a hatchet fight. And I'm not sure, but I think everybody had a hatchet but me."

"They're blue, ain't they?" said Lugs.

"Whut's blue?"

"My eyes, you asshole."

Charlie shrugged. "One of them might be. When did you guys get in?"

"Early this morning," I said. "Where did you stay last night?"

Charlie blinked a few times. "Stay?" he said.

"Jesus, Charlie never *stayed* any place in his life," Lugs said. "You know that. When you got a whole great big motel full of rooms, why make a reservation? Lissen: he's been going racing for fifteen, maybe twenty years now and he ain't never paid for a motel yet."

"Lissen, I gotta message for you from Heffer," Charlie said.

Lugs nodded. "What is it?"

"Go fuck yourself." He flopped down on one of the beds and balanced both cans of beer on his stomach. Then he looked around critically. "Not a bad room," he said. "I'll probably like it here."

Lugs pulled another T-shirt over his head. It was green and it had Day-Glo lettering in orange on the front: DAYTONA BEACH, FLORIDA. And in smaller letters: *Racing Capital of the World*. "Is this here movie in color?" he said.

"God, I hope not."

On the bed, Charlie was reflectively picking his nose. "Lissen, Lugs," he said. He withdrew his index finger, looked at it closely for a second, then delicately wiped it on the bedspread. "Lissen: it don't make no difference what you wear in the goddam movie. No way. I mean: all them little girls are going to get one look at old Charlie Heffer up there on the silver screen — lifting two tires in each hand, by God — and they're gonna cream all over themselves. Man, it don't make a shit what color your eyes are because —— "

"Well, the *lady* said they were blue," Lugs said.

twelve

e were just pulling up again, leaning back in our seats, and Jigger gave the wheel a couple of hard shakes. "You know," he said, "I think we got one of them buggers that time. She don't feel just right. What we got is a chicken caught in our landing gear, that's what we got."

In the seat right behind me, Charlie was fumbling around inside the Styrofoam chest, rattling the ice. "You guys ready for another beer?" he said.

Jigger turned right around and looked at him. "Well, hell, yes, we're ready for another beer," he said. "What the hell you think we brought you along for? Yer supposed to serve the goddam *cock*tails, you dumb bastard. Christ, you are the dumbest fucking stewardess I ever saw."

"Just answer the question," Heffer said, "and don't give me no bullshit lectures. God, and I coulda drove the truck up here just as easy. But, no, you assholes talk me into *flying* up here. I could have stopped and got me a chicken-fried steak and country gravy." He ripped the tops off the beers and handed them through the space between our seats.

Jigger turned back to him again.

"Well, will you tell me just how you are gonna drive the service truck up there when you got both hands bandaged like that? Tell me that."

Charlie looked at his hands. "Well, *a*," he said, "I kin drive that fucking truck with my *elbows* if I have to. And *b*, I got these bandages all wet anyway fishing around in this ice bucket for the beer, and *c*, I'm gonna rip them off anyway when we get there."

"I hate to break this up," I said, "but who is flying this here thing anyway?"

"I am." Jigger took his hand off the wheel and pointed at his chest. He was holding the beer in the other hand.

"Well, don't you think you ought to look every now and then to see where you're going?"

He shrugged. "Going? Jesus Christ, Stroker, that's just *air* out there anyway. You think we're gonna run into something up *here*?"

"How high are we?"

He looked at the dials. "Oh, four, five hunnert feet. Climbing a little."

"Let's go down and get some more chickens," Charlie said. "Them little bastids."

Jigger shook his head. "Well, first we gotta get rid of the one we got now. Now, how in hell is it going to look if we come into Terre Haute with a fucking chicken hanging onto our wheels?"

It had been going like this all morning: we had flown back to Indy from Florida and we had an open day and everybody had decided to sneak up to Terre Haute for the big annual Sprint car race up there. And along about three o'clock in the morning after a few shooters at the White Front it seemed like a hell of an idea to fly up there with Jigger James in his Cessna 182.

We had taken Charlie along because some clown at a table all the way across the room had smashed off the end of a whiskey bottle and then had ra'ared back and thrown it at a guy who was sitting next to us. And Charlie had reached up and intercepted the pass, thereby saving the stranger's life. Earlier, I had planned to call the Big Soft Greek and say "Guess who's coming to town," but then I forgot it. The hell with her, anyway.

By the time we had all gone downtown and gotten Charlie's hands all stitched up it was daylight, so we all went right to the airport and took off.

The doctor had shaken his head at us. Doctors do that a lot.

"Terrible," he said. "Nasty. Your hands are all caked with grease."

"Look," Charlie told him: "just go ahead and sew. If I had wanted a *manicure,* I woulda gone to a goddam barber shop."

And, finally, one more thing:

Jigger likes to see how low he can fly the plane, dipping down into sheep pastures, cow pens, hog wallows and chicken yards. This drives the chickens pretty crazy and they come flying up to beat hell. And, come to think of it, the farmers don't think all that much of it, either.

And now we had one of the chickens hung up in the landing gear.

"Tell you what," Jigger said. "I'll just slow this sumbitch down some and you climb out there and kick that chicken off there. We're almost at Terre Haute now."

"Who, me?" Charlie said.

"Hell, yes, you." And he pulled the throttles back until the Cessna started to wallow and fishtail all around, nose down.

"Well, I'll tell you what," Charlie said. "I ain't climbing out of *no* plane to kick *no* chicken off *no* landing gear. Hellfire, I don't like flying all that much anyway, you shitheads. I coulda drove the truck up here, you know."

"Then I'll do it," Jigger said.

"Go ahead."

So Jigger opened the door and climbed out, hanging on to

the door frame and fishing around in the air with one leg until he could get a tiptoe on the wheel.

Charlie leaned over my shoulder.

"W-w-w-who's flying the plane?"

"It's Jigger's plane," I said.

"Come *on*. I mean, who's flying it. Look: we're going down."

"Well, the pilot is flying the plane, but the pilot just stepped out for a minute, that's all. He'll be right back, folks."

But I reached over to the wheel on my side and steadied it up a bit until Jigger climbed back in and slammed the door.

"It was a rooster," he said. "Where's my beer, Heffer?"

"Here."

The Terre Haute airport lay just below us. Like twenty feet below. Jigger got back on the throttles.

"Lookee there," he said.

"What?"

"That hangar there. Got the doors open on both ends, you see?"

"I don't think you can make it," I said. "Specially if someone was to stand straight up when you were going through."

"Fifty dollars?"

"All right. Fifty says you pull off at the last minute."

"No," Charlie said. "No, you guys."

But Jigger banked it tight and fed it more gas, coming right around in a little circle before he leveled off. Then we took dead aim on the open hangar doors and got her down about twelve feet off the ground.

"No," Charlie said. "Awww, no." And he put his bandaged hands up over his face.

Flash! we went right through the hangar and out into the square doorway of light on the other end. I got a lightning, split-second impression of a sudden boost in noise and a quick-image pressed inside my mind of some people diving off a ladder or something like that.

Jigger brought her around again and began looking for a runway.

"Where's Heffer?"

"Well, he's either back in the hangar or here on the floor somewhere," I said.

Slowly, he brought his head up. "Did we make it?"

"No way."

And by this time we were down, rolling along smoothly, and Jigger was finishing the rest of his beer. Then he burped. "Fifty," he said.

So I got out my money and peeled back the top layers until I got down to the fifties. "Here."

"Way I figure," Jigger said, "we had maybe four feet clear on each wingtip. Did you see those guys painting in there?"

"I saw somebody; I'm not sure."

There was a sort of reception committee there to greet us: there were three United States Auto Club officials, who were wearing blazers and pissed-off looks; there were a whole lot of race fans from Terre Haute — who know that a lot of the big-name drivers come flying in with their own planes — and they were all cheering and clapping their hands. And off to one side were four guys who were all dappled with fresh gray paint. God knows, they should have been madder than hell, but they looked pretty pleased about it. Hell, *class* is recognized, even when you're up to your armpits in paint.

I pulled my duffle bag out of the back and then Charlie climbed out and bowed to the crowd. "It was nothin'," he said.

Jigger was over getting his USAC bad-behavior fine when Buzz Boyer came in.

They don't call him Buzz for nothing: he put that Cherokee right down in the tops of a grove of poplar trees off to one side of the apron.

Well, this was all due to a movie we had all watched late one night at the Speedway Motel. You know: here were these RAF pilots coming back from a mission, see, and they were all shot up, naturally. And they came zinging in, silk scarves and the usual bullshit, and they just clipped off the tops of some trees near the field and then landed, with branches and leaves flying and the ground crews cheering.

Not Buzz. He got maybe just a little bit too low and caught the landing gear and flipped that son of a bitch right over on its back on top of the trees.

"You know," said Charlie, "that's the same goddam way he drives a racecar."

They were putting a ladder up the tree to prune old Buzz out of his Cherokee when we left in the rental car.

The Avis lady had kind of dimpled up a bit.

"You goin' to win the big race, Stroker?" she said.

And then she had done that old turn-around, very slow, to run my credit card through the little machine: that little red skirt fit just right and she pooched out perfectly in back and there was a faint hint of panty-line where her little old underwear was. This is maybe the oldest move in the world — it is a special thing that only car-rental girls can do — and anybody who has just gotten off a plane and is standing there at the counter, all tired and knowing he has to go to a goddam sales meeting or something like that can see a girl do that move and tell you what frustrated passion really is. And when she came back, she slipped my card across the counter top so that the tips of our fingers touched. Oh, shit.

I got very suave:

"You bet your little bottom I'm going to win the race," I said, "and then I'm going to take you to the hot-damndest victory party you ever saw."

"Promises," she said.

"You better not be so flip about it, you know, because you're the guest of honor."

She was penciling in the rest of the information and she had given me that long, slow look, head down; so that the whole thing started with a slow sweep of false eyelashes.

"Where can you be reached during your stay in Terre Haute?" she said.

"Easily," Jigger said.

"Holiday Inn," I said. "Ask for me."

"I don't live very far from there," she said.

"I know." And I had reached across and held the flat of my hand against her cheek. This always does them in; I don't know why. It's something they do in Avis training, maybe.

"You're gonna come to our party?" I said.

"You'll call me?"

"Lissen: I'm very bad at numbers. You'll be at the race?"

"Wouldn't miss it for the world."

"Then come around to my pit afterward, all right?"

"But you'll be busy with the trophy and all."

"Look, I'll *give* you the goddam trophy. You'll be there?"

"Maybe," she said. "And maybe not."

Charlie had leaned over and goosed me, gently. "She'll be there, for chrissakes," he said. "Come on, Mister Horny, let's go."

And we went to the track.

Ahh, dear God, dirt track racing. And Sprint cars.

Understand now: this is what racing is really about, and if I live to be a hundred (which is very fucking doubtful), I will always come back to dirt track racing like religious people go back maybe to a shrine. This is the fountain of the whole game and this is what fills a man up inside and pumps life back into him. This is living life right on the ragged mother edge with everything hung right out for everybody to see — and no matter how big or rich or famous any race driver gets he will go back to a dirt track anytime and take on the hayshakers.

Lissen: there is dirt, for God's sake, the stuff that cars raced on before somebody invented pavement. There is something *raw* about racing on a dirt track — like maybe you've gone back in time and searched out your beginnings — and there is excitement hanging right there, thick in the air, and there is this feeling of, mmmm, *animal* lying just underneath.

The folks in Indiana, say, Terre Haute, don't have to have this explained to them; nobody has to print it in the sky in red letters. They crowd those old dirt tracks and they get right down there at the fence and they hang over there as the cars come splashing past — coming through the corners sideways, spraying all those clods and chunks of dirt up, and roaring — and the noise vibrates their goddam *rib cages*, man, and they come alive with the powerful sense of it and it plays mad music inside their heads. Shit, man, this is living.

Nothing has changed. Suddenly it's the goddam 1930's and you can squint your eyes and see yourself in a fucking pencil-line mustache and wearing that old leather helmet and they could have carved your jawline right out of solid Georgia marble and you finish one of these races and you swagger; I swear to God, you fucking swagger around and the goddam *hum* doesn't leave your body for months. Go back to the fountain and get filled up.

Sprint cars stay the same. Everything gets streamlined but not Sprint cars.

They're open cockpit and open wheel. They sit high and the engine is out in front where God and Frederick Duesenberg put it in the first place. The front wheels are small and the rear wheels are big and the damn old intake velocity tubes stick right up out of the hood where you can see them buggers and the nose hangs out in front with that nerf bar, giving the car a sort of look like it is smiling an evil grin.

The driver sits right up there where everybody can see him, his entire damn torso sticking up over that little bitty Plexiglas windshield; none of that lying-down nonsense like in Indy or sporty cars.

The nice thing about it is the danger: you see, if you happen to run right up on somebody's wheel, it is flat guaranteed to get you upside down; sometimes people come flying right over your head. And, always, you have got your foot on the gas and the car is trying to get away from you, skittering around — and sometimes it takes forever for the wheels to get a bite on the loose dirt and you are right up against the fence and, besides, you can't see a whole hell of a lot anyway because of the dust in the air. And, after, say, two laps you get this nifty fucking sense of invincibility and you find yourself looking back over your shoulder on the turns and driving right down for the straight-away and knocking those bastards right and left on each side of you. Jee-zuz!

Tell any race driver that, well, he's all right as far as it goes, but that he can't race on dirt — and he'll bust his ass getting there to race you. God knows, it isn't the money.

Hellfire, the First-Place purse is a whole lot less than the tenth-place car gets at Indy. It comes to maybe $600. Shit, I *spill* that much money at one of these things and my poor god-dam tax consultant (who wouldn't be caught dead at a race-track) always puts Terre Haute down as a dead loss, for chrissakes, even though I always win.

But I've got to come back. One: it cleans out my whole head. And two: just because I'm running all the big races now, I don't want any asshole to accuse me of forgetting my origins or say-ing I can't win on the dirt. And, maybe three: Terre Haute is Lugs Harvey's hometown, for chrissakes, and that explains a whole lot right there.

We keep my Sprint car on a trailer at Lugs's speed shop most of the year; sometimes he parks it out front and people come by and look at it. The goddam thing was fourteen years old when I bought it for $6,500 and it had killed two drivers and once it had run right through a first aid tent and injured four other people and one doctor. Well, he was an *intern*, really, which doesn't count as much.

Now, they had rolled the thing down and unloaded it, and I was sitting there on an oil drum, looking at it. The leather seat was starting to get a little cracky. And along came Lugs.

"I changed," he said.

Lugs was wearing some brand-new white pants and a pair of orchid-color, hand-worked cowboy boots with high goddam heels and little toes that came to sharp points. And he had on the big midget-racecar belt down over the roll of his stomach and a sort of fuchsia shirt and black leather snap-on tie.

"I give up," I said. "Who are you?"

"It's me, all right," he said. "Lissen, shithead: this is my *hometown*. Chrissakes, everybody in the stands knows that I'm a Chief Mechanic. You like this here tie?" He pulled it out about a foot on the little elastic cord and then let it snap back against his throat. "Real leather."

"Lissen: you think that little Avis girl will be around here?"

"Well, of course she'll be around. Look: are you gonna race or are you gonna fuck around? What's it gonna be?"

"In that order," I said. "How's the car?"

"The car? The *car*?" He blinked at me. "The goddam car happens to be perfect. Perfect. The car ain't thinkin' about gettin' laid after the race, for one thing."

By now the fans were really starting to flood into the old grandstand in the crisp night air and there was that fine, assuring roar all around so that a man didn't have to sit there and listen to his own thoughts.

They were filling the rickety wooden bleachers beneath that old gray latticed wooden roof and others were jockeying for position right alongside the fence, where they could look into the flying dirt and maybe catch some of it right in their teeth.

Lugs was putting in the last spark plug when I inched into

the cockpit and got myself buckled in. I pulled down my goggles and then I squirmed myself comfortable and ran the hollow of the palm of my hand over the smoothness of the gearshift. Then Lugs straightened up and looked over at me. He nodded.

I hit the button and the big Chevy mill coughed into a fine, goddam irritated bark and the old car began to shimmy and vibrate and I could feel it all through me like fine music. And I nodded back at him and then I dumped it into gear and I pulled out of there, kicking up clods of dirt and skidding it right into the first turn. The fans are right: this is a bitching sport.

Man, my blood pressure climbed right up along with the tach and, just for the hell of it, I broad-slided the old bugger right out of the Fourth Turn, my forearms all crossed over, and there was this nice, quiet singing sensation just behind my wishbone. Whoops-see; that old rascal drifted right up against the fence, spewing up rich clay, and I quick-looked into the rear-vision mirror and I could see all those heads looking back at me, smiling through mud-stained teeth.

And after I got her all loosened up, I took it out to qualify.

This is like twenty-seven Rockettes dancing on one side, see, all kicking in perfect step; and twenty-seven Rockettes dancing on the other side, all as one — and the Rockette right in the middle is flat naked. I mean: everybody is vaguely aware of the perfection on all sides, like it was being reflected in a mirror — but everybody is watching that *one* Rockette.

I was all alone out there on that reddish clay and the night-track lights were perfect on the pearlescent finish on the car and I knew that the track announcer had given the crowd the usual bullshit about the great Stroker Ace coming here to race with us tonight. The champeen himself, right here with us at Terre Haute, man, and here he comes right now!

So I waved one hand in kind of a lazy salute and I let her tear.

First official lap I got just a teeny bit high coming out of the First Turn and that old fart just plain skittered up into the loose dirt right next to the fence. This loose dirt is called marbles, which makes an awful lot of sense. So I looked around and then I wrenched it sideways and for just a few seconds the damn thing actually bobbled — just short of spinning out of control. But the tires finally got a bite of something down there and the rear end swung back around, missing the fence by maybe a millimeter. And I shot out of the Second Turn, completely sideways in one of America's great, all-time, complete fucking four-wheel drifts. I knew it was costing me time, but what the hell. There I was, drifting sideways and looking around to see that I still had four wheels and the crowd could see my head turning and my goddam forearms entirely crossed over each other and they all wet their pants.

It felt so good that I jammed it back into high gear again as I came out of Number One. If you can get the bite, which is not often, you can actually get a sort of slingshot effect coming off a turn that way. So I gave her a little bit more gas and hung on there.

And when I finally pulled back in, zapping the engine importantly, I knew I had the pole position. I waved to the crowd and shut it down.

I unhooked and got out, putting the butts of my hands down on the cowling and lifting up. Lugs went over and looked inside at the gauges, and then back at me.

"Have fun playin' out there in the marbles?" he said.

"It's bitchin'."

"Uh-huh. Well, next time, maybe you should think about last year when you took out about sixty-five yards of fence with that slingshot bullshit."

"Yeah, but I stayed right side up, didn't I?"

"How'd she feel?"

"The Avis lady?"

"The car."

"Fine. In fact, I think that old bugger has got more fire in it than maybe last year. What'd you do, mill the goddam heads some more?"

"Lissen, them heads is so fucking *thin* right now that you could hold one up to the light and read the fucking *Akron Beacon-Journal* through it. No. I just put in my own spark plugs, tha's all."

"Uh-huh. Lissen: if Champion ever finds out about your own spark plugs, for chrissakes, they'll pay you a million dollars to go away somewheres and get lost forever."

He nodded. "Serves 'em right. You want something to drink?"

"Well, what I *want* is a Seven and Seven, that's what I want. That Avis girl come around yet?"

That's when they called the start.

"Here's your cotton," Lugs said. He had rolled it up between his fingertips.

"Well, *look*, for chrissakes: you got it all greasy. Jesus H. Christ, you expect me to stick that stuff in my ears?"

He sighed. "Look: you can stick it up your ass, for all I care. All I'm telling you is: here is your cotton. Let's go race. Jesus Christ."

So I took each little black wad and jammed it into my ears and then buckled on the helmet. And I got wedged back into the cockpit. "I get syphilis of the ear and it's all your fault."

He leaned over so that I could read his lips and smell the goddam Dr Pepper on his breath at the same time. "Don't worry about syph," he said. "Just try to stay off the fucking *wall*, all right?"

Tony Hoyle was on my outside in the front row. Right behind us was Jigger; when I turned around to look at him he gave me his crooked grin and flashed me a go-fuck-yourself signal. Beside him was R. A. Wilbourne. There were sixteen cars in back of them but forget them: not one of them had a Chinaman's chance of keeping up the pace. In fact, if I could run up high again and come down out of the marbles on each lap like I had done in qualifying, not even Buzz or Tony or R.A. or anybody in Terre Haute would be able to keep up.

Lugs strolled out again, grandstanding for the crowd, and patted me on top of the helmet.

"I want you to get out there and win this one for old Lugs," he said.

"Oh, shit. You've been watching that Pat O'Brien movie again."

And then Tommy Hoffman, who also is from Terre Haute, mumbled those immortal words: "Gentlemen, start your engines." And nineteen engines roared to full throat. One didn't.

Mine.

Lugs looked startled, frozen there for just one quick second, his black leather tie afloat in the air.

"You motherfucker," I yelled. "Get this son of a bitch started. Come ON!"

He wheeled around for his long-snouted oilcan. Except that it didn't contain oil; it contained pure alcohol. And he began squirting it right into the velocity tubes while I cranked it over.

Nothing.

Coming around us, the rest of the field got underway and headed for the first turn.

And then that bugger caught on and snapped right into life, shaking and snarling and jiggling me all through. There was a burst of white smoke and I had that bastard in gear and was spinning the rear wheels even as Lugs was pulling his oilcan back and doing a little *entrechat* out of my way. And the car fishtailed first one way and then the other all the way through the first turn as I kept pouring it on.

Nothing serious, understand.

I got it completely sideways right up at the fence coming out of the Number Two Turn and, already, I was past the last two cars in the field. Then I slingshotted down, scaring two rookie drivers right into the fucking infield and — coming out of the Fourth Turn I was suddenly up high above Tony Hoyle and really coming on. So I dove down under him as we came into the front straight and then looked around and stayed right on the gas because I could see the starter poised there with the green flag in the air. And, just as he waved that son of a bitch, I got nicely straightened out and I shot right out in front.

I glanced down and saw about 6,000 RPMs on that old rascal with a lot of pedal left.

Wheeee, you motherhumpers, come and get me.

There was noise and oil spray and dirt clouds and everything great: I got sideways right in front of Hoyle as we slashed into the First Turn and headed for the highest groove. When we went into Turn Two, I was sliding so goddam hard that I was all squished over against the right side of the cockpit and I could feel the tubular steel bending my ribs inward. I glanced left and Hoyle wasn't there — yet — so I drove her down and charged down the back chute about five car lengths in front of him and the rest of the pack. I could see in the mirror that Jigger had moved down under Tony and that R.A. was right on both their asses. That's beautiful. Let them humpties fight it out for second.

Fourth lap: I had a half a straightaway lead on Jigger, who was now running second.

I was humming inside. Fine, high, musical hummmmmmmm.

Running through that fast groove was just like running on ice. Except that at just the right time I got the bite that I needed to come out of the corners. Beautiful. Steer it slightly to the right, cock it and — Jee-*zuz* — what a sensation.

It takes just a second to refocus your eyes after you cross up a car to go sailing into the corners. The perspective of every-thing goes a bit sideways and it is a shock for your optic nerves. But a blink cures that. The rest of the sensation is purest joy.

For one thing, the car suddenly feels like it has power steering. Part of this is because you are racing on loose dirt; the rest of it is because the left front wheel is completely off the ground. The car is zinging along on three wheels, all beautifully cocked — and it stays that way until you come out of the corner and line it up for the chute.

The rooster tails I was kicking up looked like a goddam unlimited hydroplane in full chase — and the crowd was absolutely bananas. And then, when I figured I had everything more or less under control, humming along, I glanced over at the pits.

Lugs was there, and I got the quickest shot of him holding up the pit chalkboard. He had smudged on it:

R. U. NUTS?

So I rocked back and forth a bit in the cockpit like I was trying to make the car go faster and I could see him laughing to beat hell and slapping the side of the pit board.

And then I came zinging past Buzz Boyer and I held out my hand at him and then turned it upside down like his airplane.

Hot damn! If I came past the Avis girl I was going to stand right up in the cockpit and unzip my fly, for chrissakes, and maybe wave it at her in a full, four-wheel drift.

And then I looked ahead.

Focus: there was R.A. just in front of me. This was fine, understand, since I was a full lap ahead of him and was about to lap him. But what was not fine was that he was right, fucking out of control. He was spinning, that's what he was doing.

Oh, shit, Ace.

Suddenly there was about four inches between us and there I was, in the marbles, which made it too late for me to hit the brakes. That little maneuver just then would have taken me right through the fence.

So I jumped right off the throttle and pulled in my elbows and subconsciously sat up as tall as I could in the seat, hoping that somehow it would make me and the car just a little bit thinner.

Then R.A. gathered it up slightly. He was still in bad shape but at least he was lower in the groove. So I twisted the wheel back left and the car came around. If I could just stay on it and maybe slide through the little opening that had appeared, I was out of it.

End of fantasy.

R.A. ran smack up over the rear wheel of Darel Warren's car and I saw the rear end start to lift.

Awww, shit, as we say. Upside-downsville.

He kept right on climbing straight up into the air, right up over where I was going to go through. Goddam.

I muttered just a little quick prayer.

Little Quick Prayer: *Stay Up There,* you Son of a Bitch.

Nothing left to do but stay on the gas and try and hunker down in my seat.

Understand, we were all going to beat hell and we were all screwed up.

I sighted up ahead and I could see a sliver of light between the upside-down car over my head and the grandstand. There was this flash-impression of R.A. trying to keep his arms inside the cockpit because he knew fucking well that he was going to come down awful hard. I know the feeling well. I also knew that I had time to get through before he came down.

Swoosh. I was through and, behind me, R.A. landed upside down with a crash that pulled everybody's pants down to their knees for miles around.

By the time I got to the front straight I was in great shape again:

All screwed up.

I had been gunning too fast and the rear end naturally broke loose and came right around on me like a whip and I just had to let it go. I went ass-end-to-backwards through the Second Turn and I couldn't get back on the gas until the nose came around again when I was out of the corner. Then the car did a little hula and slid right up against the fence, and flat stopped. So I jammed back on the pedal and got back in the race.

Hummmmmm.

Around at the front straight again, R.A.'s car had finally settled and was sitting there on what was left of the axles. All four wheels had been ripped off and R.A. was sitting inside it with a dazed look on his face and blood was coming out both nostrils. There was a wisp of blue smoke coming from the engine where oil had spilled, and there were Sprint car parts scattered all over the track.

I snaked into the pits and Lugs trotted up and leaned in, nose to nose.

"I was sure you'd never get underneath R.A.," he said.

"Lissen: just fuel this son of a bitch and then look around and see if I broke anything when I got into the wall, will you?"

Lugs had hired three locals to work the pits; three fucking local yahoos who were wild about racing.

"They'll be all right," he had assured me.

Wrong.

One guy tipped up the fueler can with the long spout and another guy ran around and looked at the tires while Lugs looked at the overall car. And then, moving fast, the fueler lowered his can and stepped back smartly. Lugs moved in and slapped me on top of the helmet.

The rest of the pack was moving around slowly under the caution flag while they cleaned up R.A.'s wreckage, so I popped it into gear and fed it gas and sped away.

Ka-boom!

The whole car was suddenly on fire and it was all around me

when I looked over my shoulder. And I knew what had happened. Oldest mistake in racing.

What had happened was that that dumb bastard hadn't snapped the gas cap back on, that's what had happened. And when I whipped away, the gas had sloshed, as gas will do.

And it had sloshed right onto the hot exhaust pipes, as gas will do.

And you know the rest. Oh, shit.

I slapped off the harnesses and put both hands down on the cowling and yanked myself half-up. The car was still rolling. And I pulled my feet up onto the seat and then I did a small snap-roll with a full twist right out the left side.

And I hit the ground on my right shoulder and flopped one more time, already putting my gloves up over my face.

And the goddam car rolled right on over my right ankle.

Crack. I could hear the bone snap; not with my ears, but in a small spot just inside my stomach and once you hear the sound you'll never forget it. And then the car went away, somewhere.

And I rolled over one more time and then lay there and blinked up at the spotlights around the track. I could hear the race going on, plain as day, and through the greasy damn earplugs inside my helmet, I could hear folks screaming.

Don't scream, folks. I'm fine. Just let me lay here for a minute and I'll get up and kick the shit out of that car. In fact, I'll take a fucking ball peen hammer and I'll smash that goddam car right into little pieces right here before your very eyes.

But just let me lay here for a minute first.

I want to wait for my right ankle to come back.

Run over by my own car. Huh.

And there was Lugs, kneeling down beside me, looking at me from up close.

"You all right? Ace, are you —— "

"I'm fine," I said. "FINE, GOD DAMN IT. Lissen: I been run over by MY OWN FUCKING CAR. You understand?"

"I can hear you," he said. "You don't have to shout. Are you all right, I said."

"Get my ankle back," I said.

He looked at it for a minute. "It's all crooked," he said.

"Well, *certainly* it's crooked, you dumb bastard. And you know *why?* Because MY OWN FUCKING CAR ran over it and broke it, that's why it's crooked."

"Well, it's broke. Busted, sure as hell."

I raised my head a little. "Well, where's the goddam ɔ ʄʊ Because I'm going to finish this here race and then I'm goiɳʓ to take that no-good fucking car and ———"

"Jee-*zuz!*" Lugs said. And he got up and ran away. I rolled over on the ground and watched him.

The car had rolled on until it had hit an empty trailer just inside the infield. It was still burning.

Lugs and the fire truck got there at the same time — it was a dead heat — just as the fuel cell burst with a dandy damn whoosh and there was flame all around. And suddenly Lugs was on fire and the firemen were spraying both him and the car with CO_2 and then Lugs hauled off and knocked one great big fireman right on his ass right there on the spot and Lugs was slapping the CO_2 off his new black leather tie and kicking at the surprised fireman.

And then a wave of pain came along and I rolled over and put most of my face down into the cool grass and breathed in deeply and smelled a great big lungful of Indiana and passed right out.

I came around to the sound of a racing engine.

I was in an ambulance and, sure enough, the goddam ambulance was in a full, four-wheel drift. Lissen, I know a full, four-wheel drift when I feel it — even when I am lying all stretched out and strapped into a stretcher.

So I raised up my head as far as I could, what with the chest-restrainer across me and all, and I yelled.

Yell: "SLOW DOWN! This ambulance ain't set up to take corners like that!"

There was a big, heavy hand on my chest and I looked around. It was Lugs, naturally.

"S'all right," he said. "That ain't just no ordinary ambulance driver up there."

"Well, who the hell is it then?"

He nodded, calmly. The ambulance suddenly wrenched and began to drift in the exact opposite direction and, under us, I could feel the suspension straining.

"It's Charlie," he said.

"I thought for just one fucking second there that you said it was Char —— "

"It *is*," he said. "First, I was fighting the whole goddam fire department of Terre *Hoot* for spraying me with that fucking foam. And then . . . and *then* some pimply faced young ambulance asshole tried to pick you up out of the grass. So, when he bent over and you yelled in pain, well, Charlie just plain kicked him right over into the infield and then we loaded you in here and Charlie just bopped the other driver a bit . . . not too hard, and said he'd drive you to the hospital. And here we are." He shrugged.

Lugs was a mess. His new white pants were black underneath and coated with foam on top. His fuchsia shirt was ruined and the leather tie had started to curl up like a goddam window shade.

Then the ambulance went into a four-wheel drift again and I passed out again.

thirteen

I really hate the part where they pull up your eyelid. Hell, all drivers crash. They hit walls at two hundred miles an hour in cars with fiber glass bodies. They are hit by other cars at God-awful speeds and the impact sometimes *packages* them right up inside their cars like they were gift-wrapped for the doctor. They get upside down. They get sideways, skidding along, leaving a trail of elbow skin on the track. Engines explode and little pieces of that very same engine take off with the aim of flying right through you. Any good driver has got scars all over him and he is dappled with shiny spots that used to be burns.

Stark naked, any good driver looks like a relief map of Cincinnati, for chrissakes.

And then they haul you off.

I have looked up at as many hospital emergency-room ceilings as anybody and the feeling is always the same: that goddamned white padded table is bumping along on its big black-rubber wheels and you lie there, thinking that a table like that ought to have a better suspension system and that you'll fix it if you ever get the chance. And you keep getting flash-impressions of hospital ceilings and doorways and every now and then a face will lean over into your line of vision and loom up close to you. Everybody talks strange:

"Nurse, get me two million cee-cees of hemo —— "

"What happened?"

"Race driver. He was —— "

"Here, hand me a frappen-staff and —— "

(Don't cut the fucking uniform, you guys. These uniforms cost money. Un-*zip* it, you dumb bastards.)

"Mmm. That's a compound fracture of the —— "

"Any evidence of head injury? Where's the damned ambulance driver? Why didn't somebody give him some *framis* on the way in here? Give me fifty units of —— "

"You getting any pulse, Doctor?"

(No way. You meatheads probably left my pulse back at the racetrack. And stop cutting on my uniform.)

"Twenty-eight over thirty-six over seven under five."

"Hmmm. Where's the swab?"

"Bone splinters in there, see?"

(Well, hell, *yes*, there are bone splinters in there. Plus some little pieces of throttle linkage and a goddam broken connecting rod.)

"There; that'll hold him for now. Is surgery ready?"

And . . .

That's the part where they lift up your eyelid.

"Shock," they always say.

(Well, shock you.)

Finally I woke up and looked around. Same hospital ceiling. Mirror and chest of drawers over on the far wall; a curtain-on-wheels to one side. So I turned my head and looked the other way.

And we were nose to nose. He had faintly minty breath.

"Doctor Furbee," he said. "Doctor Haversham Clinton Furbee. I come from an old-line Indiana medical family. I saw you in the Indy 500."

"No shit."

"No shit. You were magnificent."

"Uh-huh. Well, how am I *now?*"

He blinked and breathed some more mint on me. "Well, how does the old doctor's joke go? Oh, yes. I'm afraid you'll never play the concert violin again."

"Mmmm?"

"Otherwise," he said. "You're fine. Just fine."

"Well, if I'm so fine, then let my leg down. For one thing, I got to get up and go take a leak."

He shook his head. "Sorry. The leg has to stay in traction. Compound fracture. That means that the ragged point of the bone was sticking —— "

"I know what that means."

"Well, here. You can urinate right into this. Here now, try and roll over on your side just a little. There now. Go ahead."

"Well, are you just going to sit there and watch me whiz, for chrissakes?"

"Look, Mister Ace, I'm a *doctor*. And the only reason I'm watching is to make certain that you *can* pass your urine. If you can't" — he began to fumble around in his jacket pockets — "if you can't, then I'm going to have to catheterize you."

"My ass. There, look at *that*, old buddy."

"That's fine." He nodded. "Now, then. You also had, in addition to the compound, some severely bruised ribs and some contusions on your arms. I understand you were run over by a Sprint car."

"Not just *any* Sprint car. And how would you like a punch alongside the head?"

"Uh-huh. I see you're grouchy, which is a good sign." He leaned back in the chair and crossed his legs and carefully fixed the crease in his pants. "You know, I'm really delighted to have you here, if you'll forgive the medical irony in that statement. But delighted. I have been a fan of yours for years. Years. And —— "

"That's swell. Here. Take this thing and throw it out the window."

"I'll just set it down here and the orderly will come and empty it." He leaned over and rang the button over my head. "Seriously now. You represent much more than, say, the ordinary sports hero. Like, say, a quarterback. Or a swimming star like Mark Spitz. You are an authentic hero. You live your life on the very ragged edge of disaster. You are the *beau sabreur* of life today, the ―― "

"The Bo what?"

"Beautiful saber fighter," he said. "You laugh at death. You challenge disaster. You scoff at danger. You see, there is a little bit of race driver in every man, really. Lurking deep inside. Every man, behind the wheel of his pitiful family car, is a Stroker Ace at times. You represent all of us. There are moments, out there on the highway, when I am singing along, passing other cars perhaps, when I feel cool and . . . and *power*ful." He leaned over again, nose to nose. "I'll tell you a little secret: I have some driving gloves that I keep in my medical bag. And when I'm all alone in the car, when nobody is with me, I slip them on and drive along and pretend I'm Stroker Ace."

"No shit."

He nodded again. "No shit."

"Then let my leg down."

"I can't. But, I wonder" ― he looked around, over his shoulder ― "but I wonder if you would do me the signal honor . . ." And he bent over and opened the black leather bag beside his chair.

"What's that?"

"Miracle drug," he said, coming up with a sort of beaker of amber-looking stuff. He held it up to the light. "The miracle drug of race drivers, I am told."

"Come *on*, for chrissakes. All I got is this dumb goddam

broken ankle. I don't need no miracle drug. What I really need, in fact, is —— "

"Exactly," he said. "Exactly! This, my boy, is that old Latin panacea known as Seagram's Seven Crown. And as I told you, I come from a long line of Indiana doctors. And my dear grandfather, rest his soul, taught me early in life that there are certain times when certain strong medicine is definitely necessary. So I wonder if you'd do me the special honor of having a drink with me."

"Here. Let me smell that."

"Take it." Then he stood up and spoke into the intercom: "Nurse Polinos," he said. "Would you please bring me an ice pack and some glasses?"

And the velvety voice came back out: "Yes, Doctor Furbee," it said. "Sterile, of course."

"Of course."

Well, hot damn, and all that. The White Greek. My Girl, Big Woman branch, Earth Mother division.

Doc Furbee got up and closed the door behind her. Then he turned. "This is Nurse Polinos," he said.

"You can call me Nursie," she said.

Nursie was in uniform, understand, and it didn't mean a thing. Nothing had changed: she was all soft hills and hollows and hideaways and black hair and the top button of her uniform was undone and there was the start of a warm, dark shadow between those breasts going down into the starched whiteness.

I looked at her coming toward me and finally figured it all out: I knew where I had seen her before. Everybody has seen her before. She is one of those ladies in the big oil paintings in the museums; the one who is lying there all nude and hummocky on the bed and one leg is sort of cocked up and she is maybe idly holding up this bunch of purple grapes and there are a bunch of little bitty cherubs hovering there in the air all around her and they are all looking horny as hell. That's where I had seen her.

She put the tray down beside the bed. It had some glasses on it and some Seven-Up and a big red-rubber ice bag full of ice cubes.

". . . Stroker Ace," Doc Furbee was saying.

"I know," she said. "Everybody in the hospital knows. And we're all very excited. Good to see you again, Mister Ace." And she bent over and put her lips against my forehead, so lightly I could feel just the briefest flash of heat. And the front of her uniform swayed back and forth slightly when she stood up.

Doc Furbee was mixing the drinks. "Seven-Up?" he said. And then: "Did you put the QUARANTINE sign outside the door?"

"Yes," she said. She turned to me: "I certainly hope you'll let us all sign your cast, Mister Ace."

"How high up does this cast go, Doc?"

He shrugged. "Ummm. About not quite up to your knee."

"Damn."

"I know how you feel," he said. "Now, here. This will make you feel much better. To you, Stroker Ace, and to a speedy recovery. To the felicitous mending of your bones, which, I might add, have been expertly rejoined by one of Indiana's finest surgeons. No house calls. Wednesday off."

And we all drank to that.

"Mmmmmmph," he said. "Now. What are you going to do when you get out of here, Stroker?"

"Well, the very first thing I am going to do is to run out in front of the hospital and let a semi-truck run over my *other* ankle."

"I was the one who cut off your uniform," she said.

"God, I hope so."

She came over and stood close by the bed and, from my angle, I could look right up past the outcropping of her bosom.

The uniform buttoned down the front. About two more of those buttons would do it.

"If you ever need *your* uniform cut off, be sure and let me know," I said. "Call any hour of the day or night."

"Well, except Wednesday," Doc Furbee said.

And we drank to that.

"One more wee drink and I've got to go and make my evening rounds," he said. "Ahhh, now. You'll forgive me, of course, if I stir these with a tongue depressor. Here we are. One for you, Mister Ace. And one for you, Miss Polinos. And one for young Doctor Furbee. There."

The pain was going away, slowly, and my ankle was missing me with every other throb.

"This is a nice room," I said.

"Certainly is." Doc Furbee nodded briskly. "This is the maternity ward. And you're the only mother here." He smiled at us. "You get that little play on words, I take it? A little medical joke there."

"Doctor Furbee is really in obstetrics," Nursie said, "and gynecology."

He nodded again. "And every day when I get home from work, I stagger into the house and say, 'I've had a tough day at the orifice.' You get that one? A tough day —— "

"Lissen," I said. "You want me to take away your driving gloves, for chrissakes? And besides, if it's all the same, I would rather you didn't mention to anybody that I was in a *maternity* ward, all right? I'd never hear the end of it."

He turned at the door. "Right. And now, I'm off to — you'll forgive the expression — look *into* things. Miss Polinos, you might take Mister Ace's temperature while I'm gone. Orally, of course. And see that he's comfortable."

And he closed the door.

"I'd be a hell of a lot more comfortable, Nursie," I said, "if you were to get right in here with me."

She giggled at me — a really nifty, throaty sound — while mixing another drink. "You haven't changed," she said. "You're impossible. But it *is* good to see you, compound fracture and all. I probably shouldn't tell you this, but I do think about you a lot."

"Well, hell. I think about *you* a lot. I don't know why."

So she sat down on the edge of the bed and we drank to that. "And it's awfully nice of you to call me from time to time," she said. "Do you call other girls, too?"

"Nobody," I said. "Here, hand me that umpty-ump, the, uhh, thermometer. I'll take your temperature."

And I reached over and got the first button unbuttoned: "Whatever are you doing?" she said.

"Now, sit still. Put your hand down. This is called a boob-sensor and it's very scientific with us medical men. But you have to sit still and hold your breath until I tell you."

She sat still. But she breathed a lot. And after a few minutes, I reached back and got the thermometer out and looked at it: "Uh-huh. It's very hot in between those things."

"I know," she said. Then, softly: "I know."

So I undid one more button: "Hold *still*, will you? This is for science, remember. We're taking a survey in hospitals all around the country to find out if . . ."

She was giving off a warmish glow. "Mmmmm. What?"

"Well, I've always wondered about nurses. No, really. I've always wondered if *everything* was white underneath. You know: white slips and white, uhhh, things, and —— "

"What are you *doing*, Stroker?"

"Checking," I said. "Now, hold still. Ahhh, yes, Mmmm hmm. You know, you really smell *good*. You don't smell hospitalish at all."

"Your nose is cold," she said.

"I know. I'm warming it."

"But this isn't good for you. A man in your condition."

Ah-hah! A white slip. Just as I had figured.

So I undid another button: "Lissen," I said. "Don't forget that I threw myself in front of a goddam car just to get here to be with you."

"Poor baby." She pressed her lips to the top of my head and I could feel the surge of heat all the way down to the top of my cast.

And *White Garters,* race fans! Hot damn. A real nurse.

"That's as far as you go," she said. And she reached down and held my hand.

She had one hell of a grip for a girl. But not over the long haul. And I finally got the last button.

And the uniform sort of fell away crisply on each side of her.

"All right," she said. "You may look but you mustn't touch. No, no. What in the world is the matter with me? I mean, us? I mean . . ." She was sort of half-twisted now and talking right into my neck, breathing on it, and the words just curled right up around my chin. "You know," she said, "you smell rather good yourself."

"Mmmm hmmm. Old Downshift Cologne."

There now: ahhh, *lordy,* she was wearing a white garter belt. And white panties. Crinkly white lace.

"Don't do that," she said. "You mustn't."

"I must."

"Must *not.*"

"Uh-huh. You *know* I must."

And then she pulled away, looking at me. Directly in the eyes.

"Only one thing to do," she whispered.

"Hmmmm?"

"I'm going to have to let your leg down."

I lay on my back and looked at the ceiling. Hospital ceilings, motel ceilings, for God's sake. The whole world was coated with white gunnite, sprayed on. Other people had rooms, real rooms, where they painted the fucking ceiling any color they wanted. And all around them they had other rooms and a whole house and a lawn around it. And it was *permanent* and it was *there* and it belonged to them. And they didn't have to get up the next morning and go to Atlanta. Or Indianapolis. Or Daytona or Darlington. And they didn't know how to drive their car over fifty miles an hour and — what's more — they didn't give a damn.

And they did other things. They read books and visited the neighbors and if the guy next door was tougher, well, the hell with it. I mean: they didn't feel that they had to go right over there and kick the shit out of him. Let him be tougher.

It was one o'clock in the morning. Sometimes this is a bad time for me.

And my damned ankle throbbed.

That sumbitching Sprint car. I hoped that miserable bugger had burned right to the ground.

That damn . . .

There was a scratch at the door. It was like a cat trying to get in. And then it swung open.

"Su'prise," Lugs said.

He had both arms full of brown paper bags and he clinked a lot, like bottles. Then he shuffled to one side.

"You fucked up another set of new tires," Charlie said. "Burned them bastids right off to the rim. Here, where can I set this stuff down?"

"Put it down there on the bed," Lugs said. " 'N' then he won't have so far to reach. They got yer leg jacked up, I see."

Charlie unloaded the sacks and began searching around in them until he came up with the beer. Then he fished around in his back pocket until he found the opener he carries on the long bathroom chain and he opened it. "Here," he said. The foam splurged up and down across the bedspread.

"I got some sandwiches here somewheres," Lugs said. "Here, move that sack over by his leg. You want, uhh, ham and sliced raw onion or you want — "

"Ham and sliced *onion?*"

He nodded. "Cures broken bones every time. Goddam, just *smell* that little rascal. Whooo-eeee." He took a bite and started fishing around for another one.

Charlie rubbed the palms of his hands across the seat of his pants. "There," he said. "Hand me a sammitch."

They were both spattered with oil. And, mmmm, blood spots. And Lugs had a new Band-Aid across his two little fingers. And a greenish-purple spot under his left eye.

"All right," I said. "All right. What happened?"

They blinked.

"Well, you jumped right out of the car," Charlie said, "and then — "

"Look: I remember that part. Come *on.*"

He shrugged, chewing. Then he took a long pull at the beer.

"Well," Lugs said. "There was a little teeny hassle about stealing the ambulance. You know. But we *explained* to the police it was a matter of life and death, see, and — "

"Course," Charlie said. "I knew you wasn't *dead.* But yer leg was sure as hell crooked." Then he held up his hand, thumb and forefinger about an inch apart. "Little piece of pure bone sticking out through the skin."

Lugs crumpled up the sandwich wrapper and threw it over his shoulder. "And then it took a little while to find the pit crew," he said.

"Pit crew?"

"There was three of them," Charlie said.

"I remember."

"And we hunted all over town. But we found them fellas."

"And . . ."

Charlie shrugged again. "We *disciplined* them," he said.

"You *dis* —— "

"Actually," said Lugs, "we kicked the shit out of them. You know. For not handling the gas right and for causing your crash and all."

"Nobody," Charlie said. "I mean no-BODY gets my old buddy here in danger on no fucking racetrack." And he plopped down on the bed and slapped me on the cast.

"You ready for another beer?" Lugs said. He wiped both hands on my sheet and started searching through the sacks again.

"Oh, hell. Why not?"

He opened them and then pulled the guest chair over and eased down into it. And he put his boots up on the bedspread, and looked around. "Nice room," he said. "How're the nurses around here? I hear nurses are always horny."

"What about the car?"

"The car. Uh-huh. The car. Here, you want a cee-gar? Ain't there any ashtrays around this fucking place? What kind of a hospital room is this, anyway?"

Charlie came up with the bedpan. "Here," he said. "Use this. Yer fulla shit anyway."

"Come *on*. The car."

Lugs shrugged grandly, puffing up a little mushroom of gray smoke over his head. "Sold it." He patted his pocket. "Got your share right here on me."

"How much?"

"I'll bet that little bugger really throbs," he said. "Broken legs is like that a lot."

"Goddammit, how much did you sell the car for?"

"TWENTY-NINE FUCKING DOLLARS," he yelled. "And one word — just one fucking *word* out of you — and I'm gonna break your other leg."

"Twenty-*nine* dollars, right?"

He flicked some cigar ashes in the general direction of the

bedpan. And missed. "You get half," he said. "Less what I spent on these here sammitches and beer, of course."

"Well, thanks a lot."

"Well, thanks a lot, my *ass*. They carried that sumbitch car off in a fucking *dustpan*. I sold it by *weight* for chrissakes."

"More beer," Charlie said.

"Besides: you gotta stop this goddam Sprint car racing, Stroke. Jesus Christ, you're gonna really get *hurt* sometime assing around in them goddam Sprint cars. It's costing us money for you to come back here to the boondocks and race with fucking hayshakers. Grow up, for chrissakes."

"You wouldn't understand. I do it for a reason."

"I do understand. It's like you got to come back and prove that you still got both balls where they always was. But lissen, Stroke: nobody is questioning your balls. No-*body*."

"Lissen," Charlie said. "When do they let you out of here, anyways?"

"Mmmmm. I'll miss Trenton, I guess. But I should be ready for Atlanta if I can get them to saw off this cast and maybe trade it in for some tape. You know. In fact, I think I'll go down to Atlanta early and maybe rest up for a couple of weeks and then maybe shake out the new car a little bit."

Lugs grinned widely through the cigar smoke.

"You know," he said, "I almost got that car to where it really looks like a car. I mean: that little rascal is a *perfect* goddam-looking Dodge. Three-quarter size, of course."

"Will it fit under the template?"

"Well, hell *yes* it'll fit under the template. But I got new trick stuff in there nobody ever heard of."

Charlie was opening more beer, spraying the bed. "And I just happen to have fourteen or fifteen tires hidden away in the van," he said. "Them bastids run off one really good batch last week and I got them all."

"Can you keep 'em hidden until Atlanta?"

"Lissen: anybody touches my tires and I snatch their arm off at the roots."

"Well, tell me one thing," Lugs said. "How you gonna get any *rest* in Atlanta? You must have fallen on yer head when you jumped out of that car."

"Here, better give me another beer," I said. "Well, in fact, I'm taking this nurse down there with me. She's gonna *nurse* me back to health."

"Shee-it," Charlie said. "Taking a lady to Atlanta is like taking a sammitch to a goddam banquet."

Scratch.

It was the door again. And Nursie stuck her head in.

"This is the one," I said.

"Take her to Atlanta," Lugs said.

"You'll have to be a little more quiet," Nursie said. "Ladies are having babies all around you."

"Well, ladies do that all the *time*," Charlie said.

"And perhaps you'd better open the window a bit." She came in, moving like a big, soft Greek ocean liner through the blue smoke, and leaned over the bed. She plumped up the pillow. "There, there, baby," she said.

Lugs leaned over to Charlie and whispered. Lugs's whisper is roughly like a Pierce-Arrow warming up.

"You know," he growled. "I've allus wondered about nurses. I mean: if they wear, you know, white —— "

"They do," I said. "They do."

"Now, remember to be still," she said. "And I'll see you in the morning, right?"

"God, I hope so."

She kissed me on the forehead again and I caught that quick flash of tawny cleavage before she stood up. Tawny surrounded by white lace.

"Night, boys."

"Night."

And Lugs stared at the closed door for a long time, the cigar clenched right in the dead center of his mouth. "You know," he said, "I think maybe I'm gonna go right out and break a leg or something."

Scratch. The door again.

"There you are."

It was Shirley. Queen of All Racing. She was in a white nurse uniform. White nylon and you could see her leopard-skin underwear through it. "Look at me."

"God damn, you look *great*." Charlie whapped her approvingly on the ass. "Just like a goddam nurse."

She came over and sat on the edge of the bed and patted me on the cast. "Well, actually, it's an old waitress outfit I used to have before I got into racing," she said. "But I got it out and put it on and then sneaked up here just like a real nurse, see?"

"Have a beer." Charlie wrenched open some more, foaming them again.

"A lady drinks out of a glass," she said.

He looked around. "No glasses."

"Well, then." She took the bottle and drank deeply.

"I can see your underwear," Lugs said, approvingly.

Shirley stood up and jiggled around, shaking her bottom and spilling a little beer around in a wet arc.

"I know, I *know*. Isn't that *kicky?* You know where I got these panties and bra?"

Charlie shrugged. "Atlanta," he said.

She bent over and kissed him on the forehead. "Right," she said. "Atlanta has the prettiest underwear. Doesn't it, Strokie, honey-babe?"

"Bet your ass," I said.

"And look what else I got," she said. She opened her purse and fumbled around inside it and come up with a transistor radio. "This is to cheer you up, Strokie-babe."

"Swell."

And she cranked it up. The voice came on really loud and filled up the entire room.

". . . and now: STEPPENWOLF!" the voice said. And this really big, rocking music started.

Shirley stood there and shook it and she was a goddam rhapsody in pure jiggle.

"Uuuuuuuugh!" she said. Then she did a little bump and shook it some more. "Anybody wanna dance?"

"Me, for one," Lugs said. And he hauled himself up out of the chair and tugged his pants into place just under his belly. "Here, Ace, hold this cee-gar. I'm gonna show this little lady some plain and fancy dancing. Lookie here."

And just standing there, he began to quiver his belly in long, slow rolls, like waves coming in off Corpus Christi.

"Go, baby," Shirley said. And she began to tug at the zipper of her uniform, slowly opening it until we could see bouncing, shaky little flashes of leopard.

"Well, hellfire," Charlie said. And he drank down the rest of his beer and stood up. "Lookee *here*."

He began to shake his shoulders a lot and unbutton his shirt. "It's old Boom Boom Heffer and I'm a dancing bear. Yahoo."

Shirley was really cranking them out now and her bosoms were rising right up out of the white nylon and leopard skin with every bounce. And then she ra'ared back to do a great, big bump.

And knocked the lamp over.

This time the door really flew open. Ka-*pow!*

And it was the Head Nurse.

She shouted something.

"What's that?" Charlie said. "Can't hear you." And he slipped into just a little off-to-Buffalo.

"Catch this," Charlie said. And he pulled his shirt off and wriggled the twin bluebirds tattooed over each chest.

The old lady snatched away the radio and clicked it off.

"I *said*," she said, "what's going on here?"

Shirley stopped dancing. She stopped dancing, but she didn't stop shaking. Everything just kind of settled down in slow, soft, undulating quivers. It was a goddam sight to see.

"We're cheering up a sick friend," she said.

The Head Nurse turned and pointed one bony hand at the door.

"Out!" she said. "Everybody out! Out this instant before I call the *police*. You understand? In fact, I think I *will* call the police this instant. Out!"

"Lady," I said. "Lady, these are my friends."

"And *you*," the Head Nurse said, wheeling on Shirley. "You . . . you *hussy*. Where did you get that nurse's uniform! You're a dis*grace*. I'm going to have you *arrested* for im*personating* a real nurse. And, for heaven's sake, ZIP YOURSELF UP, young lady. The very idea."

That's when Charlie leaned back and shouted.

"Look," he shouted. "Don't you call Shirley no hussy, you old *biddy*. You keep on like this and we gonna LEAVE, you understand?"

The Head Nurse strangled a bit, still pointing at the door. "Police," she gurgled. "I'm going to call the police this instant."

Then she wheeled and sailed right out the door.

"Who's a hussy?" Shirley yelled. Shirley is slow sometimes.

"Just for that," Lugs said, "I may leave."

Charlie nodded. "Me, too."

And I nodded. "Me, too. Get my clothes out of the closet there. And somebody untie my goddam leg and get it down."

"Way to go," said Charlie.

"Well, I got a bulletin for you," Lugs said. "There ain't no clothes *in* here."

"Oh, shit, that's right. They cut off my uniform."

"They're always doing that," Charlie said. "Allus."

"Well, gimme that blanket. Come on, hurry up, for chrissakes. Oooooh, Jee-*zuz*."

"No, no," Lugs said. "Don't try to put your foot down, you meathead. Here, Charlie, grab him under the other arm. Okay? Now, *lift*."

"Where's the backstairs?"

"Over here, I think."

"You okay, Stroke?"

"Jee-*zuz*."

"Here, open that door. Come on. Lift, Charlie. That's it."

"Lissen, you guys," Shirley said. "Did you hear what that lady called me?"

fourteen

We were still spinning around the parking lot when they started arguing about the record.

Spinning: the entire parking lot was covered with loose, pea-sized gravel, all sprayed white, and the Ford LTD was going around in full-power skids one way and the other, and throwing up a rooster tail of little stones. The inside of the car was rattling with the sound of gravel under the fenders.

Hell of a song. I leaned my head back against the head-stopper and sang a few bars:

> Oh, I've just got one leg, dear,
> And a big sack of beer here;
> But one thing is clear . . .
> DEAR,
> Uhhh . . . sure as there's a Wankel,
> I've busted my fucking ankle,
> And I'll have to hold my socks up with
> suspenders,
> Because: every time I see you,
> I get,
> Gravel Under My Fenders.

What the hell. I was delirious anyway and my ankle was keeping perfect time to the music. One, two, *throb;* one, two, *throb.*

The LTD came around one more time in a full, swinging three-sixty degree turn and I finally got it figured out in my head why the car was spinning. Two reasons:

One: too much power was being applied on the loose gravel and there was no traction.

Throb.

Two: Lugs was driving it and everybody knows that Lugs is a goddam *dummy.*

Throb.

And they were arguing about the record:

Charlie had his chin resting up on the top of the front seat and his whole face filled up the space between Lugs and my shoulders. He was wearing Shirley's leopard-skin brassiere over the top of his head, with the back-snap part hooked under his chin, and the D cups poofed out on each side like big, spotted earmuffs.

"Lissen," he said, "you better get us the hell out of this here parking lot before the cops get here."

"No," Lugs said. "I'm going around here one more time. I'm not leaving this here lot until you tell me what the record is. Hold on, here we go again."

And the car came whipping around again, spraying up gravel like thunder against the chassis.

"Wheee!" Shirley said. "Sing the song again, Strokie."
Throb.

"Not until you give me another beer."

"It's right here on the seat between us," Lugs said. "You want me to drop everything and open you one, for chrissakes? Can't you see I'm *driving?*"

"Driving? Come *on,* Dummy. If I couldn't spin a car any

goddam better than *this*, I'd get out and walk. Now, really get down on the goddam *gas*, Dummy, and crank that wheel."

Throb.

"Sing it again," Shirley said. "One more time."

> *Oh, every time I see your two knockers,*
> *I get gravel . . .*
> *Under my rockers.*

Charlie's big hands came over and opened two more cans of beer, spraying the imitation-leather dashboard. "Lissen to this," he said.

> *Oh, every time I look at your ass,*
> *I get gravel,*
> *In my GAS.*

And the car came around again.

"You going to tell me what the record is?" said Lugs. "Or are we going to spin around here until daylight?"

"All right," Charlie said. "It is sixty-three miles to Indy. And the record is thirty-four minutes. Now, if you can't beat that by at least a half-hour I'm gonna —— "

"Well, hang on," Lugs said.

Throb.

We came carooming out in something of a ragged four-wheel drift just as the police car was coming in — and for just one, tiny, tiny split second there, everybody in both cars all looked into each other's eyes.

Lugs braked her hard and we did one final pirouette on the hard-top road, shaking gravel out from under the car like steel rain. And then he cranked it over tight and we came around through the Hospital Emergency entrance in a nice little circle, taking out about fifty-five feet of dahlias planted along the walkway.

By the time we hit the Interstate, just flashing under the overhead green *Indianapolis* sign, Shirley was singing:

> *Oh, who put the tire tracks in my flowers,*
> *That I worked on for hours and hours*
> *[Throb]*
> *It must have been a bunch of folks out on benders ...*

"All together now. Come on":

> *Because now I've got, uhhh,*
> *Flowers under my FENDERS.*

We made it in thirty-two minutes point sixteen seconds, sliding into the White Front parking lot in a nice, easy long, looping drift.

"Are we going *in?*" Shirley said.

Everybody looked at her.

"No, we're just going to sit out here and insist that they open curb service," Lugs said. "Of *course* we're going in. Now, come on."

"Well, can I have my brassiere back?"

Charlie thought it over: "No. It's the first time my ears been warm all season."

So she zipped up her uniform a little bit, just up to the edge of that tawny warm valley.

Outside, the car was crackling and popping and giving off strange, helpless little clicks, trying to cool off, and little wisps of steam were curling up out of the front grill.

"The car is talking to itself," Shirley said.

"Naw," said Charlie. "What that car is doing is *praying.*"

They all kept sliding in and out of focus, everybody moving wavily as if the entire White Front had been moved underwater somewhere off the Florida Keys. And little bits of conversation drifted in and out of my head, sometimes hanging there for a minute or two so I could study what was being said as though it had been printed right on the smoke over our table:

"Will you get the hell *up*? Yer sitting on Stroker's *cast*, for chrissakes . . ."

"Did you hear he was in the maternity ward?"

". . . and Lugs knocked the fireman on his ass."

". . . stole the ambulance."

Throb. Another round of beer here, Grace.

"What're you doing wrapped in a blanket, fella? You playing cowboys and Indians?"

"Who ast you? If that man wants to sit here in a blanket, it's fine, you follow me?"

"Look: I'm talking to the guy in the *blanket*. I don't like his looks, you unnerstand?"

Throb. Where's Grace with that beer?

"Uh-huh. Well, what I'm telling *you* is: leave the guy in the blanket alone."

"Yeah? Well, I don't like the looks of his fucking blanket. So I'm just going to snatch it off him and then I'm going to ram it right up yer ass, buddy-boy."

Focus: I could see Lugs sitting down, all nicely tilted back on his chair, very calm, looking up at some giant, mean hay-shaker who was standing there. The guy had big, red-knuckled hands and he was leaning over towards me.

Lugs was undoing his belt buckle while he was talking, and he was slowly pulling it out of the belt loops.

Throb.

"More beer over here?"

"Hey, Grace. Where you been?"

Throb.

Grace was all fuzzy around the edges, wavering there underwater, and she had a big trayload of beer. She smiled and the smile hung there frozen in the smoke so that I could study it.

"Maternity ward, huh? Well, here's your beer, you mother." And then she was gone, but her smile still hung there.

Throb. The bottle felt cool; the palms of my hands were hot.

"Well, I come in here for a peaceful drink, see, and I ain't gonna allow no goddam *Indians* sitting here wrapped up in blankets while I'm drinking, see?"

Focus: Lugs was still sitting easy. But his right hand had now dropped out of sight down alongside his chair. And his belt was now gone from his Levi's.

Throb. Now if I can only find a cigarette here. Must have a cigarette here somewhere . . .

Slowly, in perfect diminished four-quarter time, the two big red hands reached over for my blanket. And I looked up into the guy's face. There was a big scowl squinched down between his eyebrows and he needed a shave. He was talking to me, slowly, underwater, and I waited, listening carefully for the words to come out.

"F-u-c-k-i-n-g I-n-d-i-a-n," he said. "Gimme that blanket . . ."

I smiled up at him, trying to keep him in sight and trying to study the words he had printed in the smoke over our table.

Our faces were very close together now. And the tips of his fingers were on my shoulders. And he was looming bigger, fuzzy and bigger, very slowly, until I could see all the open pores and blackheads across his nose.

Throb. Naturally I can't have any cigarettes here because I haven't got any *pockets*, right? I wonder if this stranger has any cigarettes on him? *Throb.*

Oh, look: he's doing a nice *trick*. In slow motion.

I watched him.

His face was drawn right up close and — gently, easily, just as slowly as could be — a perfect white slash grew right along-side his right eyeline. The skin peeled back smoothly, in slow four-four time, until I could look into the new slot and see his bare cheekbone. And then, without a sound, it turned pink.

"That's *wonderful*," I said. I reached over into his shirt pocket and pulled up a pack of Pall Malls. He didn't seem to mind because he was still doing his nice trick to entertain me:

The ditch in his face turned bubbly red and, gently, a mar-velous fountain of blood began to come up out of it, sparkling and frothing in the smoky light; all glistening and throbbing in perfect time with my ankle. And then his eyes grew beautifully opaque, as though he was trying hard to hold me in focus by some slow, magic force of his own will. But the fountain of red was all lit up now from the inside, just like teeny spotlights were playing on it — and he made it grow wider until part of it covered the side of his nose. Then he sort of sighed with his mouth opening just like a Walleyed Pike and he started to care-fully put his head right down on the tabletop next to me, in the middle of all the bottles of beer.

Throb. The beer bottles parted, smoothly and quietly tum-bling without a sound; some of them giving off little foamy spurts of amber and creating neat little rivers on top of the oil-cloth.

I looked at the rivers and followed their course, pretending that I was swimming in them through the red and white checks. It was easy: the foam carried me right along.

He was a big man, but now, just a little bit at a time, he grew smaller and smaller until I could just see the very top of his head. His hair was thin on top and his scalp was pretty dirty.

And then he did the final part of his trick: he vanished. *Throb.* And the only thing left was a little red road map smeared across the top of the table, pointing a trail to where he had sunk out of sight.

"You all right, Stroker?"

Hazy focus: "I'm fine. Where are the cigarettes?"

"In your hand."

"Hey, Stroker! How you?"

"Hey . . . uhhh, Demon. How you?"

"Those dumb buggers didn't close the gas cap and his car caught fire. You hear?"

"Busted his . . . look at the cast there."

"Hey, yer sittin' on Stroker's cast again. Go get another chair, he's got to have his leg propped up."

"No, wait. Here I'll put his leg up here on the table, all right?"

Throb. Where's Grace with the beer?

"Get that sumbitch out from under the table and throw him out, will you?"

"Jesus! What happened to this guy?"

"Now, how in hell would *I* know? He just came staggering over here and did a full face-down in amongst the bottles of beer here, tha's all. Grace! You got something I can wipe this blood off with?"

Throb!

"Strokie-babe. My poor baby."

Focus: it was Shirley Cleavage. Her nipples were apostrophes hidden inside the white nylon.

"Your leg hurt?"

"It's *ticking.* Can you hear it tick?"

"Well, for one thing, you got the *wrong* leg up on the top of the table. Where's your other leg? The *hurt* one?"

"Uhhh. Oh, here it is. See, right here. Look, some guy is lying down on my leg under the table."

"More beer?"

"Hey, Grace, where you been? Here, put it right down here. Wait: help me get Stroker's other leg up on the table."

"You've got nice thighs."

"Me? Where's my blanket?"

"They're carrying some big guy out in it. He hit his head on something. Hell of a cut on his head."

"Well, he wanted the blanket anyway. Anybody got a light?"

"Strokie-babe, you're all flushed. Damn, he's got a *fever*, you guys. Here, feel his head."

"Gravel Under My Fenders."

"Come on. We gotta go."

"Hey, Stroker, where's yer pants?"

Throb. And focus: Charlie was doing a ballet, an easy, quiet half-turn in the air with both hands out and his fingers all spread out like exclamation points. And then one hand dipped down just as he was completing the full swirl and when he came out of it, swinging around slowly, he had a *man* in his hand. It was nifty and graceful and I studied it through the smoke.

Throb. Charlie and the man did a half-step, except that the man's feet weren't touching the floor at all. That's because Charlie had him all gathered up right under his nose. And they spoke their lines clearly so I could hear:

"Were . . . you . . . speaking . . . about . . . Mister . . . Ace's . . . pants?" Pause. "Shithead?"

Answer: "No . . . sir . . . not . . . me . . . uh, uh . . . no . . . sir."

And Charlie gave him a little, slow twirl like they were jitterbugging and the man swirled off into the smoke until I couldn't see him any more at all.

Throb.

"I'm hungry."

"You hungry, Stroke?"

"I want a White Castle New England boiled dinner–burger."

We were tooling along in the rain and the tires were zinging. "You feeling any better?" Demon said.

His real name is Dennis Manley Daniels and he used to steal cars for a living until he got into stock car racing. And he had sense enough to know that a name like Dennis just wouldn't do. So he had changed it to D. Manley Daniels and then, after he had won his first Super-speedway race, some newspaperman had called him Demon Daniels. And that was that.

Demon is not all that far behind me in points for the championship, mostly because he drives the entire circuit and I don't. He figures to knock me over this season, which is two things. One: a lot of shit. And two: impossible.

"Where are we?" I said.

"Charlotte coming up. How's yer leg?"

It felt a hell of a lot better. I had spent two days in the Speedway Motel: one sleeping and one throwing up. And then Demon had come by and told me that he had been in the party at the White Front and that I had promised to drive down to Atlanta with him. "Besides, you need the rest anyway," he had said.

"Rest? Chrissakes, the way you drive I could get more *rest* walking down there on this cast."

But what the hell. My helmet and gearbag with the driving uniforms were in the trunk and I was resting easy in a goddam baby-blue seventy-six-dollar cashmere pullover and one very soft Gucci loafer with the gold snaffle bit on top.

And Demon was hauling right down the outside lane on his new Goodyear iron-belted radials or whatever the hell they were, and his monster goddam Chrysler New Yorker was undulating softly up and down like a killer whale masturbating in the Gulf Stream. And Demon had a bunch of stereo speakers all over the car, probably even under the seats, and we were playing Thwacker Martin's "Busted Gearbox Blues" on the tape deck, and we had two Stroker Fast Packs on the front seat between us and I was eating fried chicken drumsticks and throwing the bones out the little vent window on my side. The good life.

Demon was going to drive all the way because — even with

his one big brake pedal that went practically the whole width of the car and his goddam automatic throttle — you could set for ninety-five and crawl into the back seat if you wanted to — I didn't feel like doing anything.

"You ate all the drumsticks," he said, fishing around in the boxes.

"Don't bitch to me, for chrissakes, talk to Clyde Torkle; he's the one who tells 'em what to pack in these here kits."

"And you mean to tell me he's paying you a whole bunch of money to put yer face on these boxes of chicken?"

"Uh-huh. A bunch. You see the billboards yet?"

"*See* 'em? Chrissakes, I can't even get out of bed of a morning and look out the window, but I don't see yer goddam ugly face on a billboard somewheres. Pole Position Chicken, my ass."

"Uh-huh. Well, how about Atlanta, asshole?"

He shrugged grandly, lifting his hands off the wheel for a second. "Atlanta? Lissen: I'll have you so far back in the fucking pack that you prolly won't even get in the goddam *race.*"

"How far back?"

Demon turned and looked at me. "All right, then. All right. So I *heard* about yer hot new car awreddy. But I got a bulletin for you: I'll suck the doors off that sumbitch and I ain't just whistlin'."

"Look: You want to go for the pole or don't you?"

"All right: FIVE HUNNERT!" he shouted. "You sumbitch, five hunnert dollars says I beat your ass out of the pole."

"That's more like it. Now, here's a drumstick. You better enjoy that bugger because it's going to be the most expensive piece of chicken you ever ate."

Still, there was the ankle to consider. Maybe I could get Lugs to design a hinge for it, right at the ankle bone.

And there was Demon to consider: he was about as wild-assed as any driver on the circuit and he got a little bit better every year. And they loved him in Atlanta, God knows.

Well, for one thing, Demon held the all-time record for driving through downtown Atlanta and he was the only driver on the circuit ever to be banned from driving in the city for *life*, in any kind of machine, including golf carts and wheelchairs. And for two more things, he had received the only $500 traffic ticket ever issued in Georgia. And before that, he had gotten the only $400 traffic ticket. It wasn't easy.

Old Demon had worked up a head of steam just somewhere outside of Bismark, North Dakota, for chrissakes, and he had hit I-75 going full-bore right through Atlanta. Every police cruiser in town had had a run at him and they had him figured at 140 miles an hour. So they had radioed ahead — way the hell ahead — and they had set up a roadblock. And then they had set up a series of cars with flashers on them to get him slowed down safely ahead of time and, finally, they had set up big floodlights on the road. And Demon had come purring right up to a stop, his stereo tape deck blaring.

"It's me," he said. And when the lieutenant opened the door, Demon sort of spilled right out into the street, not a bone in his body.

So they hauled him up and steered him away towards the Black Maria, between two big cops.

"What's a matter with you?" they said.

And Demon shrugged. "Well," he said. "I hadda couple of drinks, see, and I was trying to hurry back to the motel before I had an accident."

And then: about halfway back into town, the paddy wagon gave a couple of coughs and stopped dead, right in the middle of the Interstate. And one of the officers had climbed out and spent a lot of time looking under the hood and shaking his head. And finally he had come around and opened the doors and looked in at Demon.

"Awright," he said. "Yer a goddam race driver. Come on out here and tell me what's wrong with this here engine so's we can get going."

"Shertainly," Demon said. And he had fallen out into the street again and then, finally, lurched around and looked under the hood.

"Well?" the cop said.

"Ah-hah!" Demon said. "Here's yer problem right here." And he reached in and wrapped one hand around the ignition wiring harness and snatched it right off. Wiring, distributor cap and coil all came up. And then Demon wound up and threw it all off into the darkness. "There," he said. "It's fixed."

Then he reached in and snatched all the wiring out of the two-way radio. And he was going for the air cleaner when they finally got him stopped.

That was the $400 ticket and Demon got a real nice write-up in the *Constitution*. And when his sponsors finally found him and got him back to the track, every red-neck in the crowd gave him a standing ovation.

Next time: they caught him going through town in the *other* direction in a bad-ass Avis rental car with both back doors open and beer cans falling out about every five yards or so.

And *this* time they called for the police cruiser with the prisoner setup in back. That is, it had a regular back seat, all right, but it also had this thick wire mesh screen between the back seat and front seat where the policemen sat. And they sort of dumped him in there and locked the doors and then the two officers got in and drove off.

Demon sat there just as peaceful as could be. Then, after about ten blocks or so, he spoke up.

"Hey, there," he said.

They were so mad that they wouldn't even look back at him.

"Hey, there," he said. "How's about stopping so's I can take a leak?"

They ignored him.

"Hey, there," he said. "Lissen: I *really* gotta pee. I'm so goddam full of beer you'll never believe it. You gotta stop and lemme *whiz*, you guys."

One of them spoke without turning his head.

"No way," he said. "Yer going straight to jail."

Demon was pretty quiet for about three more blocks. And then he slowly got up on his knees on the back seat, facing the front of the car. And he unzipped his fly and he whipped it out.

"Hey, there," he said.

And he pissed right through the thick wire-mesh screen, all over both cops.

That was the $500 ticket.

Demon says about the only thing he could remember about it was the scene in the station house when they were booking him. The desk sergeant had turned to one of the cops.

"Don't stand so close to the radiator, y'all," he had told him.

"Gotta stop in at Charlotte," Demon said. "Old Sam Bisby's race driving school. After I win Atlanta I'm gonna teach driving there between races. And . . . uhh, and . . ." he glanced over at me. ". . . and, uhh, lecture."

"What?"

"Now, come *on*, don't give me no nonsense. I'm gonna show those guys how to drive and then, well, lecture them on the techniques. You know."

I let him have that one. Those were going to be some fine lectures. Besides, Sam had already asked me about teaching and we had determined right away that he couldn't afford me.

We wheeled in at the Charlotte Speedway and one of the classes was going on and there was a pretty good size group of kids clustered around the pit wall. They all had their eyes good and wide open.

The reason was that Sam Bisby and Caleb Powell were out on the track in a brace of racecars, going very goddam fast, it seemed to me. No messing around.

And down at the other end of the pits, Hank Lewers, Sam's other assistant teacher, was strapping on a helmet while standing beside a pale-green stock Dodge Charger. Demon eased the big Chrysler up and flicked down the electric window.

"Hey, Louie."

He came over and bent down and looked in at us. "Hey, Demon. How you, Stroke? I hear you busted your ass up at Terre Haute."

"Leg."

He shrugged, snapping up the helmet. "You okay for Atlanta and all?"

"I suppose. Right before the physical I'm gonna saw off this cast and tape myself right up to the balls."

He nodded.

"What you doing?" Demon said.

Louie looked out on the track. "Well, I'll tell you. Those two clowns ain't coming in, so I'm gonna take this here Hertz car and go out and chase them around a little bit. You know."

We knew all right: Hank Lewers is maybe the Number Two stock car driver in the world, present company included (which makes Demon Number Three), and he is not one to stand around when there is racing to be done.

So he popped that rascal and slewed out on the track after them. And right away, all the students could see that he was having trouble holding the Hertz car in the corners. Those skinny street tires smoked and the Aunt Nellie suspension mushed the coupe around in the groove. But he stayed right on it and, sure enough, when they came out of the Number Two, he was running right between Sam and Caleb.

They both acted a little surprised to see him there. So both of them pushed the loud button a little bit harder and left Louie for a minute. And here he came again, shagging along after them.

The students loved it.

Louie caught them one more time, driving on more or less sheer guts, just as they were going into the Four Turn.

And then: Sam drove down in front of Louie and Caleb came drifting up from the low groove. Pow! Both cars caught the little Charger broadside and parts flew off like someone shaking a Christmas tree.

Poor Irving Hertz. But Louie stayed right on it — his shoulders all hunched up, no doubt — and the three cars came right on out of the turn strictly welded together. And that's the way they came down the chute, everybody waiting for everybody else to get off the damn gas.

Man, the students were laughing and howling and hitting each other on the arms a lot. Some classroom.

One of the students was a girl, no mistaking that, driving coveralls and all, and she was clearly impressed with old Sam, who once was the best in the business before he burned out. And she sidled up to him while he was explaining what just happened, with his gray old curls tumbling over his head.

"Any questions?" he said.

"Yes," the girl said. "Do you smoke cigars when you race?"

Sam said: "No, but I will."

It was quarter past ten when we got to the King's Inn Motel in Atlanta, with Demon wearing some sort of innocent look on his face in case we passed any patrol cars.

I picked up all my mail and my laundry from the last trip: I have letters and dirty underwear at every motel along the NASCAR and USAC circuit. Sometimes it takes a whole season to get everything together.

I had:

— a check from Clyde Torkle for $7,500. Expenses.

— a check from Fire Injection Carburetion Systems for $6,000. Quarterly pay.

— a bill from the Holiday Inn in Milwaukee for $615.27 in damages. We had had a pretty good party there.

— a telegram from Lugs Harvey: ARRIVE WEDNESDAY. REST AND STAY AWAY FROM GREEK FOOD. AND NURSES. STOP.

Hell, telegrams don't say "stop" any more.

Do they?

"Stroker," the desk clerk said. He was half-leaning over the counter and whispering.

"Mmmm?"

He nodded towards the lobby. "There's a lady waiting over there for you. Brunette. Big jugs. You know."

And there she was: all tall and willowy, dark hair floating down over her shoulders, moving toward me with her gently shaking breasts plowing the way ahead — the silk and lace Greek.

Let's hear it out there for white underwear.

"Stroker! How are you . . . how's your leg?"

"Mmmmm, I think we better go and take a look at it right now."

Demon was standing there, kind of stunned, looking first at me and then at Nurse Polinos and then at her knockers and then back at me. Finally he took a deep breath.

"Hey, lady," he said. "I'm Demon Daniels."

She pulled her face out of the hollow of my neck for just one second and looked at him.

"Good for you," she said. And then she started kissing me again.

I nodded at Demon. "Boy, when you get a chance, drop my bags off at my room. That's a good fellow."

fifteen

This is the way it was at one-thirty in the morning: the long, soft black hair was splayed out across my chest and her cheek was buried somewhere just this side of my thorax and she was holding a cigarette for me so that I just had to bend my head a little to puff on it, and I was blowing smoke up toward the sprayed-on gunnite ceiling, and I had two pillows plumped up under my leg, and we had Johnny Carson on the television. Sound off.

The room looked roughly like a deer crossing.

"Stroke?"

When she talked, her lips were warm and soft right up against the big vein in my neck and I hardly had to *listen* to her. The sound of it came right in through my throat-bones and I could hear it play gently inside my head: "Stroke?"

"Mmmmmmmm?"

"I think I probably love you," she said.

"Everybody loves me. I am old Sam Cuddly."

"No, really."

"Really what?"

She raised her head just a little, until I could see one velvet brown eye. And then she moved a little, bare warm breasts trailing across my rib cage a bit, and stamped out the cigarette in the ashtray. "No. Really, I think I do."

"And I love you, too. Let's see, now, uhhh: How Do I Love Thee? Let Me Count the Positions."

She moved my hand away. "No. Come *on*, now. I want to talk to you."

"You have really got a great fanny, you know that? I mean: this here may be the greatest bucket in the Intermountain and Eleven Western states."

"You're not listening. Stop that."

"And your front-side is maybe even better. Mmmmm. Lissen: we could run that rascal through the Park Service and we could have it named officially the Pubic Arch National Monument. And then we'll have pictures made of it on postcards, you know? In color. And —— "

She was up on her elbows now, looking right at me. "I *love you*," she said. "You hear me?"

"Uh-huh. But you know about race drivers."

"No. You're the first one I've ever known. But I know about you."

"Well, race drivers are, uhh, mean, faithless, beat-up, untrue, horny, Godless, hollow and Flopsy, Mopsy, Cottontail and Peter."

She shook her head, slowly, hair tumbling down over one cheekbone. "I could be very good for you," she said. "I mean: very *good*. And you can talk all you want, but you *do* have feelings. You keep them all hidden away under a lot of old emotional armor."

"Who, me?"

"Yes, you."

"Naww. You're just in love with the glamour part, that's all. Stroker Ace and his Big Magic Racing Machine. You know: Captain *Danger*. Lissen: if you'll just move over for one second here, I'll go and get my crash helmet and wear it to bed."

"Honey, *stop* it. You do, too, have feelings but you're afraid to show them; you're afraid to admit it. You're all tough and swaggering on the outside. But you —— "

I got another cigarette and then patted all around on the nightstand until I could find the lighter. And then I began to puff little shots of smoke up at the ceiling. Hoo-Boy.

Finally: "Lissen," I said. "I got you now. This is the old motel room analysis, that's what this is. I get this very same routine in every motel room in every town around this circuit and on every racing circuit. 'You're really *different*, Stroker. You're afraid to show emotion, Stroker.' Uh-huh. It turns out that there is a head-shrinker hidden inside every girl. Maybe they all talk to each other secretly or something and they hold underground meetings and have a motto: Help Salvage Race Drivers. Lissen: I'm not *different* Stroker. I'm *Stroker* Stroker, that's all."

She blinked. "And girls drift in and out of your life."

"That's me, all right. Life's big transfer point. Just drift in, get your ticket punched, and drift on out."

"With no meaningful relationship."

"No, ma'am. Why, ah jus' love mah *car*, ma'am. Me an' ole Paint. Yessir, when all else fails, a man can trust his racecar, by God. True blue, ma'am."

"Oh, come *on*, Stroke. Now, I know you've heard all this before, I know that. But no matter what you say, there are times when you look inside yourself and you get a glimpse of your own *mortality*. And you won't admit it, but it scares you."

I put out the cigarette. "Ah-hah! Wait a minute. I *know* the part that's coming next. It goes like this: deep down inside myself I feel that someday ole Stroker will die in a flaming crash, right? And there will be broken glass and junk scattered all around and old Stroker's broken body trapped inside the flaming wreckage, right? And I refuse to let myself think about it, and so I enclose myself in all this emotional *armor*. Uh-huh. Well, *wrong*. All that routine is a rumor started by the very first girl who ever slept with the very first race driver. You know why? Well: because every girl who has ever screwed a race driver has got this really nifty mental picture inside her mind. You know what it is? She sees herself standing there in the stands watching a fireball of death out there on the Number Two Turn — with one hand at her throat and her eyes full of tears. And while she's watching the car burn, she is sort of mentally going through her wardrobe, trying to remember what she's got in basic *black*. That's all it is."

Her eyes were misting up just a bit and she was biting at her lower lip.

"That's not true," she said. "It isn't."

"Sure it is. Look: race drivers aren't bugged by any feelings of *mortality*. That's purest bullshit, honey. Nobody thinks they're going to get killed out there one day. Hell, they wouldn't *race* if they did. Chrissakes, I don't even figure I'm ever gonna get *hurt* out there; it would throw off my timing. No, lissen: men race because it's a goddam wild-assed sensation to drive a car at speed and control that son of a bitch — and beat everybody else. Racing is the fucking greatest and it is *living*, that's all it is. And it sort of burns all the other feelings out of you and, finally, you don't really give a damn for anything else but racing. And you don't give a damn especially for people, because people can't give you what racing gives you. And, sure, you get a lot of girls drifting in and out. And I promise you: you lay back there on motel beds and you watch them stand there and reach behind them and unsnap their brassieres and then pull off their pants and you think to yourself — hell, I've *earned* this. Right?"

She was crying now, without making any noises; just tears easing up out of the brown eyes and making tiny, hot drops on my chest.

"But what . . . what will happen to you?" she said.

"Who cares? Hell, I don't know and I don't even think about

it. And it isn't because I don't want to think about it. I only think ahead to the next race or maybe the next season and that's about all. Sometimes, sure, I think that I should probably get out of this thing — but racing keeps getting me back. I can't imagine myself ever doing anything else."

"No home?"

"Home? I *tried* that. Lissen: my home is really about thirty-six goddam motel rooms all around the circuit and they all look just alike. Hell, I can walk into a strange Holiday Inn or maybe a Howard Johnson's or whatever anywhere in this country and know right away where everything is. I know right where the bathroom will be and I know that the ice machine is just outside there around that corner and that the coffee shop is just across the courtyard. Now, that's home. But what you have in mind is being *good* for me — and maybe one day I will come climbing out the window of my fucking Dodge and grab you in my arms. And I will have this oily, dirty line under my eyes where the goggles fit — like Clark Gable in *The Big Wheel* — and we will walk away from the track and never look back. You know. And next thing, you'll have me in some goddam brick house somewhere and I'm supposed to be tinkering in the basement or painting the fucking *shutters*. No way."

She was slowly getting out of bed now, not hiding the gentle swing of her breasts or the soft curve of stomach. And she began gathering up clothes: from the floor, from the lampshades, from atop the TV set. Then she turned back.

"But a good woman. I mean, a *good* woman —— "

"No. Lissen: you're a good woman. Right now, you are the best woman I know. And I mean that. And you deserve more than me. I don't know, maybe some guy who is everything you want him to be and —— "

"Will I ever see you again?"

I nodded. "Very next time I run over my leg in Terre Haute."

And after she had gone, I pulled the pillows out from under my leg. And I rolled over and went to sleep.

"There, now."

Lugs finished snipping off the cast with his big, greasy tin shears and we both looked at the fresh pink scar where the bone had poked out of my ankle. "How's 'at feel?"

"Wobbly, for one thing." I shook it. "Where's the tape?"

Beside us, the new car had all the numbers on it now: a big Number 1 on the doors and top and back, and the little racing chicken painting with his crash helmet and goggles, and the Fire Injection stickers and every other sponsor sticker — all of it laid over with several coats of wax. That rascal just stood there and shook all over.

Out on the track, Demon was turning some laps and every time he came by, the roar would vibrate my breastbone and the clock inside my head. And Lugs kept cocking his head one way and the other and finally he half-stood up with the tin snippers still in his hand and said:

"That sumbitch."

"What?"

"Can't you *hear* that? Lissen: he's got to be turning 190's. I can tell that without a goddam clock. I *seen* that car at tech inspection and there ain't no way — no way — that he can be doing that good."

"Well, he's sure as hell doing it."

We listened to him come by again, mentally clicking him down. The sound was rolling back at us across the infield in regular waves: *zap*, off the throttle and then *ba-room*, down the backstraight. He was really hauling it around.

"Wait a minute," Lugs said. "You hear that? You *hear* that sumbitch?"

I listened some more: "He's wound up about as tight as he'll go."

"No. NO. Goddam, Stroker, you don't know a goddam *thing* about engines, you dumb bastard. Lissen: he has DONE SOMETHING WITH THE CARBURETOR RESTRICTOR. Why that cheating sumbitch! Lissen: that's plain *crooked.*"

I looked over at our car, maybe the all-time, classic cheater of all history. Complete with the magic Lugs Harvey catch-me-come-fuck-me suspension system. Right now, it was set normal, to pass tech inspection. Just before qualifying — with maybe a whole grandstand of a hundred thousand people watching — Lugs would reach down under it and do *something:* innocently. And the goddam Dodge would crouch right down in racing silhouette.

"Uh-huh. Anything I can't stand is a cheater, Lugs."

But he was storming out of the impound area now, over to the pit wall to watch Demon come by again. And when I had finished with the taping, I pulled on my other shoe and limped over there.

By that time Lugs was grinning, his hands jammed into the back pockets of his Levi's and his stomach hanging way out.

"Now what?"

"Ahhh, dear God, it does my pure old heart good to hear that," he said. "Yessir, them cheaters allus get it in the end. In Terre Haute — the home of honest folks like Lugs Harvey — we call that grim justice."

I looked at him some more. Chrissakes, he was absolutely beaming at me.

"Well, what the hell is so good about Demon turning laps faster than anybody else?"

He nodded and put on his Old Sage look. "Well, my boy, if you knew anything at *all* about motors, you would know that we got a carburetor restrictor plate ruling. Right? Right. And you would also know that they *seal* that bugger up and you can't remove that seal, right?"

"My turn: right."

He nodded. "Well, then. What Demon has done is to make *his* restrictor plate out of some sort of trick metal. I'm not sure, but I figure I know what it is because I've already tried that stuff and figured out it won't work."

"Well, then, why'd he do it?"

"I'm glad you asked that there question: because he's *stoo*pid. Now, here's how it works: the metal on his restrictor plate gradually dissolves or erodes under gasoline, right?"

"Ah-hah!"

"Exactly ah-hah! So that, alla sudden his goddam plate just ain't there any more and then, suddenly, he's *un*restricted. And that there big old Chrysler hemi-head of his is just ready to *eat* everybody *up*."

And, sure enough, Demon came by again in a long, low blur — really eating everybody up, indeed. And: flash! He was gone into the Number One Turn, with the zaps rolling back towards us.

"Who makes that trick metal?"

"Dupont, I think."

"Uh-huh. Better Living Through Chicanery."

Lugs didn't blink. I had just wasted another line on him.

He was listening to the backstretch, his head cocked again. And finally he nodded his Sage Nod.

"Well, he's gone and done it to *hisself* now," he said. "See, he's gotten so carried away with this toy of his that he don't know that this melting metal is coating his pistons and fucking up his valve train. Heh, heh."

"So?"

"Well, if I was *us*, I would get to hell away from this here pit wall, because about the next time he comes by here, he's gonna blow the engine. He's gonna *lunch* that sumbitch right about here."

We stepped back.

And Demon did:

He came off the Number Four Turn and got it all gathered up and then: Ka-blam! There was the sudden belch of blackish smoke and the car bucked and tossed a bit while he fought it down. And then he let it roll into the grass.

Lugs shook his head. Nobly. "That dirty cheater," he said.

Clyde Torkle was talking. As usual.

"No expense," he was saying, "no expense has been spared to give the champeen here the best car that Rain Tree Farms can scare up. Move over there, fellas, and let that little bitty guy get a picture, too. He's from *Sports Illustrated.*"

Torkle was standing beside the car, all elbows and cowboy boots and big white hat and, every now and then, Lugs would lean over and whisper to him not to touch the car. Torkle kept acting like he was going to slap it heartily on the flank or something like that.

"Hssssst!" Lugs would say.

"I know, I know," Torkle would say. And then: "Got all yer pictures, boys? Fine. Just fine. Don't forget to mention Rain Tree Farms chicken. Fastest chicken in the —— "

"Don't touch the car," Lugs whispered.

". . . yessir. Uh, well, now. Stroker Ace here is gonna take her out for a shakedown. By damn, you ever see so many folks gathered around for a shakedown run?"

Lugs finally had to drag him physically out of the way. And, still holding onto Torkle's arm, he looked over and nodded at me.

I reached down and fired it up. And about sixty-five sets of testicles shriveled right up where anybody was standing nearby. You could hear it maybe ten miles offshore.

I glanced over at Torkle, whose eyes were watering at the sound. And I dumped it into gear and spun it away from the pits. And then I punched the button hard as I could and started racing again, feeling the sweet music inside.

Too loose: it was plowing; that is, the front end was digging in too much, taking too big a bite. All right, we'd have to jack more weight on the rear end somehow. And about the time I got into the middle of the Three-Four Turn I discovered that the crew had put too weak a throttle spring on the accelerator pedal, probably hoping to save my ankle, and that sumbitch wouldn't feather properly.

Feathering a throttle is roughly like a bear making love to a football. The idea is to get on and off the gas as tenderly as possible — giving the car just enough power to hang it in the banked turn without spinning it out. It also is a dandy way to scare yourself to death.

So I came squirreling into the pits and braked it down and unsnapped my helmet in about the same motion and sat there while the Chicken King and six reporters came running up. Torkle ducked down and stuck his red face in the window at me.

"How is she, Ace?"

"*Perfect*," I said.

One of the reporters leaned over his shoulder: "Think you can put her on the pole, Stroker?"

"Well, I'm sure gonna try."

And they all walked back behind the pit wall and Lugs came up, wiping his hands with a rag. "Well?" he said.

I smiled at him wide and nodded pleasantly.

"This sumbitch is a fucking SLED," I said, holding the grin and talking low. "I thought you had it *set up*. First, the ass-end is too high and second, it's digging in, and third, the lousy throttle needs a stronger spring and four and five, it needs a lot of jacking around and, otherwise it's a general, all-around pile of shit."

He kept smiling and wiping his hands, nodding; glancing every now and then over to the pit wall where Torkle was talking to all the newspaper reporters.

"Uh-huh," Lugs said, and he smiled back at me, just with his teeth, so they could see. "The only thing that's wrong with this car is that yer a goddam *cripple*. All I need is a goddam one-legged driver, for chrissakes."

And Torkle came up again, with a gang of new reporters and some television people with their damn creepy-peepy camera.

"You gonna take her out again, Ace?"

I nodded at him, smiling while the camera lens closed in on my right eyeball. "In just a minute here. The car is *perfect*, but you know how chief mechanics are. Lugs here wants to make a couple of tiny adjustments."

Torkle nodded: "He's a perfectionist. It sure looked fine to me."

And I wrenched myself out the window so that the crew could roll it back. And we went over and sat on the pit wall, me and Torkle and the creepy-peepy and the man with the microphone.

"I'll bet this is a far cry from your first car," the man said.

"Hmmm?"

"You know: the Birdcage Maserati that you got when you were fifteen years old. How does it compare with this enormous, hulking, full-bore stock car?"

"All the difference in the world," I said. "Actually, the Maserati drove a lot like a hearse."

They laughed all around.

I cranked it off the Number Four Turn and looked down the straightaway and then glanced over at the tach, which was sitting steady on 7,200 RPMs. And then I brought the wheel around again and then really zapped the hell out of it, running up close to the wall and feeling it hunker right down, belly to the track. Out of the corner of my eye I could see Lugs punch the buttons on both of his watches.

When I rolled in, the crowd started to gather around again,

but Lugs waved them all away. "Sorry, fellas," he said, "but we got to con*fer* a minute here. Excuse us." And he and Torkle strolled up. They had four stopwatches between them.

Lugs didn't say anything: he just turned the pit board around so that I could see where the sweep hand had stopped on each watch. And then Torkle showed me his watches.

There was a long moment there while we all just breathed in and out a lot.

"Well?" Lugs said.

I unhooked my helmet and tugged it off. "Well, I would say that we're ready to go qualify this little sumbitch."

And Torkle kept blinking. "Jee-*zuz*," he said.

"I heard about you got the track record," Charlie said. He put down the two tires. "Not bad for a gimpy bugger like you."

I had unwrapped something like seventeen thousand yards of tape from my ankle and I was trying to figure out how to wriggle my toes. "What you got there?"

He looked over his shoulders, both of them, swinging his head. And then he leaned forward. "Yer racing tars. I pulled these out special. Nobody else got 'em."

"Hmmm?"

"No, really. See, we get this stock from the Goodyear *Condom* Division. Actually it's brand-new rubbers that they have left over every now and then. And then we grind 'em up."

He paused so that I could wait for his punch line:

"Best fucking compound around."

Torkle stood outside the shower, still talking, filling the bathroom with velvety cigar smoke, and he handed me the towel when I came out. "Got something for ya," he said.

The boxes were piled on the bed, all open, and there was tissue paper scattered all around the room.

"Now this — " he held it up " — this here is just a little pres-

ent from me for you settin' that track record today. I know how
you like cash-*meer*."

Present: a light-yellow cashmere pullover golf shirt. Three
buttons down the placket, or whatever that is. And a little,
teeny monogram on the right chest: a little, teeny chicken with
a crash helmet and goggles.

"And this here" — he held it up — "this here is a genuine
double-knit blazoo. See here? Lissen: this sumbitch comes right
from *Mister Guy's* in Los Angeles, buddy-boy."

"Mister . . . Guy's?"

He nodded. "All them movie stars get their clothes there.
Two hunnert and seventy-five dollars for the goddam coat, old
pal. Here are the pants. See: look here: no belt buckle; they
got these little jiggers on the side that snap. The pants go for
eighty per."

"Uh-huh. Where's the monogram?"

He smiled: "Right *here*, see? Just a little thing right here on
the pocket. Can't hardly see it."

So I took the pants and started putting them on. What the
hell.

". . . they got all yer sizes on file there," Torkle was saying,
fishing around on the bed for another box. "And any time you
need any clothes, you just call and tell 'em to whip up whatever
you want, old buddy, and just charge it to my account."

"Long as it has the monogram on it."

"Well, lookit *here*." He turned around and unzipped his fly
and pulled the front of his pants apart. "See *here*? I got the
little monogram right here on the fly of every goddam pair of
undershorts I own. See that? I mean: that's class, old pal. Hellfire, I give these shorts away as *soov*ineers to fancy ladies all
around the circuit. Now, here is the other thing I got for
you —— "

The other thing was a gold Movado watch and it weighed
about five pounds. No monograms. That's because it had little

tiny checkered flags on each side of the crystal and, inside each checkered flag, the white squares were made up of diamonds and the black squares were onyx. And there was a circle of diamonds going all around the outside of the dial and one big ruby right in the center where the hands joined. It was pretty as all hell.

"Well, goddam. That's very nice of you, Clyde."

He shrugged and held both hands out. "Lissen, buddy. Yer about the closest thing I'll ever have to a real *son*. And, besides, yer the best goddam racing driver I ever seen, bar none. Ain't nothing too good fer you. And, shee-it, we win any more races and I'm gonna run right out of *chickens*, for God's sake. Since you been with the team, the damn sales been right out of sight; hell, I got a couple hunnert people hanging around trying to get franchises and I keep running up the price on them and they still keep coming on. Here, have one of these here cigars."

"Thanks."

"Well?"

"Well what?"

He shrugged: "Look at the cigar band, dummy."

The Monogram.

We pulled up in front of the governor's mansion and turned the Caddie over to the parking attendant. Torkle gave him a cigar and then waited while I autographed a little notebook for him.

At the top of the marble stairs a small, nervous guy met us, nodding an awful lot and smiling. "So glad y'all could come to the reception," he said. "The receiving line is just over there, gentlemen. And then I suspect y'all will want to join us for a drink."

They do this every year: the Governor's Reception just before the Atlanta 500 is for all the fancy folks of Atlanta and the women all come in long dresses that show the tops of their bosoms a lot. And a string quartet wanders around the place, playing things. And there is a long table piled up with food that you have to eat with your fingers: mostly super-small crackers with a little splash of egg salad piled on and, on top of that, a little tiny goddam salty fish all curled up. And everyone gets to rub shoulders with real live race drivers.

A lot of the drivers show up in their best stuff: T-shirts with STP and GOODYEAR and SMOKEY'S: THE BEST DAMN GARAGE IN TOWN printed on the fronts.

So I followed along with Torkle, feeling like one arm was going to end up a lot longer than the other because of the new watch dragging it down.

This is the way it works: the little guy sort of sidles along with you, kind of lightly holding you by one elbow with a pretty feathery touch, setting your speed in the line. And then he introduces you to the governor and his wife and then he goes back to pick up and guide the next race driver while you stand there and make small talk with the governor of the sovereign state of Georgia.

LITTLE MAN: May I present *Stroker Ace*, the current point leader and the *defending champion* of the Atlanta 500 and our *honored guest* here this evening.

(What the little bugger is doing is *cueing* the governor, who is glassy-eyed.)

LITTLE MAN: You remember, sir, the fantastic finish of last year's Atlanta 500 when *Stroker Ace* won the *title*. And with Mister Ace is Clyde Torkle, who you know *well*, of course. Mister Torkle is president of Rain Tree Farms and sponsors Mister *Ace's* car, and, of course, was a *key* contributor to your campaign last year.

(Then the little man does a half-turn, stalling a bit while His Honor gets his bearings.)

LITTLE MAN: Mister Ace, Mister Torkle: May I present the governor and the first lady of Georgia.

GOVERNOR: Well, now, I'm certainly honored to meet *you*, sir. Welcome to Atlanta. (He shakes hands and half-turns to his wife.) My dear, this is *Stroker Ace* who, uhh, *won* the race last year.

FIRST LADY: How nice to meet you, Mister Race. My, what an appropriate name. Welcome to Atlanta, Mister Race. Tell me, have you been racing long?

STROKER RACE: Oh, about one hundred twenty-five years.

FIRST LADY: How nice for you. You must meet a lot of interesting people.

GOVERNOR: And this is Mister Clive Terkle, who sponsors Mister Ace.

CLIVE TERKLE: Pleased to meet you, ma'am. Nice place you got here.

FIRST LADY: Welcome to Atlanta, Mister Snerkle. Tell me, do you race, too?

CLIVE SNERKLE: Ever' chance I get.

FIRST LADY: How nice for you. You must meet a lot of interesting people.

STROKER ACE: Well, I think we'll join the others. It was certainly nice of you to have us over.

CLIVE SNERKLE: Well, we gotta go, ma'am. Here, have a cee-gar.

FIRST LADY: Why, thank you. How thoughtful. Good luck in the 500, Mister Merkle. And drive carefully, now.

MISTER MERKLE: Ah sure will, ma'am. And you, too.

(Enter Little Man, who carefully steered us away, over to where the big crowd is gathered in the ballroom.)

And the waitress came right over, diligently, carrying the

silver tray with the long-stemmed delicate glasses all balanced on it. "Champagne, gentlemen?"

Torkle took her gently by the elbow and pulled her up closer. "Whut's that you said?"

"Would you gentlemen care for some champagne?"

He squinched over until their faces were right up close together. And with one hand he dipped quickly into his pants pocket and came right up with a twenty-dollar bill in it. He stuffed the bill right down into the front of her uniform, all in one smooth, easy motion.

"Champagne, my ass," Torkle said. "Now, here's what I want you to do. What I want you to do is to just double right back into the pantry there, little lady, and pour two big water glasses with some *Seagram's Seven Crown,* you hear me? And then you add just a little bitty splash of Seven-Up and you just trot them right back here, unnerstand? We won't move from the spot till you get back. Here, I'll hold your goddam champagne."

The maid nodded. "Yessir," she said.

Then Torkle looked all around, peering out from under the rim of the cowboy hat. And finally he spotted Demon Daniels.

"Hey, Deem," he said.

"Hey, Mister Torkle. Hey, Stroke. How you?"

Torkle handed him the tray of glasses. "Here," he said. "Here's a little somethin' because you blew yer engine today. It ain't much, just a token of our affection, that's all."

"You heard about that?"

I nodded at him. "Lugs tells me that yer trick metal melted on you."

He shrugged, jiggling the glasses. "Well, I figgered for *sure* it would work. If I can work out a way to make that stuff work through a race, I'll blow all you bastards off."

"Meanwhile?"

"Well, *mean*while, they're putting in a new engine tonight. Lissen: you want to give me the five hunnert right now?"

"Your ass."

When the girl came back with the big kitchen glasses full of Seven and Seven, Torkle held his up.

"Here's to you, Demon. Tell me, Mister Daniels, how long have you been racing?"

Deem thought about it, adding it up in his head. "Well, when you count the years when I used to run hot cars up to Canada, why I'd say about —— "

Torkle nodded: "How nice for you. You must meet a lot of interesting people."

"What does it say on that banner?"

She looked down to where it arced high over one breast and then down across her tummy and attached on one side. "It says Miss Power Boost," she said. "You like it?"

"Well, the part where it says 'Power' goes way up and it's hard to read the rest of it."

"You like that part?"

"Umm hmmm. I like all the parts."

We were standing very close together over by the big bowl of shrimps on toothpicks. And she had that way of Georgia girls: when she talked, she ran the tips of her fingers up and down your arm, lightly; occasionally, when she laughed, she would hold onto you helplessly, as though she might fall down any minute in a little old swoon.

I was nicely full of Seven and Seven now, just stroking along, and I'm not sure just how long she had been there, holding on my arm.

"I swear," she said, "y'all get handsomer every time I see y'all. And y'all got a new little scar right there over your eyebrow. I swear."

"Mmmm. Indy Five Hundred, I think. Lissen: when did you ever see *me* before?"

She laughed and held onto my arm some more, right at the

bicep. "Why Stroker *Ace,* I declare, honey. You don't remember me, do you? Why, I was Miss Fire Valve at Indy, honey, and at Milwaukee I was Miss Charge Pack. And at Phoenix I was Miss —— "

"Jiffy Belts."

"No," she said. "Honey, Miss Jiffy Belts wasn't nothin' but an ugly little ole *brunette.* You remember? No, at Phoenix I was Miss Rocket Drive. Remember?"

"Of course. You want some champagne?"

"And you never even paid any attention to little ole me, honey. Y'all been *cruel;* why, I met you at all the parties and you always had some other girl with you." And she ran the tip of her index finger right up the middle of my stomach toward my chest.

"Another girl? Nawww, couldn't have been me. You know damn well that I'm a one-woman man."

"What woman is that, honey?"

I pulled back and looked at her banner again. "Miss Power Boost," I said. "Come on, let's get the hell out of here."

She shook her head. "Oh, Stroker, honey, I can't. Ah've got to *circulate* here in the crowd and be seen. You know: the Power Boost people and all." She looked over her shoulder and leaned in so close that the tips of her breasts were right up against my rib cage. "Lissen, honey, there's a man here from the *West Coast.* And he knows a lot of big folks in the *movies.* And he says —— "

"You're gonna be a star."

She blinked up at me. "I swear, that's what he said."

"Well, lissen: think about me. You're just about so pretty that you can always get into the *movies.* Any time. But, look: I got to go out there first thing in the morning and try to qualify for the *pole,* honey. And, lissen: I'm all tense inside and full of a feeling of my, uhh, my own *mortality.* It's dangerous out there and there are times when a man can close his eyes and just see that flaming fireball of death right *there,* honey. And he knows that he's just living from one day to the next day and that — any time — his own number might come up. Uh huh, that's *right.* And it's a lonely feeling, knowing that he has to go out there and *race* the next day. And a man goes back to his *lonely* motel room and he just lays there and stares at the ceiling — all alone — and he knows that *DEATH* is waiting just outside that door."

She was blinking up at me. She was just about ready.

"And that's when a race driver needs the comfort of a *good* woman. He needs the warmth and love that she can give him. The soft, tender moments before he must go out and race. *All alone.* And even if he dies, he'll die with the tender memory of those few sweet moments of stolen happiness. Why, a man —— "

"Y'all just wait right here," she said. "I'll go and get my coat."

It works every time.

The only thing that kept me awake was my goddam ankle: I came off the One-Two Turn cocked a little bit wrong and hurting to beat hell — and there wasn't anything to do but ram it down and hope to hell that Charlie had been right about his fucking tire compound.

And the backstraight just suddenly lined right up in a long blur and the car sort of shrugged its shoulders. Fine.

So I hammered it on into Three-Four and then, coming off, let it drift right up against the outside wall, glancing down at the tach again.

If that sumbitch was anyway near halfway half-right, things were in pretty decent shape.

Off to one side, Lugs had snapped the watches and was looking down at them. One more damn lap, old ankle. Just hang in there and we'll untape you in a few seconds here.

The car actually dove into the turns this time, like it should, and I feathered the throttle and then got back on that rascal right away and there was the backstraight again, sucking under me like a black ribbon.

Ahhhh, dear Lord, this is the fucking *life:* I stayed flat on it through the Three-Four, figuring that I might as well hang the record up there for a while, and I let the car come sliding out so that the folks in the pits could get a nice three-quarter view of that big bugger coming right at them. Then it snapped around and flashed past the flagman.

And my hangover vanished — just rolling away cleanly with the sound of the engine roaring back through the infield. By the time I got back to the pits I was feeling human.

Lugs was there, nodding. And Torkle, waving his hat. And Miss Power Boost, in her banner and little tiny spangled outfit and really big jugs and those fine legs.

". . . and *another* new track record, ladies and gennamum! Another track record by this great . . ."

The crowd closed in pretty fast: all I could see was teeth and cameras and microphones and Torkle's hat.

"How does it feel to win the pole, Ace?" The microphone got right inside the car with me.

"Tell us in your own words, Stroker Ace, how ——"

"Stroker, honey-babe," she said, "you-all are really neat."

"Go ahead and kiss him, Lucy. There! Right. One more time. Uh-huh."

"Take his helmet off. There. That's better. Move over so's I can get you both in this here picture. Come on, that's jus' right."

"Lugs, you get in there, too. That's it. Now shake hands with Stroker there. Fine. Now, hold it like that for a minute. There."

"Lucy, you lean in there and kiss him again —— "

"Don't touch the goddam *car,*" Lugs said, looking all around. "There. Like that. Now hold it."

"Honey," she said. "You're my honey-lamb, baby doll. All

those sweet things you told me in the room last night. Honey, ah'm always gonna be right here beside you all the time to see you through, like ah promised. Ah'll never leave you, ever, because ——— "

"Stroker, tell the world waiting out there in radioland just how it feels to ——— "

"Stroker, honey-sugar," she said.

I looked right into her eyes for just a flash. They were all shined up with tears.

"Lissen," I said to her. "Will you get the hell AWAY from me, goddammit? Now, go away."

"But ——— but you said ——— "

"That was last night," I said.

sixteen

About halfway across the Gulf Stream the pilot came out of the little narrow door up front and stood beside our seats. "I'm a great fan of yours," he said, "and it sure is nice to meet you. I saw on television that you got a new track record and the pole position for the Atlanta 500."

Torkle reached up and tugged at the guy's sleeve, right where the three circles of gold braid go around.

"Lissen," he said. "What I want to know is, is who is flying this here plane?" Torkle hates to fly; he starts bracing himself about three or four hours before every flight with a few Seven and Sevens — the Drink That Makes Better Fliers of Us All.

The pilot smiled at him: "The plane can find the way to Nassau by itself," he said. "And you must be Mister Torkle, the Chicken King. I recognize you from all your pictures."

"Here, have a cee-gar," Torkle said, "and go on back and fly the *airplane,* for chrissakes."

"One thing," the pilot said. "Would you mind signing this menu for my son, Mister Ace? He's a really big racing fan and he follows all your races."

I took the menu and got out my monogrammed Chicken King ballpoint.

"You sure this thing can fly itself?" Torkle said.

"What's his name?" I said.

"Randy. He's eleven years old."

So I signed my usual autograph: *Stand on It, Kid. Love, Stroker Ace.*

And I handed it back over.

"Thanks so much," the pilot said. "Uhh, may I order you gentlemen another drink, perhaps?"

Torkle held up his glass. "Wall, maybe just a little dollop," he said. "Just fill her right up with Seven Crown and I'll add the Seven-Up after we get to Nassau, all right?"

"Fine. And enjoy yourselves. The girls will be serving lunch soon."

"What's for lunch?" I said.

He consulted the menu. "Fried chicken," he said.

"Oh, for CHRIST'S SAKE," Torkle said.

Torkle was sound asleep when we landed. That was after:

— he had personally given a cigar to everybody on the plane and

— then had danced with two of the stewardesses and had shown everybody in the first-class cabin the monogrammed fly front of his underwear and

— then had autographed his eighty-five-dollar white suede cowboy hat and presented it to a schoolteacher from Grand Island, Nebraska, who had been just a little bit touched off because he had pinched her on the ass when she had gotten up to go to the rest room (he had barked at her a little bit about wearing a girdle — "You look like you just got one, big, round buttock," he had said). And also after:

— the pilot had come back out again and had to calm everybody down, and

— Torkle had shown the pilot the monogrammed fly front on his underwear, and

— the pilot had had to make Torkle zip up his pants again

and strap himself back into his seat and promise not to get up again, and

— Torkle had offered to buy the whole goddam airline and shut it down, and, finally, after

— he had given the schoolteacher his cowboy hat and had leaned across the aisle to her seat and had made a date with her for that night in Nassau. And I'll be goddamned if she didn't accept, blushing to beat hell because Torkle was promising her a night of uncontrolled carnal passions she would never forget.

"I get you out of that goddam girdle, little lady, and yer gonna shake it all around," he had said.

And now he was slumped down, blowing little frothy bubbles, smelling roughly like the bottom of a sour-mash barrel.

The race promoter had promised us four or five nights of love and laughter in Nassau, and just about every major driver on the circuit had accepted, figuring, what the hell, it was a fine way to get a little free sunshine and sex before the 500.

Here is the way it works: this thing is called Nassau Speed Week and it is essentially a bash for sporty-car types, those guys who wear silk scarves knotted carelessly at their necks and drive restored MG-TD's. They all get together at Nassau and they stage a few bad-ass, no-account races for trophies and they have a different cocktail party every night where everybody talks some foreign language and keeps brushing his hair out of his eyes with the back of one hand.

You with me?

And the racetrack out there is pretty scruffy, with the infield sort of made up of crushed coral rock and lizard holes, and the pit area isn't much better. But an awful fancy crowd gathers there and the ladies all wear these big-mother round sunglasses up on top of their heads and this is perhaps the only racetrack in the world where the loose papers blowing across the track are always cocktail napkins.

Hell. *Cruise* ships come in for this week and they unload grape-colored Aston-Martins and maybe an Austin-Healy or two and hundreds of Formula Vees.

A Formula Vee is a Volkswagen engine pretending to be a racecar: it is a class for rich folks who dabble in racing. They drive them like they are at the Nurburgring or the Spa and are liable to get into big trouble any second. And any real race driver will tell you that there just ain't no way you can get into trouble in a Vee, including driving the son of a bitch off a dock down at the waterfront.

And as if all that isn't bad enough, sports car drivers — who all work for advertising agencies with three or four names — always stand around talking about *shunts.*

Translation: a shunt is a little old dent trying to pass itself off as a crash.

What Nassau Speed Week is, is a social.

Still, the promoter had called over to Atlanta and had offered me all free expenses and $7,500 appearance money if I would show up. And we had talked it over.

"You need the rest anyway. Your ankle and all," Torkle had said. "And besides, we'll get us some of that native *poon* and change our luck."

And then he had called up someone from the Atlanta chapter of the Sports Car Club of America and had bought a bad-ass, junked-up Formula Vee for $5,400 and had someone wrap it up in a gunny sack and throw it on a cargo plane to Nassau. "I know it was too much money to pay," he said, "but we'll write it all off as a tax loss, and then, after the race, we'll take that rascal out into the ocean and sink it."

This is the way I came down into the lobby:

I was wearing my madras dinner jacket with the satin lapels, and the body of the thing is all sort of blue and black patches that look like they have bled together. And I had on this really jazzy goddam ruffled shirt that is baby light blue and a black velvet bow tie. Black pants with the satin stripe down each leg and my pre-shine loafers that cost about thirty dollars *per shoe*. Cummerbund. And my solid hammered-silver racing chicken cuff links.

Stick Shift Cologne.

Indy championship ring.

Executive-length, lightweight socks.

My own monogrammed hanky. It said *Ace* in script.

I was absolutely ravishing.

In fact, Lee Roy Harber, who was wearing clean Levi's and new cowboy boots, walked all the way around me, nodding his head.

"Yer just about the sweetest thing I ever saw," he said.

"Ain't that the truth, though?"

"You goin' to the big party in town, I suppose?"

"Well, only long enough to cut out one of those ladies with the sunglasses on top of her head and then bring her back here. And then I'm going to get right back on this elevator and go back up to my room and take all this stuff right off again and show her what a real race driver looks like. Well, except maybe the shoes. I may keep these on."

He nodded, approving the plan. "I'm goin', too," he said. "But before I get to the part about taking the lady back to the hotel, I thought I would find me a big, sturdy sporty-car driver and kick the shit out of him."

"Yeah, well, look: don't knock anybody down anywhere near me, okay? I don't want to get all messed up."

"I'll sure try," he said.

"Anyway: come on, I'll buy you a little shooter to get you started."

The bar was packed with everybody all dressed up, all of them headed for the big cocktail party in town sooner or later. There was a lot of expensive silk and the air was nice and heavy with the smell of very good perfume and all the ladies had really tiny waists and fine backsides and each one of them was wearing at least sixteen bracelets on each arm and big rings loaded down with soft-shining pearls and their finger-nails were all long and tapered, all Ferrari blood-red in that lighting. There were men in evening tuxedos and black ties — and if they didn't have on a black tie, they were wearing this shirt open at the neck and a fat, flowing scarf coming out from under the shirt. And at the bottom of each scarf it said:

Yves St. Laurent.

The men would all turn to the ladies and say, "May I get you something, my dear?"

We got up to the bar pretty quickly: Lee Roy simply took one of the men by the scarf and tugged him right away, and then Lee Roy spread out his elbows and leaned in.

"I *beg* your pardon," the man said.

"Ah'll just bet you do," Lee Roy said. And then he turned to the bartender.

"See *here*, fellow," the man said.

And Lee Roy turned and looked back at the man, squinting in the smoke. Then he slowly smiled his *wolfish* smile, the one that shows all his eyeteeth really well. And then he narrowed his eyes a little bit more. "What's that?" he said.

"Nothing at all," the man said. "Please. You just go right ahead there. I'm certainly in no hurry."

Lee Roy did the ordering: "What we want," he said to the bartender, "is two of them drinks served in a half a goddam carved-out coconut shell, with pineapple and oranges and cherries and maybe some mangoes and mint in there and the long straw and about four or five gallons of rum, right?"

We each had three of them.

"Where's the Chicken King?" Lee Roy said.

We were standing just outside in the hot Bahama night with

thick, fuzzy stars just about *this* far over our heads. Lee Roy had a half-coconut shell on top of his head like a beanie and a sprig of real mint behind each ear.

The Chicken King had the room next to mine upstairs and just before I had headed for the lobby I had stuck my head in there to pick him up.

Torkle had been buck-naked, except for one cowboy boot. He was pouring rum and Coca-Cola into the other boot and he had it pretty near filled to the top. And a great big, white whalebone girdle had been strung up to the overhead light by its laces — and, behind Torkle, the schoolteacher from Grand Island was dancing around the room singing "A Pretty Girl Is Like a Melody." The only thing she was wearing was the cowboy hat.

Well, except for the racing-chicken window-sticker decal that had been pasted just a little off-center over her belly button.

"Go ahead and start without me," Torkle had said, "I'll be along directly."

So I explained it to Lee Roy: "Now, how in hell would I know where the Chicken King is?"

"Well, I'll tell you what I'm gonna do," Lee Roy said. "What I'm gonna do is, I'm gonna go and get me another one of these here Coconut Surprises back in at the bar, see? I'll look for you in town."

So I stood there and let the stars press down on me a little more. Breathing in and out. The Bahamas smell like every funeral I have ever served at.

Ace and Sons, my ass.

I had rented a Vauxhall at the Nassau airport, which is about all you can rent at the Nassau airport, and it was a

Viva — which is badder than any car really ought ever to be. Absolutely no horsepower and tiny, with a snubbed-in nose. Two little doors and the whole thing was sort of square-rigged and came up to about *here* on me. It had really skinny little old tires and a toy stick shift. The body is made by the very same people who make boxes for Quaker Oats.

So I swung the door open and . . .

And there was Lugs Harvey, that's what.

"Ah-hah!" he said. "I know who you are! One falsh move, buddy, and I'll drill you. Where did you hide the fucking *payroll*, Humphrey?"

Oh, for chrissakes. "Come on. Move over."

He waggled a finger at me. "Oh, no. Oh, no you don't. No, *shir*. Lishen: thish here is the car that's gonna win the goddam Talla . . . the, uhh, the Talla-*dega* two-fifty and it's prolly too hot fer you to handle, even right now. And if I let you drive it, you'll only schrew it up, you humpie."

"All right, come on: what the hell are you doing in *Nassau*, for God's sake?"

He looked all around the car. "Who?"

"You."

"Where?"

"Nassau."

"That'sh right," he said. "Nassau. Uh-huh."

"Well?"

He reached down into the front seat beside him and lifted up a pineapple. "You shee this?"

"Mmmm."

"Well, then. You screw around with *me*, buddy, and I'll blow up this whole fuckin' *island*. And thash right."

Then he carefully lifted off the top of the pineapple where it had been neatly cut off, and drank out of the bottom half. And then he cleared his throat.

"I'm drinking rum and STP," he said.

"Well, come *on*, dammit. *Out*. I'm going to a party in town. Let's go."

"Me, too. I got the invitation in my crew kit when I checked in at the airport. And —— "

"*Crew* kit? Who the hell are you crewing for?"

He nodded. Several times. "Sch . . . Str . . . ummm, Schtroker Aish. That humpie."

"My ass. You're supposed to be back in Atlanta working on the car."

"You want a *ship* from this here pineapple? Here, I've drank sixteen of these rascals awreddy. Don't drink it all, now."

"Hell, yes. Hand it over."

It had a pretty heavy rum base, overlaid with papaya juice, and there were little hunks of pineapple floating in it.

I handed it back to him:

"All right, then. Come on, move over. If I don't get to that party pretty quick all the ladies will be gone."

"I can't."

"Can't what?"

"I can't move over. Lookee here." And he sat up a little bit straighter and showed me where he was wedged behind the wheel by his stomach. "Shee? So I'll drive. Don't sit on my pineapple."

I went around the other side and got in. The goddam Viva smelled like a runaway fruit salad. There were four empty pineapple shells on the floor at my feet and Lugs's tool bag was on the tiny jump seat in back. So he pumped the starter over a couple of times until the engine caught fire and we sat there and listened to it idle. Lugs swung his head around and looked at me.

"Is that all there is?" he said.

"That's it, buddy. Put that sumbitch in gear and come on, let's go. Here, give me the pineapple."

I drank some more while we bucked and lurched out of the

driveway; Lugs's feet are so big he was hitting the brake and clutch pedal at the same time. Then he got it straightened out a little and headed down the road — fat overhanging sentry palms on each side, with shafts of moonlight coming down through them. The road looked striped.

I gave him back the pineapple and he finished it off and tossed the husk out the window: "All right," I said, "you ain't told me yet what you're doing in Nassau."

He swallowed. "I'm schrewing for you."

"Crewing. *Crewing*, goddamit. I'll do my own screwing. And besides, no you're not."

But he kept right on nodding, hunched up over the steering wheel. "Look," he said. "Look: you schnuck off, that's whut you did. You and Torkle. And what do you mean, back in Atlanta working on the car? The fucking car is *perfect*. Chrissakes, yer hauling 190's in that bugger now and you got the goddam track record and the pole and what the hell else can I *do* to it? Jeez, the goddam car is so wound up right now it won't even let *me* near it; that sumbitch spits and growls at me ever' time I open the garage *door*."

"So?"

"So, thish: I jush staked that rascal down to hold it in place and I put Limpy Clawson and a twenny-four-hour guard around the garage and . . . and, uhh, here I am."

"Uh-huh. Is this all the speed you can get out of *this* car? Come *on*. Anyway: how'd you get here?"

"Charlie Heffer."

"Charlie Heffer what?"

We cranked around a corner and the whole car leaned.

"Well, Charlie hadda come over here for Goodyear, right? They're servicing thish race. Or whatever it is they call this event. And Charlie hadda bring the service truck over here and . . . and, so, I came along. And then besides that" — he took both hands off the wheel and kept the car pretty straight by steering with his stomach — "and *besides*. I heard about Torkle buying you that used Formula Vee. So I went over to the loading dock at the airport and looked at it. Chrissakes, some racecar. Hell, I'm not sure I kin even get it *started*, let alone get it in shape to run any races. Sheesh. I turn my back on you guys for just one *minute* and yer in trouble. Hell, you can't win no race in that fruitcup car, no way."

"Horseshit. If it's got wheels, I can race it."

"Uh-huh. My ass, too. Well, hell, I'll work on it tomorrow and do what I can and at leash maybe get you in the *field*. An' after that, yer on yer own. Jush don't ever let the word get out that anybody ever saw Lugs Harvey working on no Formula Vee, all right?"

Now, what in the hell can a guy do? So I squinched around in the seat and tried to get comfortable. "All right," I told him. "All right, long as you're here. Nobody asked you to come over here in the first place, you dumb bastard, but all right, you can work on the car. Now take me to the Harbor Beach Club and then go the hell away somewhere."

He was punching it as hard as he could: the road was straight two-lane going off into the darkness between these trees. Ocean on our left and the golf course on our right. The needle was sitting right over on its side, for whatever that was worth — and the little, teeny engine was having the time of its life.

Lugs was still steering mostly with his stomach and then he turned around and started pawing at the back seat. "I gotta nother one of them pineapple things back here," he said. "I stopped at a roadhouse somewhere and got six of them to go." And he twisted back around and held it up. "Shee here? The bartender had never made one of these buggers to take *out* before, so I just taped them all shut with my tape here. Unpeel that thing and hand it over."

I untaped the top and threw it out the window and we both had a couple of long swallows.

"MMMMmmmmmrrrmmph," Lugs said. Then he leaned forward and shouted down at the little hood on the car. "Anybody *in* there? Come *on,* I know yer in there."

"Gotta be somebody home," I said. "I can hear pistons."

He shook his head. "Hello, *carburetor?* Come on, *eat,* you little sumbitch, EAT!"

"Get *on* it, Harvey, for chrissakes. There's a goddam covered wagon gaining on us back there."

He hunched over some more, straining. "Thish is world famoush racedriver Schtroker Aish on the backstretch at *Dar*lington. Here he comes now, leading the field. Come on, *EAT,* you little bugger! Here comes the checkered flag and here ——"

Right-turn sign.

"Right-turn coming up," I said. "Hand me the pineapple; it looks like a ninety-degree-er."

Lugs nodded. "Here'sh the world-famous Stroker Aish in his patented *sideways* turn. Drifting to *glory.*"

"Wrong."

"Whut'd you say?"

"I said: wrong. No way you can get this cracker box into a drift. Just stay on the gas and turn the sumbitch."

"Yes, a four-wheel drift. You hear that engine gnashing its teeth?"

"Fifty dollars," I said.

"Yer on. Where'd you say that turn was?"

"Right here."

He blinked and flashed the wheel around, sucking in his stomach and staying right on the gas, hard. And then he thrashed the wheel around in the other direction, with the wheel like a toy in his big hands.

And the Viva shuddered and slammed hard into a full four-wheel drift, flat sideways and screeching into the turn. The

back window popped right out and the right side bumper
bracket snapped off and we started dragging the bumper,
spewing up a shower of sparks.

"Yaa-*hoo*," Lugs said.

The car drifted right off the road and the turn flashed by
me on my right, just like that. Too late.

And then we bucked a bit and drifted across about forty or
fifty feet of marsh grass. Lugs still had the wheel cranked hard
left.

And we drifted the front end right up the side of one of those
slanting cocnut trees. The back end snapped around and we
did a wheelie on the front wheels alone. The front bumper fell
off and clattered under the car. And then we came spinning
around again, right in the middle of the beach.

Lugs tugged the wheel back hard right again and we started
to drift in the other direction.

Sideways.

"Brake," I said. "Pop the brake just once and straighten out
the wheels."

"Yaaa-*hoooo!*" Lugs said.

We drifted sideways into the wet part of the sand and Lugs
cranked the wheel around again and popped the gas pedal.

And the Viva gathered itself up a bit and headed right for
the surf. The water was silvery in the moonlight.

"The brake," I said. "Not the gas."

"Yaaa-*HOOOO!*" Lugs said.

And he drove that little bugger about twenty-five feet out
into the ocean, headed roughly toward Omaha, with the spray
kicking up on both sides like a speedboat. And then it settled
right down, smoothly, and sat on the bottom.

The water came up to our chins. Except when the surf would
roll in, and then the water surged up over our heads and over
the roof of the car. And then the wave would suck back

strongly and the car would rock back and forth, gently as could be. The water was very warm.

A taped-up pineapple came floating up from somewhere in the back seat and bobbed right alongside Lugs's right ear. He reached over and got it in one hand.

"How . . . [splooosh!] . . . about a little . . . [sploosh] . . . drink?"

"Why not?" (Sloosh.)

He burped up a little foamy seawater. "Here. Be sure and . . . [sploosh!] . . . hold it *up*." (Sloosh.) "Hey! I can't swim, you know."

I took a quick drink in between the waves. "Too bad. I guess this is goodbye, old buddy. Here, drink fast."

"Come *on*. I mean: I really can't *swim*, Stroke."

"I heard you."

"Well . . . [glurg] . . . you gonna let me drown?"

"Hell, yes. In fact, I insist."

He finished off the pineapple and swallowed, and then put it down lightly on top of the water. The thing floated away, bobbing along, and it came floating back with the next wave, bumping against his nose. He pushed it away. "Well, you'll never . . . [mrrrrmph: glarg] . . . win Atlanta without me."

"My ass."

"No, really, And I been a good friend to you all these years, besides, buddy. And . . ."

I finally got the door pushed open, waiting until the surf was sucking back out. And I climbed out, hanging on to the roof of the car.

"And, besides," Lugs said. "YOU OWE ME FIFTY DOLLARS, YOU SON OF A BITCH. YOU SAID I COULDN'T DRIFT THE CAR."

"You're gurgling."

"Well, I'm *drowning*, for chrissakes. You gonna let yer old pal drown?"

"Uh-huh. Well, it'll cost you fifty to be rescued."

He thought about it, ducking his head under the next wave, coming up sputtering and spitting. "Nawww. Fuck you. I think I'll drown instead."

"Fifty."

"Thirty-five?" he said.

"Fifty."

"No, you go on. Just let your old *buddy* drown, you heartless sumbitch. Yer old-time pal. First, you drank all my pineapple bomb, buddy, and that ought to be worth *some*thing. Glaaaarrg. And then you just let the best goddam chief mechanic in the whole . . . glurg . . . world *drown*! Well, so long, fella. Thish is it."

When the next wave came by I bent over and looked in at him. "It's not so much the drowning that counts," I said, "as it is them big goddam mean sharks. And the alligators and CROCODILES here. And sting rays and . . ."

He beat me to the beach.

Her name was Fifi or Mimi or one of those very French sort of things and she stood exactly *this* high and I swear she couldn't have had anything on under her dress.

But she did have the sunglasses up on top of her head.

"Ahh, Strokie," she was saying, walking right through my hair with her fingers. "You are . . . how you say, you are the *sexy* man. You walk into the ballroom all soaking wet and your pants, they *cling* to you and you make the face like that naughty little boy who has been into mischief, no?"

"I took a shortcut through the ocean to get here," I said.

That had been, say, five hours ago. Now I was pretty much dried out and stroking right along and we were all entwined in the back seat of this black and gray Rolls, which was just ghosting toward the hotel.

True: I had shown up at the party all soaking wet and everybody had given me a round of applause — especially the sporty-car drivers, who thought that this entrance showed a certain touch of class. And after five or six champagnes, Mimi (or was it Fifi?) had materialized through all the smoke, all in tunnel-focus the way certain girls hit you, moving along like a half-grown cheetah in a long flowered silk gown, with her little twin-cupcake bosoms just fluttering around inside, and big pearl rings on absolutely every finger, and tiny sandals with diamonds or whatever on the T-straps.

Someone had introduced us, I think: "Oh, you are the famous Americaine Strokaire Ace who wins the Indy . . . how you say, the Indy." She shrugged. "You know."

"I know," I said.

And then the party had gone on, hammering right along, and over at the other side of the room, Lee Roy Harber had dropped some very big guy with one punch, putting a little backspin on him so that the guy had hit the wall and then came forward again off it. Lee Roy perfected this particular punch at Lenny's in Atlanta because there usually isn't all that much room to r'ar back and swing there.

I had met roughly two thousand people and they spoke all sorts of languages and they kept asking me about how it felt to be *ze champion* — and, all the time, the fluffy little Mimi kept zigging in and out of the smoke, looking at me.

The look was in French.

In English it meant: Uh-huh.

And, finally, we had talked a lot and I had looked down the front of her dress a lot and each little, tiny boob was just *this* big, with a little delicate nipple on the very tip, as though it had been put there by Claude Lelouch or one of those guys. Every time she made a move — which was a lot — the silk gown swirled around and clung for just one flash to her bucket. It was the Greatest Bucket in the Bahamas.

"My 'oosband," she had said, "is terribly jealous."

"Well, where is your husband now?"

" 'E also is terribly drunk," she had said. "You see, over there? No, there. 'E is weaving all about."

"He's very pretty," I said.

" 'E is . . . how you say . . . effeminate," she said. And then she shrugged. "And he drives the Formula Vee to assert his manhood."

"No shit."

"No, Strokaire, I am serious. Is this not true of every man?"

And I had looked at her and narrowed my eyes. This usually works pretty good. "Not always," I had said. "I drive the car because it makes me HORNY. And I finish the race and I want the . . . how *you* say . . . hot woman."

It worked: "Oh, Strokaire," she said. "You are *mean*."

I had growled a little, for effect. "I'm the meanest sumbitch you'll ever see," I said.

And now: we were in the back of this Rolls, with a silver bucket of ice on the floor and two bottles of champagne in the ice, and she had unbuttoned two buttons on my shirt and was sliding the very tips of her fingers softly in and out, on my rib cage. Her fingertips were very hot.

"What about yer old man?"

"My . . . ?" her eyebrows went up.

"Your husband. The guy with the scarf around his neck."

She shrugged. " 'E will not show up until, mmmm, say tomorrow morning. 'E does not like *women*, I think. And then he will be very repentant and 'e will not ask me what I did last night."

And we had grabbed up the ice bucket and champagne and had weaved out in front. The Rolls was parked there and the driver had been leaning against the front fender, cleaning his fingernails.

"Take us to the Royal Beach Hotel," I had said. "And try to keep the goddam car out of the water, all right?"

The driver had looked startled.

Until I gave him the wet fifty-dollar bill. After that, he would have driven us to Memphis, for chrissakes.

We wheeled in through the lobby and I had moved the ice bucket under my arm and punched the elevator button. And Mimi or Fifi had been clinging to my other good arm, looking up at me like I was Sam Stud.

Quickly past Torkle's room: the door was wide open and there was about a six-piece brass band in there and they were playing:

> *Montana, Montana, Glory of the West;*
> *Of All the States from Coast to Coast*
> *You're Easily the BEST.*
> *RAH, RAH!*

And when they got to the "*Rah, Rah*" part, Torkle was leading the cheers. There were maybe two hundred people in there cheering. Every goddam last one of them was a Bahamian native who wouldn't know Montana if somebody hit them over the head with it.

And I had closed my door.

"Oh, Strokaire," she said.

We kissed a lot while I was carrying her to the bed. And then, when I put her down beside it, she did the neatest little thing.

Neat little thing: she reached down, arms crossed, and grabbed the bottom of her dress. And then, standing up quickly, the whole thing whisked off cleanly over her head. And there she was: Mother Naked, all creamy and white.

And she looked at me. "You are *mean*," she said. "And you will *ravage* me, no? And you will take me like the BEAST and bend my poor little body to your masculine *will*. You will bruise poor little Fifi and conquer her, no? And the marks of your white teeth will sink into poor little Fifi's BODY. And —— "

"Well," I said. "Just as soon as I can get out of these *pants*, for chrissakes. Give me time."

That's when the phone rang.

God *damn*: I picked it up and the voice was talking even as I got the earpiece up close.

"Stroke? Stroke?"

"Sorry," I said. "Nobody named Stroke here. This is the linen room."

"Come on, Stroke, I know it's you."

"No clean sheets until tomorrow morning," I said. "Go away."

"Stroke! Lissen: this is Charlie."

"That's a nice name. Don't fuck it up."

"God DAMN, Stroke! Lissen for just a minute, will you? This is Charlie and it's about Lugs —— "

"Poor Lugs," I said. "He drowned four or five hours ago. We shall miss him."

"Stroke? Are you *there*? Lissen: Lugs is off over the hill in the native quarter, you *hear* me? And, lissen again: they got him!"

"Well, fine. They can cook him up and eat him for breakfast, for all I care."

"No, lissen. I mean: they *got* him. And they're gonna *kill* him. Lissen: two guys just came down here and they got their whole goddam *heads* practically cut off and they *tole* me. Chrissakes, Billy Joe Horton is all cut up and in the hospital, you unnerstand? And they got Lugs."

"Where are you?" I said.

"I'm on my way," he said.

"Fine. Me, too," I said.

And I turned to Fifi. My pants were down around my ankles.

"You're never gonna believe this," I said, "but . . ."

seventeen

Ahhh: there he was, leaning against the big Rolls, legs crossed and arms folded. He was looking up at the fat night stars over the hotel. And when I came sort of skidding up, he seemed surprised to see me.

Well, my fly was open, for one thing.

I got him by one coat lapel and brought him around a little. And I put it as briefly as I could:

"Native section," I said. "Where?"

He shook his head at me, sadly. "One doesn't go up there after dark, sir," he said. "Never."

"That's not the question. The question was: Where?"

He made a sort of a sweeping gesture. "Past the British Colonial. A bit of a right jog off Bay Street. Work up beyond the Snooty Fox and continue going over the hill. But one ——"

"Take me there."

"But, sir, I *said*, one never ——"

"Come *on*, goddammit. This is an emergency. Let's go. Here," — I fished up a pretty good pile of money " — let's go."

"No." He pushed the money away with the palms of both hands. "Never, sir. It's far too dangerous up there."

"YES."

"No."

Uh-huh. Well, well. So I glanced around him to see if the keys were in the ignition. And then I stepped back just a half-step. And then I really hit him.

You learn this by doing most of your fighting in bars: I put an awful lot of backspin on him (the way Gene Fullmer used to do without trying) and he came bouncing right back off the car door with his nose just a tiny bit crooked, and I caught him under the arms and eased him down. And then I dragged him over to the next parked car and propped him up against the front tire. He looked pretty comfortable. Certainly relaxed.

I took the Rolls out of the hotel driveway full-bore — that engine was just whispering — and got it aimed toward town. It poured right along, with the road and the sentry palms just flashing and flickering by on both sides.

Well, I'm not really all *that* used to right-hand drives on cars and, coming out of town on the other side, there were two cop jeeps right behind me, whooping through the corners.

Ahhh-haaah, Strokaire, babee, you drive the car, how you say, *terrible*, no?

Well, yes.

But the hill road did it: I finally got it figured out where everything was — let's see, the steering wheel is over on *this* side — and I started cranking and drifting it through the uphill corners, screeching through them into the soft dark.

Understand: nobody can catch me in the hills. No matter where you put the steering wheel.

And we came up over the top absolutely floating and full-sideways, me and the Rolls, and I raised up on the tips of my buttocks on the seat and looked all around.

There were a bunch of shanty houses all around in the tall, wavy grass, and the place looked pretty still in the moonlight. Hmmmmm.

But maybe that was it: there was a bigger place down the

line; still a shanty, but bigger. It had lights coming out and a sort of front porch on it and there were a few bicycles and a jeep or two parked out in front and one taxicab with the light shining on top of the roof.

You know the look right away: it could only be a whorehouse.

I came whispering down the road and cranked it in across a little wooden bridge, and then slewed it over in the grass close alongside the place. And I shut it off and listened.

Steel drums. And bongos.

Torchlight, for God's sake.

What the hell were they going to do — eat him?

That's when the window shattered right next to where I was parked. And what made it break was this great big sumbitch flying out backwards, all sort of balled up.

He landed on the hood of the Rolls and slid right across the shiny part and plopped off on the other side, doing a barrel roll across the front fender and coming up on his feet.

It was a chief petty officer and half his hash marks were hanging down like shoelaces. His shirt collar was gone and his pants were all mixed around and he was wearing only one shoe, as near as I could tell. He had his fists rolled up into big goddam craggy balls and he looked around for a few minutes until he saw me.

"Shit, oh dear," he said.

And then he wheeled and headed around the building again. It took me a second to catch him.

"What the hell's going on?"

And he got one big hand on my shoulder, shaking it. "Fight," he said, shaking his head at the building. "I mean: a real goddam *fight*, fella. Man, I'll tell ya, I been everywhere and I ain't never seen nothing like this. Shit, oh, dear, man. I been in Guadalcanal and it wasn't this bad. Man, them fucking natives won't give *up* and there's about a jillion of them. Hell, me and this other guy . . ."

Uh-huh.

"Big guy?" I said.

He nodded. "It ain't so much he's *big*, but that sumbitch is awful *broad*, I swear. And he's —— "

"Swinging a belt with a great big silver buckle?"

"Well, how'd you know that?"

I shook my head at him: "Well, I just wanted to make sure. I sure as hell ain't going in there to help out the *wrong* guy, for chrissakes. Let's go."

We pushed back in through the door. There were elbows and fists and fists with bottles in them and wild eyeballs and the whole place was snapping and snarling. Everybody was whirling and punching, roundhouses mostly, and people were flying a pretty good piece before they fell — and every now and then a bottle would zing high through the air and smash against the wall, with the booze splattering out in a sticky blotty pattern. A hell of an effect, really.

The place looked a lot like a full cattle car that had been rolling along about sixty miles an hour and then suddenly stopped. Against a wall.

First thing: a guy came wheeling up very close and tried to bite my nose right off — while standing on my bad ankle. So I feinted a little tiny bit to my right to see if he would go for it.

He did. And I brought my left knee up into him and made him a soprano right on the spot, and then pushed him away and ducked a big, floating punch from the guy behind him.

"See what I mean?" the chief said.

"Jesus Christ. Where's Lugs?" And I pulled off a native who was climbing up the chief's back. He came away in sections, like ivy, clinging to the hash marks on the chief's sleeve. And since he wouldn't turn around I had to hit him two or three short ones on the back of his head, which made him nod a lot, like he was agreeing with me.

"Slugs is in the corner, I think," the chief said. "Last time I saw him, he was braced between the bar and the piano with his back to the wall. Over here."

We did about three rounds on the way over, sidling along the other wall. Someone hit me just over the ear with a bottle — like they do in the movies — and it broke — like they do in the movies. So I squinted through the Southern Comfort and got the guy spotted. There was a reason: he was looking at the broken haft of the bottle in his hand and I could tell he was slowly getting the idea that it would make a hell of a dandy knife.

Hot damn, the guy was thinking, this thing would make me a dandy . . .

Too slow: the chief reached out one monster hand and got the chap by the throat and just cut off all his air.

Then he dropped him and then I began to get pretty goddam mad about the Southern Comfort — damn I *hate* Southern Comfort — and so I just settled down and started to hit everybody. *Everybody*: any sumbitch came anywhere within range and I hit him. Someone tore the sleeve right out of my shirt and I wheeled around and hit that bastard right in the thorax so hard that his eyes rolled around about twice before he went down. And then I kicked him in the nose. And the next man up had the broken-off leg of a chair in his hand and I waited until he raised it up and then I hit *him* under the fucking arm so hard that it dislocated his shoulder and his arm went crooked. And when he turned his head to figure out why he couldn't get his arm down, I shifted over to my left and hit him in the ear and he just plain disappeared.

"That's better," the chief said. He had one guy way up over his head with both hands and he was looking around for a place to throw him. "I was thinking for a minute there you was some kind of candy-ass. Let's go and get Slugs."

I was really pissed: "It's Lugs, *Lugs*," I said. And then I bent down and laid an uppercut on the next guy and it brought him right up on his very tippy-toes, all goggle-eyed, with foam coming out both barrels of his nose. Behind him, a little woman came wheeling around with a *real* knife and I kicked her in the stomach.

Well, hell, I was wearing my Guccis. It wasn't as if I had boots on.

And then I hit two more guys with very quick, short punches, trying to get the goddam Lenny's-of-Atlanta backspin on them — and I broke a knuckle each goddam time.

Then someone was clinging to my leg, biting me right up high under my left buttock — very mean bites — so I had to stop punching for a few minutes and *unwrap* that bugger. When he finally slid to the floor I stamped on him until he lay still, with his hands over his mouth. That's because I was stamping on all his fucking teeth.

"Over here," the chief said. "Hey, Slugs."

And I locked one guy under my arm and was in the process of pinching his head off, looking around for the voices.

And Lugs and I were nose to nose.

"Ooooga-boooga," he said. "Ain't this the goddamdest pit stop you ever seen?"

Chrissakes, he looked like he had just been attacked by a band of folks with beer-can openers: his face looked like a street guide to Akron, Ohio, and he was sweating to beat hell through tiny lines of blood and Southern Comfort.

His Levi's were half torn off and he was barefoot and naked to the waist and one hand was wrapped with the end of his belt, with the big silver buckle swinging free.

Otherwise, he was fine.

"God damn, Lugs . . ."

"Just a sec," he said. And he did a lazy little half-twirl with just the upper half of his body and the belt buckle cut this glittering, sparkling arc through the air.

There was an attacker coming in at the time and — for just the twinkling of a second — the man looked right into the silver buckle, where the little midget racecar was hammered out. And then his head snapped back and his nose seemed to be mostly all over the place.

"What were you saying?" Lugs said.

"I got news for you," the chief said. And he put the butt of his hand up against someone's face and pushed. The guy went out the window in a back-gainer.

Someone hit me on top of the head with another fucking bottle and I swear I felt my liver bounce at least twice. Jesus *Christ*.

"Ooooga-boooga," Lugs said. "Here they come."

"That's what I was trying to tell you," the chief said. "What I was trying to tell you was: they're *two platooning* us, for chrissakes. Ain't no way we kin lick the whole fucking *island*. Shit, oh dear, man."

When finally I got it sorted out who hit me over the head — well, he was still holding the bottle, for one thing — I hit him between the shoulder blades. That was because he had his back to me.

He bent over to cough up some blood and I reached around him and snatched the bottle. Now, then . . .

"Jesus, don't hit him with it," Lugs said.

"*Hit* him? I'm gonna knock his fucking head off with it."

"No you don't," Lugs reached over and got it. "I need a drink first." And he unscrewed it and looked around him quickly. And then tipped it up and gurgled down several swallows.

"Mmmmrrrrrmph," he said. "Here now."

So I took the bottle and broke it over the guy's head.

They were coming in waves now and I was having a hard time getting my back against the wall. Out of the corner of one eye I could see the silver swinging and Captain Buckle was stretching them out. And I caught one incoming guy with a short, meat-ax sort of chop and broke two knuckles on the other hand. Stereo, for chrissakes.

"Shit, oh dear," the chief said.

About all I could see now was platoons coming in.

And then we heard it.

Understand, now: there is no other sound in the world like a four-wheel drive truck when it is really hauling.

"Ooooga-boooga," Lugs said. "Lookee there."

I pushed one guy away and looked across the room.

The whole fucking wall was coming down. And, gradually, through splinters and breaking timbers and shattering glass and plaster and lathes snapping, the *whole goddam grill* and nose of a truck appeared, churning inward. And then the hood. And then the cab. I could see the lettering on the door now.

It said: GOODYEAR RACING TIRES. And in smaller letters it said: SERVICE TRUCK.

"Shit, oh dear," the chief said. "What is *that?*"

Lugs swung the belt again and snapped it back, red-flecked. "It damn well better be Charlie," he said. "Or else that fucking truck is sleepwalking."

And here it came, driving right across the dance floor, horn honking and roof lights flashing and full four-wheel drive grinding — and folks diving out of the way on all sides. Right across the floor. Towards us.

Charlie rolled down the truck window and looked out.

"God damn," he said. "I thought I'd *never* find you. Chrissakes, I've driven through every house in this whole fucking *village*. Get in here, will you?"

"Where you going?" the chief said.

Charlie looked over at Lugs. "Tell that big Navy cocksucker

that if he don't get *in here* we ain't going noplace. What the hell is this — a goddam *sight-seeing* tour?"

He zapped the engine up a little while we got in.

Someone was hanging onto the door. And, since I was the last man in, I half-turned in the seat and kicked him in the forehead until he finally let go.

And Charlie popped that rascal into gear.

We drove it out through the wall, tearing down beams and snapping the dry wood. There was a little bit of a drop-off and we hung there for a minute until the front wheels finally took hold. And they pulled us out. We wheeled around the side again, slewing just a bit in the wet grass, and headed for the road.

The chief held out both hands and turned them over this way and that, looking at the cuts. "Shit, oh dear," he said.

"Hey, Charlie," Lugs said.

"You can thank me later," Charlie said.

"I wasn't gonna thank you," Lugs said. "I just wanted to know if you got anything to drink in here?"

It was way too easy: I took it out of the esses and straightened it around a little bit — and then cocked it towards the straightaway. Just behind my head, the pretend-Volkswagen was chopping and coughing and spitting up droplets of oil. It was doing a death number at just a little under 110 miles an hour.

But I was leading the race. Every time I came around they had me on the chalkboard and I had enough time to look all around the stands for Mimi. All the spectators were under silk umbrellas and drinking things from frosted glasses and waving at each other. And, occasionally, watching the race. Where they were lined up alongside the fence I could come down the main straight and sight along twenty-seven yards of bared midriffs and take a bearing on a line of belly buttons.

Mimi's husband was the guy in the pink car and matching helmet and scarf. He had spent most of the race off somewhere in the crushed coral, slewing all around — and then he kept popping back up on the road at unexpected spots. He was really asking for it.

Next time around he finally had his machine upside down, and it was about time, for chrissakes. So I eased back and held my position under the yellow flag and fed it through the hairpins and back one more time.

I figured out roughly where the pit was and brought it in sideways just for the hell of it, looking around for Lugs and unsnapping my helmet.

And the Free World's Greatest Chief Mechanic strolled up to the car. With a big black Bahamian policeman on each side of him. Stripes, buttons, white hats and all.

"How's it running?" he said.

"Running? The sumbitch is dying, that's what it's doing. I thought you said you could make it last through a whole race."

"It'll last, all right," he said. Then he fidgeted with the butterfly bandage that was holding his left eyebrow together. "So you go on and finish without me."

"Without . . . now, how in hell can I do that?"

"Well, *try*, for chrissakes."

"Well, why?"

"Well, for one thing," he said. "I'm under arrest."

"What the hell for?"

"There is a long list of charges," one of the cops said.

"I didn't ask you."

Lugs held out both hands, palms up. "Well, what is happening is, I'm being *deported*. I mean, it's either that or they throw my ass in jail for the next eleventy-seven years or something like that. How's the oil pressure?"

"Terrible. What do you mean, deported?"

"I been banned from the Bahamas for *life*."

"In the middle of a fucking *race*?"

"Them brakes holding up okay? Lissen: they awreddy got Charlie. Picked him up at the hotel and put him on the eleven o'clock plane. Didn't even change clothes or nothing."

One of the officers leaned forward. "We are sorry. But this is the way it must be. You look very good, racing out there. We are fans of yours, you know."

"Well, then let my mechanic *go*. Chrissakes, I'm WINNING this here race. You understand?"

"We understand. But he must go."

"How's the clutch?" Lugs said.

"THE GODDAM CLUTCH IS TERRIBLE. Jesus Christ."

"See you in Atlanta," Lugs said.

"Lissen, you guys: can't anybody *hear* me? I'm leading the *race*. Now, just put my mechanic down for just a few more laps here and then you can throw him off the goddam cliff, I don't care. We're racing here. *Racing*."

The officer shook his head under the white helmet, making it bob back and forth. "Don't touch the car," he told Lugs. "No, no."

Lugs scratched his head some more. "Just maybe let me check the clutch?"

The officer shook his head again "No."

"How're yer knuckles?" Lugs said.

"My fucking knuckles are *killing* me. Chrissakes, I'm steering with the *palms* of my hands and I'm winning this chicken-shit, humpty dog-ass race and you won't let me go race."

And then the policemen closed in, gently, and they all did a more or less military turn with Lugs in the middle and they all began marching away, headed for the fence and the parking lot.

"Wait a minute," I said.

They turned back, poised.

"Well, how about this: I'd like to report that my rental car was stolen. How do you like that? A Vauxhall Viva. I had it parked in front of the hotel and it was flat *stolen*, you clowns. What are you going to do about that?"

The officer smiled. A very sad sort of smile. "We have recovered your Viva, sir," he said. "And appropriate action is being taken."

"That's better."

"In fact, I think that perhaps *you* will be deported this afternoon, sir."

Lugs looked at them. "Banned for life, right?"

"Perhaps not for life. We shall see."

"Well, kiss my ass," he said.

I finally got both palms on the cowling and lifted myself up. "Well, if I don't get life, I ain't going."

"See you at Lenny's," Lugs said.

And they all walked off.

I was sitting on the tire, trying to cut my driving gloves off with a screwdriver. The knuckles on both hands were still swelling and they were all out of line underneath the split skin.

That's when the Chicken King came walking up.

"Sorry I missed the party," he said. Then he plunked one boot up on the other tire and took off his hat and wiped at his forehead with a handkerchief. "Seems to me that I heard you come back into your room once last night. And then I think I heard you go back out again in a pretty big hurry. But I never did hear you come back. Hell, I just got up a few minutes ago myself."

"Mmmmm."

"But I'll swear, that little old schoolteacher was just something *else*."

"Mmmmmm."

"She really was." And then he stopped talking and looked

around. He looked out at the track at the other Formula Vees buzzing by. And he looked around the pits. At the car. At me. At my hands. Back out on the track again. At the pits. And finally he wrinkled up his forehead.

"Lissen, Stroke," he said. "Is everything all right?"

eighteen

You've seen the signs at motels everywhere: it's that sign out by the highway as you go by. First there is the name of the motel and then there is this white-lighted area, sort of a billboard, where they can put in their own message for the folks. You know: *Holiday Inn*. And below that, in black letters, it will say: WELCOME TEXACO DEALERS. Or: WELCOME RACE FANS. Sometimes NIGHTLY, THE RED RIVER VALLEY BOYS IN OUR LOUNGE.

Uh-huh. I came off the freeway and started to crank it into the driveway and there it was:

KING'S INN

And below that it said:

STAND ON IT, STROKER!

Home again. It really sort of gets you right here, doesn't it? Some day, maybe after I run out of ankles and knuckles and eyeteeth, I may open my own string of motels in towns where they have racetracks. And I'll hire this really nice little old lady to stand at the door. She will have on a calico dress, and over that she'll be wearing this Ladies Aid Society apron, and she'll have a dab of flour on the end of her nose and tiny brown sunspots on the backs of her hands and every now and then she'll reach up with the back of her wrist and brush aside a little straggle of gray hair that has tumbled down over her forehead.

And when folks check in at the motel, why she'll just come right over and welcome them, especially racers.

"Why, it's old Johnny Go Fast," she'll say. "Welcome *home*, Johnny. Come on in and have a piece of boysenberry pie. It's just hot out of the oven, honey."

Yessir. And if the guy puts down his bag and looks puzzled and says, "Well, I'm not Johnny Go Fast; in fact, I'm not a *racer*. I'm —— "

And Grannie will say, "Hit the fucking road, sonny."

About the time I was rounding the corner, swinging my gearbag and whistling the harmony part to "Busted Gearbox Blues," I could hear the noise. Hoo-Boy.

Understand, there are party noises in motels all the time. Hell, people un*wind* at motels. But there is no party noise in the world like a NASCAR party. You could tape it and maybe play it over a hospital loudspeaker system, say, and get everybody to move their bowels at the same time.

That's when Charlie stuck his head out of my room. Mostly because my room was where the party was going on. Then he pulled his head back inside.

"He's HERE," he yelled. "All together, now."

They were singing when I walked in:

> *Oh, I'd rather take a real lickin'*
> *Than eat that fuckin'*
> *Pole Position Chicken,*

Because anybody who eats it,
Is chickenshit,
Soooooooooooo,
Shove a drumstick up yer ass,
And win the race with class.

Turbo put a drink in my hand. "We just made up that whole song," he said. " 'Bout two hours before you got here. Unnerstand you got into a whole peck of trouble down there."

"Mmmm. Where the hell were you when I needed you?"

"Hell, I got thrown out of there *last* year, remember?"

This is home: all the drivers were there, sitting all over everything, and there were gearbags and helmets all around and they had run in a clutch of ladies from downtown and J. R. Hoffman had organized a titty contest. The girls were in the bathroom taking their tops off:

One of them stuck her head out the door.

"Ready?" she said. "How shall we come out?"

Hoffman thought it over. "How about three abreast?" he said.

So I took my drink and I worked my way over to the wall, stepping over people, and got my back against it. And then, slowly, a little bit at a time, I slid right down until I was sitting on the floor with my legs stretched out. The glass and ice felt gentle and cool against the palms of my hands.

And I looked all around, through all the soft violet smoke and elbows and haze of guitar music hanging in the air, all mixed in with the occasional flash of jiggling girls with breasts the size and shape of crash helmets. Uh-huh.

Every now and then the door would open and someone would come in. And a soft roll of cool night air would stream across the carpet against the bottoms of my legs. Every now and then a car would screech around in the parking lot and every now and then someone would drop a bottle out in front and the sound of the shatter would freeze there in the air for just an instant. Off to my left, the bathroom door would open and close and the toilet would flush — in no special order. Now and then somebody fell down.

Back home again in . . . wherever the hell this was.

"You're Stroker Ace, aren't you?"

Let's see here. Ahh, yes: it was a little, tiny girl, blond and frizzy-headed, up against my shoulder. She was sitting cross-legged and she had a drink held in both hands on her lap. Her shoes were off and she was wiggling her toes inside her silk stockings.

"Yes, I'm Stroker. Now promise not to tell me the story of your life, all right?"

She nodded. "I'm Sally-June. Can I at least tell you where I'm from?"

"Mmmm hmmm."

"I'm from downtown. With the rest of the girls."

"Then how come you're not up there dancing and carrying on and cavorting and all that?"

She looked down at her chest, shaking her head. "I don't really have very big boobies," she said. "And, besides, J.R. won't let me. He's real mad at me. Really."

"How come?"

"Well," she said. "I just don't know. But, see, I'm wearing this little old black brassiere. See here? Well, and I got on this panty girdle here. See it? And it's white."

I looked at it and shook my head.

"You, too?" She said. "I swear, I just don't under*stand*. I mean: old J.R. is really *mad*. And he told me to just come right over here and sit down, that's what he told me."

"I'm not surprised. J.R. is nothing if he's not a purist."

"Now what does that mean?"

So I explained it to her. "Well, look: goddam, if you are gonna do a thing, you got to do it right. That's the way it is in NASCAR. And in life, I suppose. Hell, I don't show up to drive a race wearing *half* a damn driving uniform. Or without a helmet. That's all it means. Hell, we get enough things done half-ass in real life without this. Everybody out there — I mean on the outside — does things with no class, Sally-June. You understand? It's important. Now, if you're gonna drive a race-car, you come prepared to drive a racecar, that's all. Do it right. And who ever heard of a whore in a black brassiere and a *white* panty girdle? Damn, it's indecent."

She was sort of snuffling. "I'm sorry," she said. "Look I'll go take it off, all right?"

"Which one?"

"Well, which one do you want?"

"Let me think about it for a little while, hmm? And, meanwhile, why don't you go and get us another shooter? Put some Seven and Seven in there. What are you drinking?"

"Gin and Dr Pepper," she said.

"Jesus Christ. That figures."

Lugs was down to his boxer shorts. They draped right down to his knees and there were little, teeny pictures of cars all over the fabric. Little red, boat-tailed Stutz Bearcats. "Here's yer drink," he said. "And yer wanted on the phone."

I put the flats of my hands against the wall and worked my way up and then, when I figured I was more or less in a standing position, I waited for the room to come off the Number Four Turn. There, now. Straighten that rascal around. The music was really pulsing very big and there was too much dancing going on around the edges of the room, so I walked up and across the bed. What the hell; it's my bed.

Except that J.R. was under the covers and I walked pretty much diagonally across his shoulders and down his back and across his fanny and on off the other side. The lady he was with stuck her head out and looked around.

"Thanks," she said. "I needed that."

Phone. I took the cord in both hands, sloshing my drink a little bit, and played it in a bit at a time until it finally went right under the easy chair. So I got down on my stomach and crawled in and picked up the receiver.

"Ace Funeral Home," I said.

"Stroke?"

It was Nursie. Ahhhh, big, soft, double-breasted Nursie: "I know you're busy," she said.

"Oh, no. Just sitting here watching television."

"It isn't important," she said.

"No, no, You go right ahead. Uh-huh."

"Well . . . nothing, really. I just wanted to know how you are."

"Fine. Fine is how I am."

"Mmmm. Well, uhh. How's your ankle?"

I turned back and looked over my shoulder from half under the chair. "Well, right now there's a naked lady dancing on top of it. Excuse me, Nursie. Say, Naked Lady? Yer dancing on my goddam throttle-foot. Thanks. Now, uhhh —— "

"Oh, nothing," Nursie said. "Nothing important. I just wanted to know how you were and to tell you that I'm thinking of you. It seems that I'm always thinking of you."

And Charlie came over and stood on my other foot, looking down at me, over his stomach. "Hey," he said. "Hey — you know we gotta race tomorrow?"

"All right," I said. "Let me try it: we gotta race tomorrow."

"Be careful," Nursie said. "Won't you."

"Hey," I said. "Do you know I gotta race tomorrow?"

"Yes," she said. Then there was a long pause. "I know."

"Well, then, wait a minute. I'm gonna go and get another drink. Now, don't go away."

And I hung up the phone and backed out, looking over my shoulder and steering as best I could. And when I got it roughly out into the middle of the room, I spun it around a little bit and got up.

"Where you been?" Lugs said.

"Talking to my girl. She's under the chair. Here, put another shooter in here, all right?"

"Hey, Lugs. Here. Over here."

Focus: it was Boots Hooper and he was coming out of the door to the adjoining room. He stood there and looked through all the elbows and heads and shoulders until he spotted us. "Hey, Lugs. Get over here. Yer up next."

"Hot damn," Lugs said Then he turned back to me and put a fatherly hand on my shoulder. "It's Julene Meyers there in the other room. You know: Miss Panther Tail or whatever the hell it is she is. She's in there doin' her specialty. Hot damn, and it's *my* turn."

"I don't think you ought to," I said. "After all, I got to race tomorrow."

"My ass." And he shouldered his way through to the door. And then he picked up one big hand and knocked a very dainty, soft little knock.

And Julene came to the door.

"It's me," Lugs said. "Here I am."

She looked at him, all up and down. And then she shook her head, back and forth.

"I know you," she said. "I seen you around the track."

"Right. It's me. America's sweetheart."

"Oh, no," she said. "I don't do it to no *mechanics*. What kind of a girl do you think I am?" And she peered over his shoulder. "Ain't there any *drivers* out there?"

He just stood there for a long minute. And then this sort of reddish, purple tide began creeping up the back of his neck. And then he stepped back one half-step. And, slowly, he balled all his fingers into one great big fist. And he drew it back. And back and back.

That's when Charlie looked up and saw them.

"Jesus *Christ*, Lugs," he yelled. "Don't hit her in the mouth!"

Just off to one side — pasted up against the concrete wall, *smeared* against it — the car was burning. Coming down from it, spilled oil was streaked along the track. Down in the infield, further along the backstretch, two more cars were twisted together, locked up, and the emergency crew was working on them.

This was half way: 250 miles.

I checked all the gauges and looked over for Lugs, boiling out of the last turn and trying to hold my position. He was half-kneeled down by the pit wall and he had the board held up, pointing it toward me. It said:

PIT.

And this time around, a flagman-fireman was waving us down lower on the turn. It looked like J. R. Hoffman was still inside the car, but I couldn't be sure.

And the engine began to load up at that speed, no matter how much I zapped the thing. Damn.

I got my helmet off coming down the pitline and then braked right up against Lugs's belly. He came running around.

And I yanked down my mask. "Loading up," I said. "This sumbitch is loading *up*."

"I know, I *hear* it. What's going on back there?"

"It's J.R. He's burning. Can you do anything with this engine?"

He shook his head. "Not now. I got it just right. Now, lissen: soon's the green comes on, you punch the shit out of it and it'll clear up in two laps. Blow it out. You hear?"

I nodded. And, beside us, Turbo came stringing in, riding

his clutch and pumping that bugger as hard as he could to keep it alive.

Lugs swung around and waved the fuel crew back and swung back to me. He jerked his thumb toward the track and sidestepped, all in one move. And I took it out, punching the button as much as I could along the pitline.

They had the fire powder along the track now and the wrecker had put over its big pinchers and lifted Hoffman back over the wall from the outside.

And, coming off the Four Turn, we got the green.

And I really hit it: the big rascal barked just once and then I came slingshotting down, ducking right under Hack Downing, who had just seen the goddam light flicker on. And we went through the turn all nicely stretched out.

So much for old Hacko. You gotta be there when the bell rings, you humpties.

The whole fucking front straight was loaded up with junkers and independents and God knows who-all — every one of them plowing along nose-to-tail. And they all had the groove closed off.

Hang on, knuckles: I swung it around and came howling right down alongside the pit wall, out of the groove and *inside* and all hunkered down and passing the field. And at the end of the straight I backed off for just one blip and then cranked the wheel left for just a flash.

End of flash: I whipped it right again and let the ass-end skitter up and then got back on the gas and locked up my knuckles and kneebones and both kidneys. And I came around half-sideways, with two cars above me in the foam.

When they saw me, they both began to fishtail.

If you're ever going to stand on it, stand on it now.

And I came out of it under Lee Roy Harber and right up over Demon Daniels, ticking him on the right front fender as I came past.

This time: coming down the straight, I had the groove all cleared of the hayshakers and I got a quick blur of the crowd all standing right up, all leaning into me.

Next time around. The pit board:

J. R. Okay.

And then, about twenty-five thousand laps later:

E. Z!!!

My ass. You want to race, you bastards? We'll race.

That's when the throttle stuck.

In the full-bore position. Awww, shit.

This is the sort of thing that is fine maybe between Wendover and Wells, Nevada, where there aren't all that many high-speed curves. But, please, not here.

It took forever to get it braked down and I came out of the turn all cocked for the pits and straining at the wheel. And I stuck my arm out through the mesh-netting and waved Lugs out of the way.

He jumped sideways and then jumped back and came running up with the crew. They fell on it and began pushing me back toward our pit, with Lugs jogging alongside, pulling at the hood pins with one hand.

"Throttle . . ."

"I know," he said. "I can hear. I tole you to take it *easy*, for chrissakes."

Outside, Turbo came by, really on it, and I could see

him glance over at us. And then he was gone, with the sound rolling behind him.

"Come ON! Let's go."

He slammed the hood down and hooked it up again. And then he nodded.

He was still halfway through the nod when I hit that bugger and aimed it down the line.

With reason: I had had about a three-quarter lap on Turbo and maybe a million-lap lead on the rest of the field when the throttle grabbed.

Let's see, now. Where are you, Turbo?

And a few laps later the throttle froze right up again. Full blast.

I was coming down the backstraight, balls clenched, and there was no way — no way — to back off it. And Turbo was going out of the backstretch.

QUESTION: You gonna do it to him, Ace?
ANSWER: I insist.

He had that race-winning hunch on his shoulders when I passed him on the main straightaway, with my throttle all locked up and the car hammering out black smoke. Out of one eye I saw the checkered flag and out of the other I saw the One-Two Turn that left only one thing to do.

One thing: burn out the brakes. Hell, you've won the race anyway.

And the championship again.

So I burned them right out and finally got the bugger stopped in my usual spot in the back infield. And I sat there and waited for Lugs.

While I was waiting, I leaned my head out the window and threw up a lot.

The Chicken King filled the paper cup up over the top and let the champagne foam up over his whole hand and back down his wrist. That's because he was looking at me, hard.

"Are you serious?" he said.

I took the cup and nodded at him. And then I took a long drink. "Bet your ass," I said.

He sighed and threw the bottle out of the back doors of the tire van, then reached down and got another one.

"Well," he said. "I didn't like champagne all that much anyway. Goddam foreigners. You're serious?"

"That's what I said."

Outside it was dusky and the sun was just about down. There was nobody left on the track and the wind was stirring up waxed-paper sandwich wrappers and cardboard chicken containers and bouncing along empty brown paper bags. There was just a touch of magnolia coming from somewhere across the backstraight.

"Tell me again," Torkle said.

So I told him again: "Look: I went down to the hospital to see J.R. and they wouldn't even let me *look* at him. Hell, he's *alive*, but there aren't many spots left where he has any skin left."

"Ah'll bet that fire lit his cigar," Torkle said.

"I'll just bet it did."

"Go on."

So I went on: "Well, I was coming back from the hospital and I had to stop and throw up again. I told you about the first time, right after winning the race. And then I drove past the motel and it's the same goddam thing, Clyde: CONGRATU-LATIONS, STROKER ACE. Not a sign there that says 'Sorry About That, J.R.,' or anything like that. But maybe that's not what's really pissing me. What has got me is that I've done all this. Chrissakes: *I've done* it and now, and now I'm doing it over and over — except that I'm doing it on *stomach lining*. You follow me?"

He nodded. "I follow you."

"Well, look: what scares me is *not being scared*, you understand? Somewhere at one of these tracks, I don't know, maybe Atlanta, maybe Charlotte . . . who knows, I lost it all. Everything. All my *feelings* got burned out. I just flat don't *feel* any more — and what does that make me? I mean: really. Hell —— "

"Stroke —— "

"No, lissen: I go racing now and it's all catch-me-come-fuck-me. Kiss my ass. Hell, J. R. Hoffman left about fifty-five feet of rib-skin along that wall before he ever caught fire and every time I passed where he was burning, you know what I was thinking about? Well, I'll tell you: I was thinking, *oh, shit, the engine is loading up*, that's what. Chrissakes, where did I lose it all? Lissen again: racing is the only thing that gives me any kick at all any more and I can't race but *once a week*, maybe. When I'm racing I'm alive and when I'm not racing, I'm just waiting to get into something again and drive it fast. Sometimes I used to get a little scared. I don't any more."

"You just get meaner," Torkle said.

"Bet your ass I get meaner. And that's why I quit."

We both sat there and looked at each other for a long time, sipping at the victory champagne. Finally he filled the cups again, spilling about half a bottle, and then he cleared his throat.

"My boy," he said, "about the time you told me you was going over to the hospital instead of to the victory party, I knew this was coming. In fact, I prolly knew it maybe even months ago, and that's just because I just flat love you, you fucking meathead. And I've tole you that I want you to quit. Hell, we've *won* the goddam championship twice. And you're rich. And if you ain't got any feeling left, well, then, you can just not have any feelings in *comfort*. Here, lemme fill that sumbitch up again one more time."

I held it out: "So we're through."

"I know. We're still partners. And we're both getting out of racing. Later tonight, we'll take a couple of five-pound sledges and we'll go beat that goddam car down into a garbage can, all right?"

We shook hands. And then Torkle stood up.

"Come here," he said. And he walked over to the big open back doors. "I wanta show you something."

"Now what?"

"Well, about the time I figgered you was gonna quit racing, I bought you a farewell present. Now, *there ain't no little chicken decals on it*, all right? It's over here behind the van."

We climbed out.

Farewell present: it was a pure white Cadillac Eldorado. Convertible.

"Look at the door there," he said.

In little, tiny, really small painted gold script it said: *The Former Stroker Ace.*

"Well, God *damn*," I said. "You knew all along."

"Now look inside," he said.

I did. It was pure white. All of it — fluffy white ermine fur seats, front and back. And a white tooled-leather dashboard and white, leather-wrapped steering wheel. Shining white knobs on all the panel switches. And down in there: white, thick pile-fur carpeting all over. The inside door panels were white velvet. It was the damndest thing I have ever seen.

He handed me the keys.

"Here," he said. "Now, get yer ass out of here. If yer smart, you'll drive this sumbitch straightaway right up to Terre Haute and park out in front of that there hospital and blow the fucking horn until that nursing lady comes out. And then you'll drag her ass right in there and drive off with her." And then he sort of wiped at his eyes with the back of his knuckles. "Now, go 'wan. Go away and leave me alone."

And he climbed back up into the van, never looking back, and pulled the doors shut behind him.

I sank into the front seat and plugged in the key and cranked it over, and the engine sounded like soft ice cream. Vanilla, I suppose. And then I wheeled it out from alongside the van, not looking to either side. And whipped it out onto the service road.

Let's see: Terre Haute.

Well, hell, why not? Walk right into the maternity ward — maybe rolling along with a sort of small limp — and find the soft Greek. And say something suitable. Like, "All right, then. Mend me."

They caught me at the main gate. They were waiting there.

"Hey," Charlie said.

"Goddam, where you *bin*," Lugs said.

Charlie had his tire kit, the one with grease all over it, and he threw it into the back seat. And then he swung the door open and climbed in. He plunked down in back and put his boots up on the back of the front seat. The boots with the red Georgia clay all over them.

"Get *in*, for chrissakes," he told Lugs.

And Lugs threw his toolbox down on the floor in front and climbed in. He was still wearing his racing Levi's and T-shirt, and he leaned right back and stretched his arm out along the back of the front seat. This was his greasy arm — the one he had tried to unstick the throttle with.

"Let's go," he said.

I looked at them both. And I switched off the ignition. "I just quit racing," I said.

And Lugs nodded.

"That's *this* week," he said. "Now, next week we got Charlotte and we're gonna teach them bastards a terrible lesson. We'll blow them off so bad you won't believe it."

"I think I got a beer or maybe two still left in here," Charlie said. I could hear him popping open the cans — and then I could feel the foamy spray spattering up over the seats and against the back of my neck. "Here." And he handed one over.

"Well?" Lugs said.

"Come *on*. Let's go," Charlie said.

Lugs nodded at me. "Where to, dummy?"

I reached down and fired it up again and listened to the engine. Then I zapped it just a tiny bit and let the RPMs come up, watching the needle on the tach. And then I pounded it harder until the whole car shook. It was pure power.

"All right," I said. "All right: Charlotte. We'll suck the doors off any sumbitch who comes near us."

Lugs nodded, listening to the engine. And finally he said:

"All right. Yer wound up about high enough. Now stand on it."